Dangerous Men

Dangerous Men

The SAS and Popular Culture

John Newsinger

Pluto Press
LONDON · CHICAGO, IL.

First published 1997 by Pluto Press
345 Archway Road, London N6 5AA
and 1436 West Randolph, Chicago, Illinois 60607, USA

British Library Cataloguing in Publication Data
A catalogue record for this book is available from the British Library

Library of Congress Cataloging in Publication Data

ISBN 0 7453 1216 0 hbk

Designed and produced for Pluto Press by
Chase Production Services, Chadlington, OX7 3LN
Typeset from disk by Stanford DTP Services, Northampton
Printed in Great Britain

Contents

For Eddie, Jack and Lorna

Acknowledgements

I am grateful to three journals for allowing me to rehearse some of the arguments presented here: *Race and Class*, *Irish Studies Review* and Robin Ramsay's *Lobster*. The Library staff at Bath College of Higher Education have been of immense assistance, and I am especially grateful to Maggie Collins and the Inter Library Loans service. A number of friends and colleagues have helped by tolerating the 'SAS bore' in their midst, in particular, Alan Marshall, Olga Gomez, Brian Griffin, Sally Trueman-Dicken, Jerry Clifford, Bobbie Anderson, Graham Davis, Margaret Ward, Richard Musgrove, Terrence Rodgers, Iftikhar Malik, Paul Hyland and Neil Sammells. Special thanks to my editor, Linda Etchart and Roger van Zwanenberg of Pluto Press for his advice and encouragement. They have no responsibility for the mistakes, opinions and prejudices that appear hereafter. Lastly and most importantly my thanks to my typist, Margaret Tremeer, for goodhumouredly and patiently putting up with my inability to produce a final draft.

Abbreviations

BATT	British Army Training Team
ELAS	Greek National Liberation Army
FLOSY	Front for the Liberation of Occupied South Yemen
GPMG	General Purpose Machine Gun
INLA	Irish National Liberation Army
LRDG	Long Range Desert Group
MCP	Malayan Communist Party
MRF	Military Reaction Force
MRLA	Malayan Races Liberation Army
NCO	Non-Commissioned Officer
NLF	National Liberation Front (of Yemen)
PFLOAG	People's Front for the Liberation of the Occupied Arabian Gulf
RUC	Royal Ulster Constabulary
SAS	Special Air Service
SAF	Sultan's Armed Forces
SBS	Special Boat Squadron
SIG	Special Identification Group
SOE	Special Operations Executive
SRS	Special Raiding Squadron
UDR	Ulster Defence Regiment
YAR	Yemen Arab Republic

'Around the World three letters send a chill down the spine of the enemy: SAS. And those letters spell out one clear message: don't mess with Britain.'

Michael Portillo
10 October 1995
at Conservative Party Conference

Introduction

On 30 April 1980 six armed members of the Democratic Revolutionary Front for the Liberation of Arabistan forcibly occupied the Iranian Embassy at Princes Gate in London, taking 26 people hostage. They demanded the release of 91 Arab prisoners held in Iran and their transportation to Britain by plane. If this demand were not met, they would begin killing their hostages. While the police opened up negotiations, the SAS deployed a Counter-Revolutionary Warfare unit that began planning and preparing an attack on the building. The terrorists were persuaded to abandon their deadline and changed their demand to one of safe conduct out of the country for themselves and their hostages. They demanded a plane to fly them to an unnamed Arab country. The British believed their most likely destination was Iraq, indeed the whole episode was regarded as Iraqi sponsored.

The police negotiators played for time, prolonging the negotiations as long as possible. There was going to be no deal, no safe conduct, no plane, but it was hoped that the longer negotiations continued, the less likely the terrorists were to shoot anyone. On 5 May the terrorists' patience ended. At 6.50 in the evening they killed a hostage, Abbas Lavasani, the Embassy press officer, and dumped his body outside in the street. While the police negotiators were making promises of safe conduct if no one else were harmed, the SAS stormed the building. It was 7.23pm. According to James Adams, it had been made clear to them that 'they were to take no prisoners'.

The SAS broke into the building front and back, with the team at the rear abseiling down to the first floor balcony and to the ground floor. Stun grenades and CS gas were used to disorient the terrorists, while the SAS went through the building, killing them. In one room, a terrorist opened fire on the hostages, killing one and wounding two others, before he was killed himself. Elsewhere, they threw down their weapons and tried to hide among the hostages. They were identified and shot with the exception of one who was hidden by the hostages until they were outside the building. This saved his life. The official justification for the shooting of those terrorists who tried to hide among the hostages was that they were all carrying concealed weapons, although according to the testimony of the hostages themselves, they had thrown their weapons away by the time they were shot. One of these men was shot over 80 times. This, as James Adams observes with admirable understatement was 'a surprisingly high figure, given the SAS emphasis on minimum force'.[1] The whole operation took 17 minutes.

The assault was a success. More important, it was a stunning propaganda coup both for the Thatcher government and for the SAS. The actual breaking into the Embassy was shown on TV, turning the SAS from a shadowy undercover unit about which little was known into soldier heroes, exposed to the full glare of publicity and championed as the best of British manhood.

Writing only days later in the *Observer*, the spy novelist, John le Carré, was one of the few to complain of the astonishing triumphalism that seemed to grip the politicians, the media and public opinion. It was like 'a Guy Fawkes bonfire that refused to be put out'. The storming of the Embassy had, he wrote, awoken 'the sleeping psychopath in all of us'. It was a 'Tory triumph' carried out by 'Mrs Thatcher's Army', indeed the SAS had gone into action 'wearing her personal colours'. He warned that there were people on the right who believed that you needed conflict to keep the country together and he feared, correctly as it turned out, that Thatcher might be one of them. Far from celebrating, we should 'be scared stiff by the sight of shock troops storming into London streets, and a little ashamed of having them billed as our national – racial? – champions'. His was virtually a lone voice.[2]

Of course, John le Carré was absolutely right. The storming of the Embassy was just the sort of success the Conservative government wanted and Thatcher, in particular, exulted in it. She went to watch the TV film of the operation with the men who had taken part, fresh from the killing, and sat on the floor among them. No senior politician has appeared so openly to delight in violence since Winston Churchill over the Siege of Sidney Street in January 1911. Whereas that episode saw Churchill held up to public ridicule, Thatcher was to thrive on this one. It was the first demonstration of her 'Boudicca syndrome', a perverse militarism that made her the most warlike Prime Minister since Churchill. As far as she was concerned Britain had for too long been paralysed by memories of the Suez fiasco of 1956. She was determined to restore the country to its rightful place as a world power, showing no mercy to terrorists and standing up to the Russian menace. Her disastrous handling of the hunger strikes in Northern Ireland and her apparent condoning of SAS 'shoot-to-kill' operations in the province, were an indication of this, but it was to be the Falklands War that really gave her the chance to show what she was made of. Her tough, aggressive, militarist stance was not only intended to bolster the British position internationally, although in practice it only increased dependence on the United States, but was also an important and neglected factor in strengthening her position at home, both inside the Conservative Party and in the country at large. Thatcher presided over a rise in popular militarism that was to outlive her period in office.

The heroes of the SAS, her own particular favourites, were a crucial part of this popular militarism. Their exploits were celebrated in a growing body of popular books (novels, autobiographies, histories, handbooks), magazines, and more recently videos and TV programmes. They became, in the words of Patrick Bishop and John Witherow, 'a metaphor for efficient violence, in which Britain, rather short of heroes, took pride'.[3] Interestingly enough, it was only after Thatcher's downfall and in the aftermath of the Gulf War that the explosion of SAS material reached its peak. There were a number of reasons for this. The SAS became the last symbol of British greatness when the Thatcher miracle of the 1980s had come to be seen by many people as a shabby conjuring trick. While the quality of life might have been deteriorating under the Major government, nevertheless there was still something that the British could excel at, at which the British were best. Britain had the best elite force of fighting men in the world. The SAS had become the last symbol of British national virility.

The emergence of the SAS as the soldier heroes of the 1980s tells us less about the SAS than it does about Britain in that decade. The SAS had fought in Malaya, Borneo, Aden, Dhofar and Northern Ireland in the course of the 1950s, '60s and '70s, but these had been wars conducted without public triumphalism. They were certainly not used to further any political cause back home. The Britain of Clement Attlee, Harold Macmillan, and Harold Wilson did not need soldier heroes. This changed in the 1980s when the SAS found themselves enlisted as Thatcher's Praetorian Guard, their exploits, both past and present, celebrated as part of the Conservative Party's ideological offensive against the post-1945 political and social settlement.

While this high profile for the warrior was something of a novelty in the postwar period, it has plenty of precedent in Britain's imperial past. The soldier hero has been held up for public admiration throughout modern British history. From Francis Drake to General Wolfe, from Admiral Nelson to Sir Henry Havelock, from General Gordon to Lawrence of Arabia, the soldier hero has been seen as Britain's champion, representing the nation on the field of battle. He has embodied all that is best in British manhood. As Graham Dawson has argued in his outstanding book, *Soldier Heroes*, these men occupied 'the symbolic centre of English national identity'.[4]

One significant gap in Dawson's discussion, however, is that he focuses on the celebration of men who are without exception officers. He does not discuss the celebration of the common soldier that was becoming significant towards the end of the nineteenth century. This derived from another potent imperial source, seriously neglected in Dawson's study: Rudyard Kipling. He wrote poetry and stories of the common soldier, of men who, no matter how humble their origins, crude their manners or coarse their language, were nevertheless heroic defenders of queen and country. The contemporary celebration of the SAS derives from both these sources, embracing both Peter de la Billière and Andy McNab.

What we shall attempt in this volume is a preliminary examination of the immense and still growing body of material that celebrates the SAS. An effort will be made to put it into perspective and assess its significance as a cultural and political phenomenon. The first chapter will look at the actual record of the SAS as a military unit, arguing that it has in fact become a myth, with its reputation far outdistancing its military effectiveness. The degree of attention it has attracted in the 1980s and 1990s, from this point of view, reflects the need of sections of British society for heroes rather than the significance of their military contribution. The second chapter looks at the growing number of memoirs and autobiographies that have been written by former members of the SAS. These have come in two waves: the first after the Second World War when they were submerged in a whole number of personal accounts of irregular warfare. At this time the SAS was just one of a number of such units. The second wave began gathering momentum in the early 1980s and has culminated in recent bestsellers such as Peter de la Billière's *Looking for Trouble*, Andy McNab's *Bravo Two Zero*, Chris Ryan's *The One That Got Away* and even Jenny Simpson's *Bite the Bullet*.[5] The third chapter examines the books (histories, illustrated histories, fitness and survival handbooks), magazines, films, videos and TV programmes that have celebrated the SAS. The SAS survival manual or handbook, in particular shows the way that these cultural artefacts relate to contemporary social fears and impinge on political debate. The fourth chapter looks at SAS fiction, at some of the numerous SAS novels that are in print at the present time. While these are in the main novels of counter-revolution, there are a number that try to negotiate their way around this.

Without any doubt, what we are confronted with here is a significant cultural phenomenon that deserves urgent study.

CHAPTER 1

The Myth of the SAS

The SAS has established a popular reputation as a body of warrior supermen, capable of taking on overwhelming odds to accomplish the most dangerous tasks in the most inhospitable terrain. They, together with their publicists and apologists, have given credence to a belief that in war, whether it is conventional or unconventional, small groups of highly trained, highly motivated elite soldiers can actually make a difference between victory and defeat. From the Western Desert in 1941 to the Gulf in 1991, from the jungles of Malaya to the streets of Belfast, the SAS has supposedly made a significant, sometimes vital contribution to British success. How much of this is myth and how much is reality?

In this chapter we shall consider the extent to which contemporary accounts and assessments of the SAS reflect the ideological concerns of the Thatcher and post-Thatcher years rather than providing a realistic appraisal of their importance. The contention is that the history of these 'dangerous men' as it came to be understood and celebrated in the 1980s and early 1990s was, in large part, an aspect of the Thatcherite project and served a significant ideological purpose in her attempt to remake Britain. Military prowess was an essential part of Thatcher's attempted redefinition of British national identity and the SAS served her purposes admirably. She was concerned to lay to rest what she characterised as the Suez syndrome, and the SAS storming of the Iranian Embassy in May 1980 was one of the first steps in this direction.

What we confront with the SAS can best be seen as a contemporary myth that is certainly politically and culturally potent but actually serves to conceal the real nature of modern warfare whether waged against the Afrika Korps in the Western Desert, Communist guerrillas in Malaya, the IRA in Armagh or Iraqi troops in the Gulf. This chapter will attempt to separate out the myth from the reality.

The Founding Myth

The traditional account of the founding of the SAS tells of how Lieutenant David Stirling had 'the idea' and was able to convince his superiors of its viability. In the summer of 1941 he was stationed in the Middle East, a member of Layforce, a commando under the command of Brigadier Robert Laycock. Layforce had carried out a number of unsuccessful raids from the sea against enemy installations on the North African coast and was facing disbandment. Stirling responded to the failure of these seaborne raids by developing the idea of parachuting small sabotage squads behind enemy lines in order to mount surprise attacks on selected targets, most notably airfields. He reasoned that a comparatively small force delivered to its objective in this way would be able to cause a completely disproportionate amount of destruction and disruption. Indeed, Stirling believed that such a force would be of strategic importance and would consequently have to have direct access to the commander-in-chief rather than operating through the normal chain of command. He had already begun parachute training and had injured himself in the process.

How was a mere lieutenant to bring his ideas to the attention of the commander-in-chief, General Sir Claude Auchinleck? In the British Army it is certainly not the custom for senior officers to entertain proposals from young lieutenants. The traditional version of events is that related by Virginia Cowles in her 1958 biography of Stirling, *The Phantom Major*.[1] According to her account, Stirling, while still on crutches, broke into Middle East Headquarters in an attempt to get to see Auchinleck. While hiding from a sentry, he blundered into the office of the deputy chief of staff, General Neil Ritchie. He handed Ritchie a pencilled memorandum outlining his ideas.

Three days later Stirling was summoned to meet Auchinleck and received permission to raise a small raiding force consisting of six officers and 60 other ranks. This force would be known as 'L Detachment' of the Special Air Service. The name was invented as part of a deception operation intended to convince the Axis command that British paratroops had arrived in the Middle East. Stirling himself was promoted to captain.

This version of events is almost certainly apocryphal, the founding myth of the SAS. Much more pertinent when considering how the likes of Stirling, a 24-year-old lieutenant, could convince Ritchie and Auchinleck to let him establish his own private army is his background and social connections. Lieutenants did not get to put proposals to generals unless that is they came from suitably elevated backgrounds – and this Stirling most evidently did.

David Stirling was born in 1915, one of the Stirlings of Keir, an old Scottish Catholic family. His father was General Archibald Stirling, a former Conservative MP and Deputy Lieutenant of Perthshire and his mother was the Honourable Margaret Fraser, a daughter of the 13th Baron Lovat. His brother, Peter, was third secretary at the British Embassy in Cairo in 1941 and his sister Margaret was later to marry the Earl of Dalhousie. Stirling had attended Ampleforth, the elite Catholic public school and despite, or perhaps because of, the fact that he lacked any academic distinction, had gone on to Cambridge. There he confined his activities to the turf and was sent down. On the outbreak of war in 1939, he, together with his other two brothers, Hugh and Bill, joined the Scots Guards, a regiment that testified to their rank in society. Clearly it was this background that secured Stirling a hearing and permission to establish the SAS.

The War in the Desert

Recruitment and training began almost immediately. Stirling was concerned to establish an elite of tough, self-confident and ruthless soldiers capable of operating independently deep behind enemy lines. Organised into squads of four men, they had to possess great powers of endurance, quick reactions and to be skilled in the use of weapons and explosives. Each squad was meant to be a balanced unit with its members possessing among their number expertise in navigation, first aid, radio operating, demolition and later on vehicle maintenance and driving. At this stage, the intention was still to parachute in, attack the objective on foot and then rendezvous with patrols of the Long Range Desert Group (LRDG), who would bring them out in their vehicles.

The first raid was a complete disaster. Stirling proposed a simultaneous attack on five airfields near Tmimi and Gazala as a preliminary to the 8th Army's planned offensive, Operation Crusader, which was to begin on 18 November 1941. It was intended to parachute in five groups on 16 November and to attack the airfields the following day. On the 16th the weather was atrocious with gale force winds, but Stirling was determined to go ahead. They parachuted into a sandstorm, landed miles from their objectives and most of their number were either killed or captured. Stirling subsequently claimed that one party did actually put in an attack on a target airfield, but as no one from that squad was ever seen again there does seem to have been an element of wishful thinking. Of the 63 officers and men taking part in this first operation only 22 were brought back by the LRDG.[2]

This fiasco determined Stirling to change his method of entry. From now on they would go in with the LRDG, approach and attack their target on foot, then rendezvous with the LRDG who would bring them out. The SAS flirtation with parachuting had been both costly and short-lived. Before the end of the year a number of successful raids had taken place: on 6 December they claimed to have destroyed 24 aircraft at Tamet, on 18 December 37 aircraft at Agedabia and on 24 December another 27 aircraft on a return visit to Tamet. Stirling's 'idea' had been vindicated.

The reliance on the LRDG continued until July 1942 when Stirling acquired a number of jeeps and 3-ton trucks on which he had mounted twin machine guns, front and rear. Instead of penetrating enemy airfields on foot, the SAS now had the fire power to shoot them up in wild forays. In an attack on an airfield at Fuka on 26–7 July, Stirling's 18 jeeps bristled with 68 machine guns. He claimed that they had destroyed some 40 aircraft in this attack.

Clearly these raids were not considered decisive enough by GHQ in Cairo which required a more dramatic assault in the run-up to the El Alamein offensive. A large-scale attack on harbour installations in Tobruk and Benghazi, Operation Agreement, was planned for September 1942. The idea originated with Stirling, but was taken out of his hands. Instead of dispersed small-scale raids causing maximum damage at minimum loss, a number of simultaneous large-scale attacks were to be mounted. Stirling was to attack Benghazi with over 200 men in 80 vehicles. At the same time Tobruk was to be attacked by both land (by 80 men of the Special Service Regiment, another of the Desert private armies, under Colonel John Haselden) and sea (by some 400 commandos under cover of naval bombardment). Diversionary attacks were to be made on the Italian-held fort at Jalo by the Sudan Defence Force and on the airfield at Barce by the LRDG. According to Stirling, the plan violated all the lessons learned by the SAS over previous months and the disaster that followed was inevitable.

The SAS group was ambushed en route to Benghazi and, with surprise clearly lost, Stirling called the raid off. Under continual air attack and pursued by enemy forces, they fought their way back to the British lines, losing some 50 men and 40 vehicles in the process. The attack on Tobruk was even more disastrous with the Special Service Regiment wiped out, its commander, Colonel Haselden, among the dead, some 300 of the commandos landed from the sea killed or captured, and two destroyers and four motor torpedo boats sunk. The attack on Jalo by the Sudan Defence Force was humiliatingly driven off. Only the LRDG raid on Barce, using the methods pioneered by Stirling, was successful, destroying or damaging over 30 aircraft.[3]

Despite this setback, the SAS prospered. In the aftermath of Operation Agreement, L Detachment became 1 SAS Regiment, incorporating the Special Boat Service (SBS) and the survivors of the Special Service Regiment. The new regiment was organised into five squadrons, an HQ squadron and four combat squadrons, A, B, C (a French squadron) and D (the SBS). By the end of 1942 its total strength was 83 officers and 570 other ranks and Stirling had been promoted to colonel. He was already planning to establish a second SAS regiment under the command of his brother, Bill, with himself in command of what would have been an SAS brigade.

Meanwhile raiding continued, but with the Axis on the defensive in North Africa counter-measures against them became more effective. B Squadron was virtually wiped out between December 1942 and January 1943 and Stirling himself was captured at the end of January. He spent the rest of the war as a prisoner.

There can be no doubting the courage of the SAS, operating hundreds of miles behind enemy lines at continual risk of death or capture. Indeed their exploits often read as if they are *Boys' Own* adventure stories. As well as courage, there was also ruthlessness. Stirling himself on one occasion machine-gunned sleeping Italian soldiers, while the most effective of the SAS commanders, Paddy Mayne, was, as one of his men admiringly described him, 'the best professional killer I have ever seen'. Mayne was given to violent rages that on a number of occasions saw him physically assault fellow officers and other ranks. He seems to have positively relished killing, especially with a knife. On one raid Mayne personally stalked and stabbed to death over a dozen sentries set to guard individual aircraft. Another SAS officer, the Dane Anders Lassen, also seems to have positively enjoyed killing men with a knife.[4] Both were men of great courage, Mayne receiving four Distinguished Service Orders and Lassen three Military Crosses and a posthumous Victoria Cross. But they were also ruthless killers, ideal men to wage war.

The question remains how great a contribution to Allied victory in North Africa did the SAS actually make? The military historian, Philip Warner, in what was the first history of the regiment, *The Special Air Service*, published in 1971, states quite categorically that the SAS had an influence on the outcome of the Desert War. According to his account they had destroyed something like 400 enemy aircraft, reducing Axis air strength at the time of the Battle of El Alamein in October 1942 by more than half.[5] On the other hand no one else seems to have noticed their vital contribution to victory. The problem is highlighted if we consider two books by John Strawson, a former major general as well as a military historian. In his *A History of the SAS Regiment* published in 1984 he joins in endorsing Philip Warner's assessment of the SAS contribution, indeed these claims 'can be sustained and more'.[6] The difficulty is that in his earlier account of the Desert War, *The Battle for North Africa*, published in 1969, he does not even mention the SAS.[7] The later book was written at the invitation of the SAS regiment and very much reflects the high profile it achieved in the Thatcher years, while the earlier book is a more considered account of the Desert War that focuses on the decisive factors contributing to the Allies'

eventual victory rather than romanticising the part played by one
particular unit. In fact, it is reasonable to treat SAS claims with
some scepticism. This is not to doubt the courage of the men
involved but to consider whether they actually destroyed 400
aircraft rather than destroyed *or* damaged that number, how many
were frontline aircraft and so on.

The Desert War was won because of the overwhelming material
superiority that the Allies had established by the autumn of 1942.
At the start of the Battle of El Alamein the British had 910 tanks
opposed by the Afrika Korps' 234. Despite suffering heavier losses
than the Germans, with reinforcements arriving all the time, the
British advantage actually increased in the weeks after the Battle.
As far as the establishment of Allied air superiority and the successful
interdiction of Axis supply lines is concerned, the credit belongs
to the Desert Air Force. Between November 1941 and September
1942 2,370 single-engined fighters arrived in the Middle East to
reinforce the Allies, while the total German production of single-
engined fighters for all fronts in this same period was only 1,340.
No more than a quarter of these, and probably not that many, were
despatched to the Middle East. It was this material advantage that
was decisive, not the heroic efforts of a few hundred SAS. Barrie
Pitt's verdict on SAS activity in his history of the North Africa
campaign, *The Crucible of War*, seems inescapable: 'such operations
were only peripheral to the main conflict. They might occasionally
affect its course, but the decisive battles would still have to be fought
out by massed armies.'[8]

Liberating Europe

After David Stirling's capture 1 SAS was divided into two separate
formations: the Special Raiding Squadron (SRS) under Paddy
Mayne's command, and the Special Boat Squadron (SBS) under
Lord Jellicoe. At the same time 2 SAS, the second regiment, under
the command of Bill Stirling, had become operational. Both the
SRS and 2 SAS fought in Sicily and Italy while the SBS was active
in the Aegean. At the end of 1943 first the SRS, which reverted to
the designation 1 SAS, and then 2 SAS were transferred to Britain
in readiness for the invasion of France. The SBS remained in the
Mediterranean. In Britain an SAS brigade was formed consisting
of the two British regiments, two French SAS regiments and a
Belgian SAS regiment with an effective strength of some 2,500 men.
After the Normandy landings, the brigade was committed to
operations behind German lines, raiding out of secret camps,
cooperating with the resistance, including the Communists,
collecting intelligence and harrying enemy lines of communication.[9]

Once again this was a buccaneering sort of warfare straight out of
Boys' Own.

At the end of 1944 an SAS squadron under Roy Farran was
returned to Italy where it fought alongside the Communist resistance.
Farran has told the remarkable story of this episode, 'the culmination
of SAS experience in the last war', in his various memoirs,
including *Winged Dagger* and *Operation Tombola*.[10] The rest of the
brigade which came under the former Chindit Mike Calvert's
command in March 1945 continued operations in Belgium, Holland
and Germany up until the Nazi surrender. Men of 1 SAS took part
in the liberation of Belsen concentration camp, according to some
accounts, shooting a number of SS guards in summary execution.[11]

In the course of operations in France, Belgium, Holland and
Germany, the SAS brigade had suffered 330 casualties, many of
them having been executed after being taken prisoner and tortured.
They claimed to have inflicted 7,733 casualties and to have captured
4,784 prisoners. They had derailed 33 trains, cut the railway lines
164 times and captured or destroyed some 700 vehicles.[12] Certainly
this was an impressive performance given the strength of the SAS,
but once again it was of peripheral importance. The Battle of
Normandy and the German retreat from France, for example,
witnessed the destruction of some 60 German divisions with
German losses of 265,000 men killed or wounded and 350,000 taken
prisoner. Clearly the issue in Western Europe was decided by the
clash of great massed armies. The scale of the fighting completely
dwarfed the contribution the SAS brigade made. This is not to
denigrate their exploits, but to put those exploits in perspective.

After the German surrender, preparations were put underway
for the brigade to take part in the war against Japan. This prospect
was ended with the atomic bombing of Hiroshima and Nagasaki.
In October 1945 when the SAS was disbanded, the two British
regiments ceased to exist, while the French and Belgian regiments
returned to their own armies. Not until the onset of the postwar
crises of empire was the SAS to be reconstituted to play the counter-
revolutionary role that it retains to this day.

The first indications of its future counter-revolutionary role had
already appeared even before the end of the war. While the SAS
fought alongside Communist partisans in France and Italy, in
December 1944 the SBS was involved in British attempts to
suppress the Communist-led resistance, ELAS, in Athens. A
shooting incident in Crete had already cost the lives of two SBS
men at the hands of an ELAS sniper, nearly precipitating a serious
clash. Much more serious were developments in Greece itself.
Here a number of SBS men were captured during the Athens
fighting and held prisoner for a month: three were killed and
another twelve wounded. According to James Ladd in his history

of the SBS, this was 'the first brush ... against urban terrorists'.[13]
More properly it was the first deployment of British troops against
a popular revolutionary movement in the Cold War. It was to be
followed by many more.

One question worth at least briefly considering here is why, if
the SAS were relatively unimportant, so much attention has been
devoted to their activities over the years since the war. The answer
is quite simple: the story of the SAS in the Second World War is
an adventure story. Young ex-public-school boys, the cream of the
British race, leading their men in daring, sometimes foolhardy
exploits against a brutal enemy. While the war might in reality have
been decided by the massive application of overwhelming force,
the adventures of the SAS showed young men, through their
courage, quick wits and skill with arms, taking on the enemy in
overwhelming numbers and defeating them. As Philip Warner
enthuses, their exploits could have been invented by John Buchan
and men like Stirling, Mayne, Farran and the rest could have
stepped out of his books. This romantic view of war has always
proven more popular than the clash of great armies. In the 1980s
it was to become a potent weapon in the arsenal of Thatcherism.

The SAS was to be revived in 1947, but as part of the Territorial
Army, the military reserve, rather than the regular army. The unit
incorporated a long-standing Territorial force, the Artists Rifles and
was designated 21 SAS (Artists). Not until the height of the
Communist insurgency in Malaya was the SAS to be re-established
as part of the regular army.

Palestine Interlude

Before that there was involvement by former SAS personnel, most
notably Roy Farran, in the fighting against Zionist guerrillas in
Palestine. Here the British confronted extremely effective terrorist
organisations in the shape of the Irgun and the Lehi (better known
as the 'Stern gang') that had the broad support of the Jewish settler
community. The army had completely failed to suppress the Zionist
resistance and in an attempt to turn the tide special police units
were established to hunt down and eliminate the terrorists. Bernard
Fergusson, a former officer with the Chindits in Burma and
subsequently head of Combined Operations, was brought in as an
Assistant Inspector General of the Palestine police. He proposed
the establishment of a special mobile undercover counter-terrorist
force that would operate clandestinely in Jewish areas and carry
the war to the enemy. Two units were established, one of them
commanded by Roy Farran. They were given 'a carte blanche',
according to Farran, and the notion 'filled me with excitement'.[14]

He headed a squad of ten men, five of them former SAS, who went into Jewish areas, hunting terrorists. This method of operating was to provide a model for later counter-insurgency campaigns including most recently that in Northern Ireland. In Palestine the results were disastrous.

Farran was accused of having kidnapped, tortured and killed a seventeen-year-old Lehi supporter. He was arrested and promptly escaped to Syria, but was persuaded by Fergusson to return and stand trial. A statement he had earlier prepared admitting the crime was ruled inadmissible and Fergusson refused to give evidence on the grounds that he might incriminate himself. Predictably Farran was acquitted, but the British had suffered a serious propaganda setback. The special police units were disbanded.[15]

What this experience revealed was the inescapable tendency for such covert special units to become a law-to-themselves and to engage in shoot-to-kill methods. While in some of Britain's postwar counter-insurgency campaigns such activities were to attract little attention and less criticism, in Palestine and later in Northern Ireland where the insurgents had access to the international media, they were seriously to backfire.

The Malayan Emergency

The Communist rebellion that broke out in Malaya in 1948 was caused by the frustration of hopes for peaceful political and social change. During the Second World War when Malaya had been occupied by the Japanese, the British had allied themselves with the local Communists who had waged a guerrilla war against the occupation forces. Once the Japanese were defeated, the Communists expected the British to recognise them as a legitimate political force. They looked forward to social reform, a rapid advance towards democracy and the granting of independence – expectations that were heightened with the election of a Labour government in London. Accordingly, instead of resisting the British return, the Communists actually collaborated in the restoration of British control. Instead of mounting an armed insurrection, they disbanded their guerrilla army and concentrated their efforts on building up a strong trade union movement and establishing a leftwing political alliance uniting Malaya's three ethnic groups: Chinese, Malays and Indians. Communist efforts at establishing a multi-ethnic alliance were absolutely crucial. At the end of the war the Malayan Communist Party (MCP) was overwhelmingly Chinese in ethnic composition. In a country where only 38 per cent of the population were Chinese and 49 per cent Malay, MCP success at winning over the Malays was always going to be decisive.[16]

The British responded to these developments with a policy of divide and rule. They allied themselves with the Malays' traditional rulers, the rajahs and sultans, who had generally collaborated with the Japanese, against their former resistance allies. An attack on the citizenship rights of the Chinese population was combined with warnings that the MCP intended to establish a Chinese ascendancy. Communist hopes of peaceful reform and democratisation were quickly dispelled as the British made clear that their future plans for Malaya did not include tolerating the existence of either a strong trade union movement or a multi-ethnic leftwing political alliance. Far from reforming British imperialism, the Labour government actually intensified the exploitation of countries like Malaya. The reason was simple: the British desperately needed the dollars that Malayan tin and rubber could earn and nothing was to be allowed to get in the way.

The British responded to widespread social unrest with increasing repression, driving the MCP further to the left. Those within the party in favour of armed insurrection had come to the fore when on 19 June 1948 the British struck first. A state of emergency was declared, the MCP was banned and a widespread round-up of its members was launched. By the end of August over 4,000 people had been detained.[17]

The MCP was taken by surprise. Although it was in the process of preparing for an armed insurrection, preparations were still at a very early stage. Not until 26 June were the Communists able to mount their first retaliatory attacks. They faced the problem of rallying their forces for a revolutionary war with the full weight of colonial repression bearing down on them. The MCP took sanctuary in the jungle and set about organising a guerrilla army, the Malayan Races Liberation Army (MRLA) and re-establishing its clandestine rural support network, the Min Yuen, that had earlier sustained it against the Japanese. The MRLA enlisted some 5,000 men and women as fighters, most of them unaccustomed to the jungle, poorly trained, armed only with light weapons, but highly motivated. This force was too weak to set about establishing liberated zones, but it did launch a campaign of assassinations, raids and ambushes. By the end of 1948, the guerrillas had killed 149 troops and police and wounded another 211. More important, the MRLA had begun seriously to disrupt the colony's economic life.

By the end of 1949 the MRLA had managed to seize the initiative. Incidents were averaging 400 a month and British morale was low. The guerrillas carried out hit and run attacks, striking and then disappearing into the jungle. The British responded with large-scale cordon and search operations, combing the jungle with hundreds of troops and police, searching for an enemy that had long since slipped away. Unable to find the guerrillas, the British became increasingly brutal towards the local Chinese who they knew were sustaining them. Far from intimidating the people, these methods only increased support for the MRLA.

What broke this cycle of repression and resistance was the strategy developed by the new Director of Operations, General Sir Harold Briggs, who arrived in Malaya in April 1950. The so-called 'Briggs Plan' conceptualised the war as a competition in government, a competition for control of the local population. Instead of trying to hunt down the MRLA, the British at last placed the colonial administration on a war footing and set about establishing control over the Chinese rural population, the squatters, the tin miners and plantation workers. In June 1950 an ambitious resettlement programme was launched. It was carried out with considerable ruthlessness, so that by the beginning of 1952 over 400,000 Chinese squatters had been forcibly resettled in heavily guarded 'new villages'. Despite later rhetoric about 'hearts and minds', this was all about establishing control. It was the turning point in the conflict, giving the British the strategic initiative and putting the MRLA on the defensive, increasingly fighting to survive rather than to win. The success of resettlement left the MRLA effectively isolated, cut off from its source of recruits, food, supplies and intelligence. At the same time, the British introduced new infantry tactics in their pursuit of the guerrillas. Large-scale cordon and search operations were increasingly replaced by small unit operations, patrols and ambushes. The turn of the tide was not immediately obvious, however. In 1950 the MRLA killed 393 troops and police and in 1951 404. Their most spectacular success came on 6 October 1951 when they ambushed and killed the High Commissioner, Sir Henry Gurney. British morale reached rock bottom. The guerrillas themselves, however, recognised that they were already on the defensive.[18]

The SAS was re-established in Malaya in August 1950 at a time when the British had still not wrested the initiative from the MRLA. The man behind this was Brigadier Mike Calvert, who had briefly commanded the SAS brigade in Europe in 1945. He argued the need for a specially trained force that could penetrate the deep jungle, operate there independently for long periods and isolate the aboriginal Orang Asli population from the MRLA. In fact, this owed considerably more to his earlier Chindit experience than to anything the SAS had previously undertaken, but nevertheless when the new unit was formed it was designated the Malayan Scouts (SAS). From the very beginning the new unit had an explicitly counter-revolutionary purpose: to help suppress the Communist insurgency. This was a far cry from its wartime experience of cooperation with the Communist resistance in Europe.

Calvert recruited the first men into 'A' squadron but proved unable to shape it into an effective fighting force. He was in poor health and drinking heavily and the squadron became a byword for indiscipline and inefficiency. While 'A' squadron was establishing its unsavoury reputation in Malaya, a special mobile raiding force was recruited from the Territorial unit, 21 SAS (Artists) in London for service in Korea. In the event, the Korean War became stalemated and the squadron was despatched instead to Malaya, becoming 'B' squadron. The new arrivals, very keen to keep alive the warrior ethos of the wartime SAS, were horrified by what they found. Calvert effectively handed over command and the force was whipped into shape, dropping the Malayan Scouts designation and becoming 22 SAS regiment at the end of 1951. The two men most responsible for establishing the SAS as an effective fighting force at this time were Major Dare Newell and Major John Woodhouse. When Woodhouse returned to Britain in 1952, he introduced the SAS selection procedures that were to enable it to establish itself as an elite formation. To many Woodhouse is the real founder of the modern SAS with even the likes of Denis Healey, a future Labour minister of defence, somewhat over-enthusiastically describing him as 'the greatest guerrilla warrior yet produced by the West – a man to compare with Ho Chi Minh'.[19]

How important was the SAS contribution in Malaya? According to Peter de la Billière, who served there as a junior officer in 1956–8, 'the decisive factor was the introduction of the SAS'.[20] This is a classic example of special forces' egoism and quite grotesquely exaggerates their part in British success. The SAS specialised in deep jungle penetration, contacting the aboriginal population and establishing forts, either killing or driving away the MRLA. They performed great feats of physical endurance, became expert at jungle craft and successfully harassed the Communist guerrillas. But this only became really important as part of the mopping up process once the tide had already turned. Moreover, even as far as jungle warfare is concerned, it is important not to exaggerate the prowess of the SAS: the troops who were recognised as performing most effectively in jungle operations were the Fijians, the East Africans and the Gurkhas. Of the 6,398 Communist guerrillas killed by the security forces in Malaya in the course of the Emergency, only 108 were killed by the SAS. In no way was the SAS contribution decisive. They played only a minor role.[21]

The most important factors in the British defeat of the Communists were the Briggs Plan, the overwhelming resources available and the support of the Malay population. The forcible resettlement of the rural Chinese that Briggs initiated effectively cut the guerrillas off from their supporters. This was combined with increased repression. The police and military had wide powers of arrest and detention, could impose curfews, collective punishments and food controls. There was effective censorship. Altogether during the Emergency 34,000 people were to be interned without trial and another 15,000 were deported. More people were brought to trial under the draconian Emergency laws, receiving long prison terms or even the death penalty. Capital punishment was extended to a wide range of offences and altogether 226 rebels were hanged. This repression was imposed by a massive security apparatus. Eventually over 40,000 police, 40,000 special police, 100,000 auxiliary police and 250,000 home guards were raised overwhelmingly from the Malay population to fight the MRLA. They were supported by over 40,000 troops (British, East African, Fijian, Australian, Gurkha, Rhodesian and Malay) together with squadrons of heavy bombers and fighter bombers. The MRLA's protracted resistance in the face of these overwhelming odds was a remarkable epic of courage and endurance that so far lacks a chronicler.

Underpinning the administrative and security effort, however, was the political settlement that the British came up with. The decision was taken, under the new High Commissioner, General Sir Gerald Templer, to speed up progress towards independence. The British decided to surrender power to the traditional Malay rulers, confident that they could continue to exercise control informally. To this end, Templer encouraged an alliance between the Malay rulers' United Malay National Organization and the Chinese businessmen's Malayan Chinese Association. This provided the political foundations for victory in the counter-insurgency campaign. The British successfully established a political base that proved stronger than the MCP's.[22]

The war continued, even after Malaya became independent on 31 August 1957. By now, however, the MRLA was being remorselessly hunted down. In 1958 only ten police and troops were killed by the guerrillas, whose own losses were 153 killed and over 500 who had surrendered. The growing number of surrenders indicated a collapse in MRLA morale and signalled the end. The MCP leadership and a surviving guerrilla remnant escaped over the border into Thailand.

The Storming of Jebel Akhdar

The effective end of the Malayan Emergency posed a question mark with regard to 22 SAS. What role was there for a unit that specialised in deep jungle operations? There was a very real danger of either amalgamation, perhaps with the Paras, or of disbandment. Instead the SAS was saved by an inconvenient tribal rebellion in a British protectorate, the Sultanate of Oman. Here, the slave-owning

Sultan, Said bin Taimur, ruled as a medieval tyrant over a backward, desperately poor, Arab kingdom, kept in power only by British support. For many years the interior of the Sultanate had been outside of royal control with the tribes instead offering allegiance to a religious leader, the Imam. This had been of no great concern until in the 1950s the Saudis and the Americans began encouraging the Imam Ghalib bin Ali to establish an independent state. They hoped to exclude the British from the exploitation of any oil reserves that might be discovered in the area. In 1955 the Sultan's army marched into the interior and drove the Imam Ghalib and his brother Talib into exile in Saudi Arabia. The Sultan's rule was not popular and in 1957 Talib returned to raise the standard of revolt. With some 600 followers he installed himself on the Jebel Akhdar.

The Jebel is a sheer limestone massif 50 miles long and 20 miles wide with peaks rising to 10,000 feet. At 6,000 feet there is a fertile plateau with settlements that could feed and house the rebel forces. There were plenty of caves in which they could shelter from bombing. The only approaches onto the plateau were through narrow ravines which could be easily defended. It was, according to one military historian, 'one of the greatest natural fortresses in the world'.[23]

David Smiley, the commander of the Sultan's army, requested that British troops be sent to help storm the Jebel, but this was out of the question at the time. In the aftermath of Suez, it was considered too politically sensitive to commit large numbers of troops. Instead, Frank Kitson, a staff officer at the War Office, put forward a proposal for a counter- or pseudo-gang operation similar to those he had himself carried out against the Mau Mau in Kenya. A mixed force of British soldiers and 'turned' rebel prisoners would infiltrate onto the Jebel, preparing the way for the Sultan's troops. This too was rejected. Instead, the SAS were brought in to see if they could take the Jebel without any large-scale commitment of British troops. There is considerable justification in Kitson's contention that this campaign was to ensure 'the continued existence of the Special Air Service'.[24]

Almost without exception, the occupation of the Jebel is ascribed to the almost superhuman powers of endurance, military skill and courage of the SAS. A handful of these brave, resourceful men successfully took a fortress that would otherwise have required a major military operation. What these accounts leave out is that the Jebel had been under heavy air bombardment for weeks before the SAS arrived. Movement in daylight became virtually impossible and by night extremely dangerous as the inhabitants of the plateau had their homes and crops destroyed and their livestock killed. Air Chief Marshal Sir David Lees in his account of the campaign gives some idea of the scale of the bombardment: in the week ending 12

September 1957, for example, four-engined Shackleton heavy bombers dropped 148 1,000 lb bombs on the plateau, while roving Venom jet fighters fired 40 rockets and a large quantity of cannon ammunition. Later in the month aircraft off the carrier HMS Bulwark joined in the attack. Within the confines of such a small area this relentless bombardment 'against simple agricultural tribes' continuing week after week was, Lees admits, 'a terrifying experience'. Even before the SAS arrived the villagers were pleading with the Imam and his brother to surrender.[25]

D squadron of 22 SAS arrived in Oman on 18 November and immediately began aggressive patrolling to clear the lower slopes of the Jebel. In December they attempted their first incursions onto the plateau but met with stiff resistance. The SAS commander, Colonel Tony Deane Drummond, decided that reinforcements were needed and so on 9 January 1959 A squadron was flown in.

The plan of attack involved the SAS breaking onto the plateau from the south west while diversionary attacks fixed rebel attention elsewhere. It worked without a hitch. Only two men were left guarding the approach the SAS used. Once they were successfully established on the plateau in strength, the Imam's forces melted away. While the rebels had been effective in harassing the Sultan's army, they were not equipped for a stand-up fight with elite troops with close air support. The SAS had successfully broken the back of the rebellion with the loss of only three men killed and one man wounded.

Smiley was subsequently to complain about the way 'the SAS received the entire credit for our success', while the Sultan's army, which he commanded, was 'totally ignored, although they had suffered the highest casualties'.[26] This was to become a regular feature of operations involving the SAS. Nevertheless, there is little doubt that the SAS had accomplished the capture of the Jebel far more economically than would have been possible for other troops. The operation was an important turning-point. According to Peter de la Billière the regiment 'had demonstrated that a small number of men could be flown into a trouble spot rapidly and discreetly, and operate in a remote area without publicity – a capability much valued by the Conservative Government of the day'.[27]

Confrontation

The unofficial war that took place in Borneo on the frontier between Malaysia and Indonesia was arguably the most important British military victory in the postwar period. Not only was the Indonesian offensive defeated and Malaysia saved from domination by its more powerful neighbour, but the defeat also played an important part in precipitating the downfall of President Sukarno and the bloody destruction of Indonesian communism. At the height of the conflict, Britain had 59,000 military personnel stationed in Malaysia, its largest military force in the Far East since the Korean War. The naval presence was built up to some 80 vessels, including submarines and aircraft carriers, and for a time V-bombers 'visited' Singapore, 'an event which raised the prospect of the ultimate deterrent against any Indonesian escalation of the conflict'. This concentration of forces was instrumental in containing the conflict. Despite this the cost was still estimated at £256 million.[28]

Sukarno's objective in launching the confrontation in 1963 was to try to prevent the successful establishment of the Malaysian Federation which he regarded as a British strategem to contain Indonesian influence in the region. To this end bands of local volunteers led by regular Indonesian troops began raiding across the Borneo frontier. The first attack at Tebedu on 12 April 1963 saw two policemen killed. The Indonesians had little difficulty infiltrating armed bands into Malaysian territory. There was an ill-defined 900-mile frontier that stretched along mountainous terrain covered in dense rain forest to be defended. This presented the British with enormous problems. The key was effective intelligence and here the SAS was to play a significant role.

John Strawson, who for a while commanded British forces in Western Sarawak, writes in his *A History of the SAS Regiment* of the 'indispensable contribution' it made. Its role consisted of 'surveillance, intelligence gathering and the so-called "Hearts and Minds" campaign so necessary to win the loyalty of the Sarawak peoples'.[29] It established small outposts on the border, patrolling and seeking to enlist the support of the local tribes who could provide warning of any Indonesian incursions. In the event of Indonesian bands being discovered, they could attack small bands themselves, but if they were too strong reinforcements were to be called in and placed in contact with the enemy. This was dangerous, arduous work involving considerable endurance and great courage. The SAS operated in small detachments, two or four strong, with the emphasis put on surveillance rather than combat. In the event of contact with the Indonesians, they were to 'shoot and scoot' rather than stand and fight. While the bulk of the fighting was carried out by the Gurkhas, who made the major contribution to British success, nevertheless the SAS made an important contribution to intelligence gathering on both sides of the border.

At the end of September 1963 a large band of Indonesian raiders, perhaps 200-strong, penetrated fifty miles to attack a military post at Long Jawai. They overran the post, killing two Gurkhas, a policeman and a Border Scout. This setback for the British was retrieved by the speed of their response. On their way back to the border, the Indonesians were repeatedly ambushed by Gurkha patrols helicoptered in to intercept them. Over twelve days the Indonesian force was put to flight with perhaps 50 of their number killed. At the end of December another strong Indonesian band overran the village of Kalabatan, killing eight Malay soldiers. Once again Gurkha troops were helicoptered in to harass their withdrawal and only a handful straggled back across the border.

The following year Sukarno committed large numbers of regular troops to the conflict, establishing permanent military bases just over the border from Malaysian territory. The British responded offensively with General Walter Walker being authorised by the Labour government in London to launch 'Claret' operations, raids into Indonesian territory intended to make their bases untenable. These raids were eventually permitted up to 18,000 yards into Indonesia. To secure the Malaysian side of the border a network of strong well-defended British forts was constructed, serving as bases from which aggressive patrols could be mounted and from which the 'hearts-and-minds' campaign could be stepped up. The most serious Indonesian incursion took place at the end of April 1965 when a strong force of regular troops attacked the British base at Plaman Mapu which was held by the Paras. Only after heavy fighting were they driven off. May and June saw a succession of clashes as the Indonesians stepped up their efforts and the British responded once again with cross-border raids of their own. The last serious incident occurred in March 1966 when the Gurkhas ambushed an Indonesian raiding party in the Bau district, killing nearly 40 of them. By now the confrontation was effectively over and formal agreement between the two sides was finally reached in August 1966.

Without any doubt, the Gurkhas played the decisive part in the conflict.[30] They had outnumbered the British troops in Borneo by 2 to 1 and had lost 43 men killed and 87 wounded compared with British losses of 32 killed and 71 wounded. The SAS had three men killed and two wounded, a figure which quite usefully puts their involvement in perspective. The number of Indonesian troops and irregulars killed was officially 590 but the real figure is generally believed to be substantially higher. The role of the SAS was clearly a subsidiary one, 'small beer' as the then Colonel Anthony Farrar-Hockley put it, but still important in helping other units bring the Indonesians to battle.[31] What is interesting is that despite Denis Healey, the Labour minister of defence's typically modest claim that the Borneo campaign was 'one of the most efficient uses of military force in the history of the world', the war was actually fought in comparative secrecy. There was none of the patriotic celebration of British military prowess that was to become a hallmark of the

1980s.[32] Indeed, the histories that celebrated the heroism of the SAS in Borneo, most notably Peter Dickens's *SAS: The Jungle Frontier* and Tony Geraghty's *Who Dares Wins*, were themselves only published in the 1980s.[33] The part played by the Gurkhas has never received the same degree of publicity; presumably the fact that British success was mainly due to Asian mercenaries was not something people wanted to hear.

The Two Yemens

At the same time as the confrontation in Indonesia, Britain was also involved in attempting to put down rebellion in the recently established Federation of South Arabia. This had been set up in February 1959 in an attempt to neutralise the destabilising influence of the port of Aden, with its strongly nationalist trade union movement, by placing it under the domination of the petty sheikdoms of the South Yemen interior. The ploy was fatally compromised in September 1962 by a military coup in North Yemen where the ruling Imam was overthrown and the Yemen Arab Republic (YAR) proclaimed. The republican government of Abdullah al-Sallal received the enthusiastic support of President Nasser of Egypt and in turn began to provide assistance for the nationalist cause in neighbouring South Yemen. These developments caused the British grave concern and led to covert intervention in the North, covert intervention in which the SAS was to be heavily involved.

Towards the end of October 1962 Neil McLean, a Conservative MP with secret service connections, crossed into the YAR to establish contact with royalist rebels and report back to London on their prospects of overthrowing Sallal. This was the first step in a major covert operation that was to be organised by the founder of the SAS, David Stirling, together with old Arab hands like David Smiley, and a number of temporarily detached SAS personnel, most notably Johnny Cooper. The royalist rebels were, over a period of years, to be assisted with weapons, funds and advisers, successfully tying down a large number of Egyptian troops.[34]

This affair launched Stirling on a brief career as a mercenary captain, undertaking to provide ex-SAS personnel for regimes and causes believed to be compatible with British interests. In fact, he was to prove too much of a maverick as far as the Foreign Office was concerned. Later he was to dabble in British domestic politics, first of all through his Better Britain Society and subsequently becoming involved with TRUEMID, a rightwing organisation set up to fight leftwing influence in the trade union movement.[35]

While Johnny Cooper and his comrades were busy assisting the royalists in North Yemen, the British found themselves in increasing difficulties in the South. By the end of 1963 rebel tribesmen, supporting the Yemeni National Liberation Front (NLF), had taken control of the Radfan mountains and cut the strategic Dhala road. In January 1964 a Federal Army expedition had temporarily reopened the road but the decision was taken to mount a major British expedition to pacify the Radfan once and for all. One aspect of the operation involved the surprise seizure of an elevated feature known as 'Cap Badge'. A nine-man SAS patrol was despatched to reconnoitre the area and prepare a dropping zone for the paras who would then occupy Cap Badge. The plan seriously miscarried. The patrol was discovered and came under heavy attack. Only continuous air support kept the rebels at bay and gave the seven survivors of the fiasco the opportunity to break out under cover of darkness. Hunter jets supporting the patrol fired 127 rockets and 7,131 cannon rounds. This setback was compounded by later reports that the heads of the two dead SAS men had been paraded across the border in the YAR.[36]

Eventually, after heavy fighting, the Radfan rebels dispersed leaving the British in control of the area. To a considerable extent, however, the British success was illusory, comparable to American successes in Vietnam. Overwhelming force, including the use of air power against the local civilian population, had driven the guerrillas off but there was no effort to consolidate this success. One recent study of British counter-insurgency methods has commented on the fact that in the Radfan there was an 'absence of anything like a hearts and minds campaign'.[37] The military philosophy underlying the Radfan campaign was essentially punitive, with the local population regarded as an enemy to be punished and intimidated rather than as a source of potential collaborators to be won over. Later, when John Watts of 22 SAS was assigned to the Mishwari district, he asked the district officer for one or two reliable Arabs to act as guides and, much to his disgust, was told that there were no reliable Arabs.[38]

Meanwhile, the British faced an escalating campaign of urban terrorism in Aden itself where two competing nationalist organisations, the NLF and the Front for the Liberation of Occupied South Yemen (FLOSY), were both active. While never particularly effective militarily (in 1965 only five British soldiers were killed), this struggle was politically decisive. The British failure to defeat this threat was to doom the Federation to destruction. The problem was that the British had virtually no support among the Arab population and were forced to operate without any effective intelligence. The SAS contribution was the 'Keeni-Meeni' squads that operated along the same lines as Roy Farran's special police patrols in Palestine. Small mobile squads of SAS men capable of passing as Arabs patrolled Arab districts, making arrests and engaging in shoot-outs. There is every reason to believe that the bloody fratricidal conflict that developed between the NLF and FLOSY was at least in part fuelled by these activities with SAS men disguised as Arabs kidnapping and shooting activists from both factions. Sometimes lone soldiers in uniform acted as bait in an attempt to lure Arab gunmen into an attack so they could be captured or killed. The interrogation of prisoners was the only source of intelligence available and it was here that SAS interrogators perfected the methods of sensory deprivation that were to be considered legitimate in Aden but as torture in Northern Ireland. On one celebrated occasion an SAS undercover squad shot it out with an undercover squad from the Anglian regiment, seriously wounding two of them.[39]

The British counter-insurgency effort in South Yemen and Aden was doomed by the lack of any popular support for the Federation. They had failed to find a viable political settlement and instead had relied on the traditional rulers. These proved to be cardboard figures in the face of the rise of Arab nationalism and were swept away. Confronted with this political failure, the Labour government determined to cut its losses and withdraw.

The final humiliation for the British was the mutiny of the Federation Army and the Arab police, both heavily infiltrated by the NLF, in mid-June 1967. This cost the lives of 22 British soldiers and left the town of Crater temporarily in rebel hands. The British regained control but even the pretence of defeating the NLF was now gone. The withdrawal from the interior began. As the British pulled out of the sheikdoms, they fell to the NLF. The last British troops and officials finally left Aden on 29 November 1967 and the victorious rebels proclaimed the People's Republic of South Yemen. The counter-insurgency methods that had succeeded in Malaya, failed in South Yemen. Here the population was overwhelmingly behind the nationalist cause and the traditional rulers were weak and isolated, completely dependent on British support. The political settlement that underpinned British success in Malaya was not available in South Yemen and the result was a British humiliation despite the repression, the shooting and bombing, despite the efforts of the SAS.

Dhofar

The expulsion of the British from South Yemen created a crisis in neighbouring Dhofar, a province of the Sultanate of Oman. Here the Sultan had faced a guerrilla war conducted by the Dhofari Liberation Front since 1962. Now the revolutionary government in power in South Yemen began aiding the Dhofari rebels, who moved sharply to the left and in 1968 became the People's Front for the Liberation of the Occupied Arabian Gulf (PFLOAG). By the summer of 1970 they had control of about two-thirds of Dhofar and had penned the Sultan's forces into a coastal enclave around the capital, Salalah. Afraid that Dhofar was going to fall, on 23 July 1970 the British deposed Sultan Said bin Taimur and installed his son, Qaboos bin Said, a former British army officer, in his place. While the British had been quite content to back the reactionary Said in the 1950s and 1960s, now they recognised that a reforming Sultan would be necessary to stave off revolution. Dhofar and Oman could not be left to go the same way as South Yemen: there was oil at stake.

An SAS team under John Watts had already visited Dhofar to advise on the campaign against the rebels before the coup. They returned for a war that, according to Peter de la Billière, was 'the most important and far-reaching ever fought by the SAS. Our involvement ... rolled back and finally dissipated the tide of Communism which threatened to overwhelm Southern Arabia.'[40] According to Tony Jeapes, an SAS squadron commander in Dhofar, what followed was 'a model campaign ... one of the most successful campaigns of recent years'.[41]

The key to success lay in the pacification of the Jebel, the mountainous hinterland that ran parallel to the fertile coastal plain. This was the PFLOAG's stronghold. The intention was to establish a military presence there, cut the rebel lines of communication with South Yemen and consolidate military success through a 'hearts and minds' programme. To achieve these objectives Qaboos proceeded to modernise his armed forces and to increase dramatically expenditure on welfare and development projects. This was only made possible by the increasing oil revenues that were enriching the Sultanate. Without these resources, the war would certainly have been lost.

What part did the SAS play in the pacification of the Jebel? Operating as British Army Training Teams (BATT), they raised the firqats, a local militia that was recruited from surrendering or defecting rebels. The regime offered considerable inducements to change sides and the increasing radicalisation of the PFLOAG had alienated some of its supporters. The PFLOAG's hostility to Islam was used against them to good effect. The first firqat was ready for action in February 1971.

The 'hearts-and-minds' campaign initiated by the SAS was not a soft-hearted exercise in sentimentality, the work of uniformed social workers. Alongside the clinics and schools, the reforms and concessions, and the financial inducements that were intended to win over 'hearts', there was also the successful use of armed force to focus 'minds'. The inhabitants of the Jebel had to be convinced of the government's power, of the ability of the army to inflict punishment if assistance was provided for the rebels, of the fact that the Sultan was going to win. Only in this way would their 'minds' be won over. In Dhofar, this use of force involved the waging of war against the civilian population of those areas under rebel control, the bombing and shelling of villages, the destruction of crops and killing of livestock, the poisoning of wells.[42]

In October 1971 a mixed force of two companies of the Sultan's Armed Forces (SAF), two SAS squadrons and five firqats established a stronghold on the eastern Jebel. The following year, in April 1972, another stronghold was established at Sarfait on the Yemeni border. The government had taken the offensive. The PFLOAG responded with a daring counter-attack. In mid-July a force of heavily armed guerrillas, about 300 strong, equipped with two 75mm recoilless rifles, a rocket launcher and a number of mortars, attempted to overrun the seaside town of Mirbat, some 40 miles from Salalah. Taking advantage of monsoon cloud cover which would prevent air support, they hoped to capture the town before reinforcements could arrive. They did not intend to hold it but were going to execute collaborators before retreating back to the safety of the Jebel. This would be a humiliating setback for the Sultan and hopefully would force him to withdraw troops from the Jebel to defend against any further incursions.

Mirbat's defences consisted of two forts, one held by 25 gendarmes and the other by 30 soldiers, and a fortified BATT house occupied by Captain Mike Kealy and eight SAS. There was a 60-strong firqat billeted in the town itself. In the early hours of 19 July the guerrillas assaulted the gendarmes' fort but their attack was broken up by fire from the SAS house. Even after their initial failure, it still seemed likely that, given their numbers and firepower, the rebels would succeed. The weather let them down. The cloud cleared enough for jets to provide air support, pounding them with cannon and rocket fire, and for helicopters to fly in SAS reinforcements. The guerrillas were caught in the open and driven off. They had suffered a serious defeat in a five-hour battle in which two SAS and two gendarmes but perhaps as many as 70 guerrillas had been killed.

According to most accounts the battle of Mirbat was the turning point in the Dhofar war. John Watts described it as 'the beginning of the end' for the PFLOAG; Tony Jeapes considered it a milestone; and for Peter de la Billière it was 'a shattering reverse' for the guerrillas and 'the turning point' in the war.[43] In his history of the SAS, *The SAS: Savage Wars of Peace*, Anthony Kemp argues that 'the successful defence of Mirbat broke the back of adoo resistance ... the rebels had been decisively beaten'.[44] These claims are wild exaggerations. The PFLOAG had suffered a serious setback, but it was one they could certainly have recovered from were it not for the relentless pressure maintained in the Jebel by the SAF. Final victory in the war was not to be claimed until the end of 1975, three-and-a-half years away, and even then mopping up operations continued until the middle of 1976.

Why then the emphasis on the Mirbat engagement? Part of the reason is clearly the way that this particular incident emphasises the role of the SAS. The heroic stand by a young officer and his men, taking on a far superior force in an exotic Arabian setting is just the sort of thing to set the blood racing and bolster national pride. It summons up all the romance of empire. Mirbat has become another Rorke's Drift. In Michael Dewar's words, it 'is a wonderful tale of derring-do'.[45] Once again the SAS are shown to be the cream of British manhood. As well as this validation of British masculinity, focus on Mirbat also handily inverts the reality of the war whereby Goliath is able to successfully pass himself off as David. Instead of the hardpressed PFLOAG guerrillas being worn down by superior forces with complete air superiority, the dominant image of the war is one of a handful of SAS heroes holding off waves of Arab fanatics.

There was still to be much heavy fighting before the war was over. The brunt of this was to be borne by the Sultan's Armed Forces and an Iranian battle group that arrived as reinforcements at the end of 1973. The guerrillas' lines of communication were successfully cut by the construction of the Hornbeam Line and the Demavand Line and the Jebel was pacified. By October 1975 the last offensive was launched to clear the border area. After heavy fighting in the battle for the Shershitti cave complex the surviving rebels retreated across the border and the war was virtually over.[46]

While the importance of the battle of Mirbat may have been exaggerated, the SAS did play an important role in consolidating the Sultan's control over areas retaken from the rebels. They were the inspiration behind the Civic Aid programme that brought schools, clinics and mosques to the Jebel, built roads, established markets and introduced agricultural improvement schemes. By June 1975 35 wells had been drilled and 155 miles of road opened up. A measure of success was the growing number of defectors from the rebel camp and the growth of the firqat that by the end of the war numbered around 3,000 men. The SAS played a vital part in securing the rear, ensuring that the guerrillas never returned. This success was subsequently tarnished by revelations of embezzlement by SAS personnel that left the regiment with 'the smell of corruption hanging over it'.[47]

One important consequence of the Dhofar victory was that it ensured that the SAS had a post-colonial future as, in effect, mercenaries, hired out by the British government to friendly foreign regimes to advise and assist in the suppression of crime, unrest and rebellion. Since the end of the 1970s the SAS has appeared in this mercenary capacity as far afield as the Gambia, Colombia and Cambodia. This last and most notorious involvement saw the Thatcher government send SAS advisers to help train the Khmer Rouge guerrillas that were trying to overthrow the Vietnamese-backed Cambodian government. The British were doing the United States' dirty work because what the US Congress would baulk at, the British parliament would swallow.[48]

Into the 1980s: The SAS and Thatcherism

The coming to power of Margaret Thatcher in 1979 and the subsequent Conservative domination of British politics throughout the 1980s and most of the 1990s was accompanied by a popular militarism in which the SAS was to occupy a central place. It was at the forefront of 'the war against terrorism', a war which Thatcher was to make a personal crusade. This was to turn the SAS 'terminator', dressed in black, face masked, into a popular icon. In the Falklands War, which was to become one of the pillars upon which Thatcher's political success rested, instead of their role being played down and kept secret, as in Borneo and Dhofar, it was to be quite deliberately celebrated. The regiment began courting publicity, although as far as possible this was to be publicity on its own terms.

The SAS engagement with terrorism had begun in Aden with the 'Keeni-Meeni' squads, but this was to become a permanent commitment in the early 1970s. The key event here was the Munich Olympics shoot-out in September 1972. Seven armed Palestinians, members of Black September, took over a dormitory occupied by Israeli athletes in the Olympic village, demanding the release of political prisoners in Israel. The West German government gave them safe conduct out of the country, but then the police mounted a fumbled attack at the airport. In the ensuing battle all eleven Israeli hostages, the seven Palestinians and one West German policeman were killed. All this took place on live television. These events prompted a number of European governments, including the British, to establish specialised anti-terrorist units, ready to handle similar incidents. In Britain, the SAS set up its Counter-Terrorist team.[49]

SAS training in counter-terrorism has become, along with their selection process, an important part of the SAS myth. The Close Quarter Battle house or 'Killing House' where teams relentlessly practise hostage rescue and terrorist killing with live ammunition, has become well known, part of the regiment's folklore. Over the years a variety of celebrities and notables, politicians, members of the royal family, newspaper editors, have all experienced the fear and excitement of the Killing House. This practice has not been without casualties: an SAS sergeant has been accidentally shot dead during training and apparently the amount of lead in the environment of the Killing House has been considered dangerous to health.[50]

The rise of international terrorism in the 1970s was itself a myth propagated by Western governments and the media to justify authoritarianism at home and counter-revolution abroad. Terrorism never constituted a serious threat to any Western state, but its exorcism provided a wonderful opportunity for governments to demonise their enemies and pose as the protectors of the people. This was certainly the case as far as Britain was concerned.[51]

In December 1975 the mere suggestion of SAS intervention was celebrated in the media as enough to produce the surrender of four IRA members under siege in Balcombe Street in London. Two years later SAS involvement in the Mogadishu rescue proved once again that they were the best. In the early hours of 18 October 1977 a West German anti-terrorist team stormed a hijacked aircraft at Mogadishu airport in Somalia, killing three terrorists and capturing a fourth. Two SAS men were present as advisers.[52] The incident that established the regiment in the popular imagination as the frontline against terrorism was, however, the storming of the Iranian Embassy in Princes Gate on 5 May 1980. Overnight, the SAS became popular heroes. They emerged from the shadows to become symbols of Britain's national revival, of restored greatness. Thatcher embraced the regiment which throughout the 1980s was almost to become her personal bodyguard. She saw what they could do for her and they saw what she could do for them. The regiment was to prosper as never before. With an increasing involvement in domestic intelligence and security operations, the SAS became, according to one account, 'an adjunct of the Security Services' with an increasingly 'political role'.[53] Its future was absolutely secure. The British success at Princes Gate contrasted sharply with the humiliating failure of the US Delta Force hostage rescue attempt in Iran the month before.

Victory in the Falklands War in 1982 saved Thatcher from political oblivion. Her domestic unpopularity, presiding over the return of mass unemployment, seemed likely to doom her government, but the loss of the Falklands would have made this result absolutely certain. Instead the war and the wave of jingoism that accompanied it guaranteed her victory in the 1983 general election and made her position inside the Conservative Party virtually unassailable for another seven years! For the SAS, Operation Corporate, the retaking of the Falklands, was the first involvement in conventional warfare since 1945. There was a determination to push the regiment into the limelight, to grandstand, to ensure that this was remembered as the SAS's war. The publicity resulting from the storming of the Iranian Embassy was seen as being of considerable benefit to the regiment and now this could be magnified many times over by suitably daring headline-grabbing operations. The SAS played the major part in the recapture of South Georgia in April, but even here overconfidence, the belief that superfit troops could master any environment, nearly produced disaster. An SAS troop commanded by Captain John Hamilton was landed in the most appalling weather on the Fortuna Glacier, found the conditions too severe and so aborted its mission. Two helicopters were lost lifting them off. This was not the sort of publicity the regiment wanted.

The threat to the Task Force posed by the Argentinians' Etendard jets provided the SAS with the opportunity to strike a dramatic war-winning blow. Plans were prepared for a daring raid on the Rio Grande air base at Tierra del Fuego. Two Hercules transports would land at the base and the men of B Squadron would storm out to blow up the Etendards, destroy their Exocet missiles and kill their pilots. The SAS director, Peter de la Billière, was strongly behind this mission and persuaded Thatcher to give it the go-ahead even though a raid on the Argentinian mainland would have seriously escalated the conflict. The plan was not so well received by the men charged with carrying it out, indeed many of them thought they were being asked to take part in a suicide attack. One senior NCO, a veteran of the Aden, Borneo and Dhofar campaigns, was hostile enough to resign from the regiment and a number of others considered joining him. 'We're all going to die to fulfil an old man's fantasy' was one veteran's view. Dissension within the squadron was such that only hours before the operation was due to get underway, de la Billière relieved the squadron commander, a quite amazing state of affairs. A preliminary reconnaissance mission had already resulted in the loss of a helicopter in Chile and there is every likelihood that if the raid had gone ahead the result would have been a complete disaster. In the event it was called off after it was discovered that Argentinian radar cover was better than earlier believed. There must be a suspicion that this was an excuse to abandon a foolhardy mission that had already seriously damaged morale in the regiment. But disaster was still to strike. On 19 May a helicopter carrying 20 men from D squadron crashed into the Atlantic and all were drowned.[54]

The most important role that the SAS played in the Falklands was unfortunately not particularly glamorous. Even before the main invasion took place on 21 May, SAS teams had been secretly landed in East and West Falkland to gather intelligence on Argentinian strength and dispositions. They established themselves in covert hides, where some patrols were to remain for weeks, and relayed information back to the Task Force. One such outpost was discovered by Argentine troops on 10 June and its commander, the unfortunate Captain Hamilton of Fortuna Glacier fame, elected to fight to the death. Once he had been killed (only four days before the end of the war), his companion more sensibly surrendered.

The SAS did carry out a number of successful raids during the war: on Pebble Island on 14 May, destroying eleven aircraft, and a diversionary raid at Goose Green on 20 May to assist the San Carlos landings the following day. Colonel Michael Rose, the commander of 22 SAS, had proposed what would probably have been another suicide attack this time on Port Stanley, with SAS troops disembarking from helicopters, guns blazing, but this suggestion was never taken up. Once the main land force was ashore, the SAS role was one of mounting deep penetration patrols to provide the conventional units with intelligence of enemy strength and dispositions. There was one last attempt at grabbing the headlines on 13 June when the SAS attempted an overland attack on Port Stanley but was somewhat ignominiously driven off. The following day Argentinian forces surrendered.[55]

While the SAS might not have succeeded in making the war its own, it had in fact played an important supporting role, although the fear was always whether this was enough to justify its continued existence. More successful was its cultivation of the journalists accompanying the Task Force, in particular Max Hastings of the *Daily Telegraph*. On one occasion, he was actually given access to the SAS secret satellite link with London to file a report.[56] Nevertheless, the SAS had been overshadowed by the Paras and the Royal Marines. De la Billière was later to make sure this did not happen in the Gulf. Moreover the war had further cemented the regiment's relationship with Thatcher. The SAS could be relied on.

The War with the IRA

The war in Northern Ireland had its origins in the Catholic working-class revolt that challenged the Stormont regime in 1969. This revolt was provoked by the failure of promises to reform the sectarian state and the repression of protests against this failure. At the time, the Irish Republican Army (IRA) was not a military force. It had effectively abandoned the armed struggle and, after the pogroms, this led to the formation of a breakaway, the Provisional IRA. There had been an earlier IRA campaign against the North that had lasted from 1956 until 1962 before the republican leadership conceded defeat. On this occasion the IRA had lacked significant popular support, so much so that even the introduction of internment had not rallied the Catholic population to their cause. The situation was very different in 1969–70. The Provisionals launched their campaign at a time of popular revolt, when large numbers of young Catholic men and women were actively looking for a way to hit back against the Stormont regime and its British backers.

While the rise of the Provisionals made a military campaign inevitable, there was certainly no necessity for the war to prove as bloody and protracted as it in fact has. The Labour government had sent troops into Belfast and Derry in August 1969, determined to conciliate the Catholic population and to ensure even-handed treatment of the two communities. In reality, its reforms were too little too late and even so they met with fierce Protestant resistance. Even if Labour had remained in power in 1970 a military campaign was certain but not on the scale it was to assume. It was the Conservative government, which abandoned reform in favour of repression, that was to provide the Provisionals with the ideal environment for the launching of a guerrilla war. The security forces, troops and police went from an attempt at even-handedness to action to restore the authority of the discredited Unionist government. They cracked down on the insurgent Catholic working-class communities and met with fierce resistance. It was during these months that the Provisionals established themselves as the defenders and champions of the Catholic working class, consolidating a position in their communities that was strong enough to sustain them through a quarter of a century of struggle.[57]

The Falls Road curfew of 3–5 July 1970, which left five Catholics dead and many more injured, was the turning point. As Paddy Devlin, a staunch opponent of the Provisionals, complained, the actions of the British troops on the Falls Road and elsewhere had successfully turned the Catholic population 'from neutral or even sympathetic support for the military to outright hatred'.[58] The army resorted to colonial methods of counter-insurgency in what was formally part of the United Kingdom – with disastrous results. On the one hand it was legally and politically inhibited from the level of repression that had been possible in Malaya, Kenya or Aden, which contributed to its lack of success, while on the other it was repressive enough to alienate and antagonise the Catholic population, thereby contributing to the success of the Provisionals.

The introduction of internment in August 1971 produced a dramatic escalation in the level of conflict. Whereas in the four months before internment 4 soldiers, no policemen and 4 civilians had been killed, in the four months after 30 soldiers, 11 policemen and Ulster Defence Regiment members and 73 civilians were killed. The disaster was compounded by revelations that the SAS had carried out in-depth interrogation of a selected group of internees. These techniques, which amounted to torture, had been routinely used in other counter-insurgency campaigns, but in Northern Ireland provoked an outcry and seriously discredited the British government. The last major episode completing the alienation of the Catholic working class was the Bloody Sunday massacre on 30 January 1972. Soldiers of the Parachute Regiment attacked unarmed demonstrators in Derry, shooting 42 people, killing 14 of them. It is worth remembering that it was this incident that was to legitimise IRA bombing of British cities. Together internment and Bloody Sunday fuelled the Provisional offensive that was to bring Stormont down in March 1972.

What part did the SAS play in these events? Officially the SAS were not deployed in Northern Ireland until 1976, but this is little more than a convenient fiction. As the Provisional IRA's offensive escalated in the early 1970s, the army responded with the increasing use of undercover squads along the lines of the 'Keeni-Meeni' squads used in Aden. Brigadier Frank Kitson established a specialised covert unit, the Military Reaction Force (MRF) which carried out surveillance operations and was implicated in assassinations and sectarian attacks in Befast. SAS personnel on detachment were attached to the MRF. During this period SAS teams were on a number of occasions brought into the province for special operations but were withdrawn once these were accomplished. The in-depth interrogations that accompanied the introduction of internment were carried out by SAS interrogation teams. Later in 1974 when the surveillance unit, 14th Intelligence Company, was formed, it had SAS personnel attached. It was only in 1976, however, that the Labour government formally committed SAS troops to South Armagh. They had some initial success, even raiding across the border into the Republic, and at least temporarily disrupted the IRA's organisation in Armagh. The following year saw them deployed throughout the province. Between 1976 and 1978 the SAS killed ten people in Northern Ireland, seven IRA volunteers and three by-standers. The proportion of 'mistakes' was considered embarrassing and the regiment lowered its profile. The SAS did not kill anyone else in Northern Ireland until December 1983.

While the SAS might have become less lethal, the same could not be said of the RUC undercover squads active at this time which were SAS-trained and stiffened with ex-SAS personnel. In November and December 1982 these squads shot dead six unarmed men in three separate incidents. Clearly a shoot-to-kill practice had been put into effect, a practice that was condoned by the authorities even if there was no formal shoot-to-kill policy. The furore caused by these shootings and the subsequent Stalker affair led to the SAS once again taking on the role of executioner. Whereas in the period

1978–83 the SAS had successfully arrested IRA volunteers including those carrying weapons, between 1983 and 1985 they shot dead ten men including those not carrying weapons. As Mark Urban has pointed out, either the SAS had changed its practice or IRA members had suddenly started committing suicide by invariably making threatening hand movements when challenged, whether or not they were armed. In effect, the SAS were summarily executing IRA volunteers, shooting them down from ambush without warning – Big Boys' Rules! One reason for the change in SAS conduct suggested by Urban is that the unit had been effectively taken over by ex-paras, men more into macho violence than subtlety. This is only part of the story.[59]

It had become absolutely clear by the end of the 1970s that the security forces could contain but not defeat the IRA. In the 1980s the IRA were to kill 96 British soldiers compared with the 103 they killed in 1972. But while the IRA had been successfully contained, an end to the conflict would require a political settlement, including political concessions to the Catholic population that would be sufficient to undermine support for the armed struggle. Such concessions were made difficult to achieve by Protestant intransigence. In these circumstances, British strategy from the mid-1970s onwards became one of, as far as possible, lowering the level of conflict in the province. This strategy received a serious setback with the hunger strikes of 1980–1, which actually created the danger that Sinn Fein would become the dominant political force within the Catholic community. The hunger strikes gave republicanism a great boost, sustaining the IRA campaign throughout the 1980s. However reluctantly, the staunchly Unionist Margaret Thatcher was forced into a policy of concessions to the Catholics and to the Dublin government in order to counter this renewed threat. The result was the Anglo–Irish Agreement of November 1985 that outraged the Unionists and prepared the way for the eventual IRA ceasefire of August 1994. There is no doubt that while her government was committed to this policy of containment and concession, Thatcher herself still longed for a military solution. While the painfully protracted efforts at moving towards a political settlement continued, efforts dependent on a low level of conflict, the SAS continued summarily executing IRA volunteers without any regard for the impact this might have had on the political situation. The SAS was continuing to alienate Catholic opinion when the whole British strategy was to conciliate it. From this point of view, the SAS can be seen as part of the problem rather than as part of the solution in Northern Ireland.

Two incidents demonstrate this. First the Loughall ambush of 8 May 1987. Eight IRA volunteers attacked an unmanned police station and were all shot dead by the SAS, together with a passing motorist. Certainly these men could have been arrested while they were preparing their attack but the decision was taken to let it go ahead and to kill them. Three of the volunteers were finished off after they had been wounded and captured. This was celebrated as a famous victory by the British media, but while it was a serious blow to the IRA it provided the republican movement with fresh martyrs and raised the level of tension in the province. This was even more true of the Gibraltar shootings of 6 March 1988 when the SAS killed three unarmed volunteers in what amounted to a public execution sanctioned by Downing Street. As far as the Provisionals' working-class supporters were concerned this was plain murder. Ten days later when the three were being buried at Milltown Cemetery in Belfast a lone loyalist gunman attacked the mourners, killing three more people and injuring another fifty. When one of these three victims was being buried on 19 March, two undercover soldiers were seized by the mourners, handed over to the IRA and shot. This is a classic demonstration of the way the undercover war feeds on itself. If the three IRA volunteers in Gibraltar had been arrested, then subsequent events that dramatically raised the level of tension and left another five people dead would never have taken place. Thatcher's response to these events was to press for a return to full-scale repression with the banning of Sinn Fein and the reintroduction of internment. This would have meant an end to the Anglo–Irish Agreement and an escalation in the level of violence in pursuit of an illusory military victory. She did not get her way.[60] In the period from 1990 to early 1992, the SAS killed eleven more IRA volunteers, the last four being shot dead from ambush during an attack on an RUC station at Coalisland on 16 February. The Coalisland shootings were to be the last SAS killings in Northern Ireland. By now Thatcher had fallen from power and the new prime minister, John Major, withdrew their carte blanche as part of the process leading up to the IRA ceasefire.[61]

One other area of SAS activity about which we know little for certain is SAS involvement with the loyalist paramilitaries. While the security forces' concentration on the IRA left the loyalists with a comparatively free hand to wage war on the Catholic community, this was not the end of the matter. There was British involvement with the loyalist murder gangs, an involvement in which SAS personnel, on detachment, certainly played a part. A series of loyalist attacks on members and supporters of the Irish National Liberation Army (INLA) in 1980–1 were so professionally carried out as to suggest SAS involvement in training those responsible. On 4 June 1980 John Turnly was assassinated by Protestant gunmen, one of whom at his trial claimed that he was working for the SAS, naming a Sergeant Aiken and a Corporal McGow as his contacts. The attack on Turnly was followed on 26 June by the assassination of Miriam Daly and on 15 October by the assassination of Ronnie Bunting and Noel Lyttle. The following year, on 16 January 1981, Protestant gunmen seriously wounded Bernadette and Michael McAliskey in a botched assassination attempt. Interestingly they were actually arrested at the scene by SAS soldiers, one of whom saved Bernadette McAliskey's life by applying first aid.[62] Later revelations concerning the British agent, Brian Nelson, showed the extent of British penetration and manipulation of the Protestant paramilitaries.[63] The activities of the loyalist murder gangs (the Ulster Volunteer Force and the Ulster Freedom Fighters) in the early 1990s played a significant part in bringing about the IRA ceasefire of August 1994. By this time the sectarian dimension to the conflict was coming to predominate with Protestant gunmen killing more people than the IRA. The political road seemed more attractive to Gerry Adams and the republican leadership than prolonging a struggle which offered no prospect of victory. What the final outcome will be remains to be seen.

The Gulf War

The war against the IRA was vitally important in building up the SAS's terminator image: these were the men who could defeat terrorism, however inaccurate and misleading this notion might in fact be. Their reputation fed off popular frustration at successive British governments' failure to end the conflict and off a very real horror at the casualties caused by the IRA bombings both in Britain and in Northern Ireland. While government might appear impotent, the SAS, unrestrained by legal restraints or liberal inhibitions, could deal out justice. Even this potent myth of the SAS avenger was to be overshadowed by the extraordinary publicity the regiment was to receive during the Gulf War, largely courtesy of its former director, General Peter de la Billière.

De la Billière was preparing for his retirement (he had actually taken a course on butchery!) when Iraqi forces occupied Kuwait. In *Storm Command*, his account of the Gulf War, he recalled how the news 'set my adrenalin racing ... this seemed to be a task for which my whole life had prepared me'. He determined to seize the chance to end his career with a full-scale war.[64] A key factor in his appointment to command British forces was Margaret Thatcher's great admiration for him. In her memoirs, she remembers that she wanted 'a fighting general' and insisted on de la Billière against Ministry of Defence opposition. She had known him since the Iranian Embassy siege and the Falklands War and had complete confidence in his readiness to commit his forces to battle. Her admiration for him was wholeheartedly reciprocated and her downfall came as a great shock to him. He sent her a personal letter of commiseration.[65]

He makes clear in his account that he intends to 'demonstrate the importance of individual human beings in warfare'.[66] Despite all the technology, wars are still fought and won by the men and women who put their lives on the line. In fact, what we get is another exercise in special forces' egoism with the exploits of the SAS taking up as much space as the rest of the air, land and sea forces under his control put together. There was to be no repeat of the Falklands: the Gulf was to be the SAS's war. This did not derive just from his obsessive commitment to the regiment that had been his life, but also from the nature of the Gulf War. The conflict was so one-sided, the American technological advantage so great, that when the land battle actually came, it was little more than a massacre, more reminiscent of Omdurman than El Alamein. He describes how his 4th Brigade in the 100 hours of the land offensive knocked out more than 60 Iraqi tanks, 90 armoured personnel carriers, 37 artillery pieces, and captured over 5,000 prisoners. All this without suffering a single fatality from Iraqi fire. It is very difficult to turn such a battle into a celebration of heroism, endurance and self-sacrifice. De la Billière does not even try. Instead he focuses on the exploits of the SAS patrols that operated behind Iraqi lines. Here they played a part in the hunt for the Scud missile launchers that were targeting Israel, very much a politically-inspired sideshow, but one allowing for plenty of heroics and daring. The actual effectiveness of this Scud hunt is hotly disputed.[67]

A proposal that an SAS squadron should parachute into Iraqi-occupied Kuwait City, jumping from a Hercules at between 400 and 600 feet, was never put into effect. This would have been a suicide mission, but would certainly have got the regiment plenty of publicity! De la Billière was successful, however, in persuading the US commander, General Norman Schwarzkopf, a man extremely sceptical with regard to the use of special forces, to agree to patrols and raids behind Iraqi lines. Once the SAS was involved, the US Delta Force soon followed.

Operating behind Iraqi lines, the British were still the underdog, overcoming vastly superior odds by sheer guts. This was where British manhood could show what it was made of, where cause for national pride could be found in abundance. Here British superiority over the 'ragheads', as the Iraqis were known, could be established without the interference of technology. Whereas the entire land offensive is covered by de la Billière in 23 pages of text, the heroic exploits of one lone SAS corporal, Chris Ryan, take up 15 pages. Separated from the rest of his lost patrol, Bravo Two Zero, he fought his way to safety. While there is no disputing the courage and endurance of this particular soldier, what is of interest is the ideological purpose his feat is made to serve. After one of the most one-sided wars in modern history in which Iraqi troops endured weeks of bombardment followed by a devastating and overwhelming attack that left perhaps 100,000 of them dead, the image we are left with is of the lone British soldier, hungry and cold, being hunted across the most difficult terrain by blood-thirsty Iraqis yet making good his escape. The Gulf War is redeemed, transformed from a massacre into a tale of individual heroism. And, of course, de la Billière's own determined effort at making the war the SAS's war has been reinforced by the enormous success of Andy McNab's account of the lost patrol, *Bravo Two Zero* and Chris Ryan's own account *The One That Got Away*.[68] Moreover, this SAS aggrandisement actually conceals the military lessons that the West learned from the war, lessons which had to do with air power and armoured warfare and nothing to do with special forces. The American commander, General Norman Schwarzkopf, does not even mention the SAS in his account of the war.[69]

CHAPTER 2

Telling it like it was: the SAS as Autobiography

Military memoirs are a literary form that has received little critical attention, at least in part, one suspects, because the experiences recounted are so uncongenial to most students of literary and cultural studies. This is unfortunate, because it involves the neglect of a significant, even a central component of British national culture, of British national identity. The military memoir has been throughout both the nineteenth and twentieth centuries a consistently successful publishing endeavour. Moreover, in recent times, it has been given an enormous boost by the Falklands War and this shows no signs of abating.

This literature of soldiering and war is particularly important because of the way in which it identifies militarism and imperialism as central concerns of British national identity. They are not peripheral matters that can be treated as marginal, eccentric, or be ignored, but are at the heart of Britishness. While the police might well be generally unarmed at home, throughout the rest of the world British influence and power always rested on the bayonet and the gallows, on the machine gun and the bomber aircraft. This paradox often goes unnoticed, let alone explored.

What we are concerned with here is one particular body of military memoirs that have been published since the end of the Second World War: those written by officers and men of the SAS. They are the recollections of elite soldiers, a chosen few who supposedly embody all that is best in the British warrior, in British masculinity. Whatever else might be wrong with the country, however low Britain's international standing might sink, however much the economy might decline relative to other countries, the SAS are still regarded as the best soldiers in the world. They are capable of extraordinary feats of endurance, of mastering any environment no matter how inhospitable, of triumphing over any odds. Their courage, skill, adaptability and ruthlessness – their professional effectiveness – is legendary; they are respected and feared by friend and foe alike.

The publishing history of SAS memoirs falls into two distinct phases: the period immediately after the Second World War and the period since Margaret Thatcher took office in 1979. A number of wartime memoirs were published after 1945 and into the 1950s, celebrating the British capacity for unconventional warfare and its contribution to the liberation of North Africa and Western Europe. Thereafter the regiment lapsed into silence and secrecy, going discreetly about its counter-revolutionary work from Malaya to Aden, from Borneo to Oman. All this changed quite dramatically with the storming of the Iranian Embassy in May 1980. Suddenly, the SAS were publicly celebrated as a symbol of British renewal, as an embodiment of all that was best about Britain. There followed a flood of memoir literature that continues to this day. This second phase saw memoirs looking back over the whole postwar period as well as dealing with the events of the 1980s and 1990s. Moreover, many of the memoirs of the Second World War period were republished and some hitherto unpublished accounts at last emerged. This remarkable celebration of British militarism has gone largely unremarked.

For our purposes the memoirs will be considered in three distinct groups although inevitably there is some overlap. First, there are the memoirs about the regiment's exploits during the Second World War. Inevitably these are informed by the extent to which this was a war of liberation fought against an enemy of unprecedented brutality and murderousness, as well as a clash of empires. In this conflict, the SAS was always very much the underdog, operating behind enemy lines, fighting alongside the resistance and risking torture and execution if captured. This literature often pays tribute to the courage and fortitude of the common people in the face of the most fierce repression. It reflects, in however mediated a form, the notion of the Second World War as a popular, democratic war of liberation fought against Nazi tyranny.

Some of these wartime memoirs overlap with the second category which is made up of memoirs of the colonial and conventional wars fought since 1945. These are memoirs of counter-revolution, of imperial retreat and retrenchment, of enforcing the New World Order. The change that took place in the role played by the SAS in the Second World War and subsequently is perhaps best demonstrated if we consider their part in the liberation of Belsen in 1945 alongside their part in helping to train the forces of the Khmer Rouge in the 1980s. The wheel had gone full circle. From being participants in the crusade against Nazism, the SAS became counter-revolutionary mercenaries, prepared to go anywhere and kill anyone. This change is reflected in the tone of the memoirs.

The third and last category are memoirs of the war in Northern Ireland. This deserves separate consideration because it involves accounts of the most protracted postwar conflict fought in part of the United Kingdom. Here the SAS takes on an enemy that continues to strike at the very heart of Britain. Both these last two categories of literature are, it must be insisted, a product of the 1980s, of the fascination with military prowess that was an important feature of the Thatcher years and after.

All of these memoirs will be looked at for the way in which they construct notions of masculinity and male camaraderie, the way in which they celebrate the thrill, the 'high' of combat, the way in which they contribute to the construction of notions of Britishness, and, of course, for what they have to say about the conduct of Britain's wars. The changing character of the memoirs reflects changes in British politics and society, in British self-perception: from the moment of triumph and liberation in 1945 to the desperate clutching at military reputation that has been a feature of the 1980s and 1990s.

The Appeal of War

One point worth considering before we proceed to a discussion of the memoirs themselves is the appeal of war. While the conventional wisdom is that war is hell, the uncomfortable fact remains that there are significant numbers of men who are irresistibly attracted to it. In his important study, *The Warriors*, J. Glenn Gray discusses the various attractions that war holds for some men. The attraction of war as spectacle should, he insists, never be underestimated. While much of war is ugly, there is also colour and movement, variety, panoramic sweep, sometimes even momentary proportion and harmony. The spectacle of battle can overawe men and hold them in a spell, lost in its display of power and magnitude. Astonishment, wonder and awe are part of our being and war offers them what he describes as 'an exercise field par excellence'.

The second appeal is the experience of comradeship. While danger certainly heightens any experience, in war it has a communal significance that binds men together in a way that nothing else can. Many veterans, he argues, are prepared to admit that the communal experience of combat was the high point in their lives. Despite all the horror, the exhaustion, the discomfort, the stress, communal participation in the chances of battle has its unforgettable side, a feeling of liberation that it is hard for anyone who has not experienced it themselves to understand. In combat, comradeship becomes an ecstasy. Our species has, he contends, a longing for community but at the same time an awkwardness about achieving it. The extreme experience that war involves brings men together in a way that no other experience does, enables them to discover what he somewhat lyrically calls the mysteries of communal joy. Comradeship reaches its peak in battle. This appeal is, of course, routinely recognised in studies of men in combat, but J. Glenn Gray is its poet.

Both of these first two appeals can be satisfied in other ways, but there is a third appeal, the delight in destruction that can only be satisfied in war. Many men become possessed by a lust to kill and destroy when in combat, a lust that can become an appetite. The army introduces young men, many of whom never suspected the existence of such passions within them, to what he calls the mad excitement of destruction. They are taught to enjoy killing and learn to take delight and satisfaction in it, a delight that often has sexual overtones. Not all men by any means experience this particular appeal of war, but enough do to keep the elite military units supplied with soldier killers. While J. Glenn Gray suggests that this lust lies dormant within certain men, merely waiting to be awakened, almost like a biological drive, my own emphasis would be on a historical understanding of the construction of masculinity and of the effect of socialisation into military institutions. How else to explain the continual involvement of the British in armed conflict right across the globe for the past two hundred and more years, while there are other countries that have hardly ever gone to war in the same period?[1]

This exploration of the appeal of war is a necessary starting point for the consideration of the SAS memoirs and some of the issues raised will be taken up as we proceed. One important distinction needs to be made here, however, between the memoirs of the Second World War and those of the post-1945 period. The former were often written by men temporarily enlisted in the army for the duration of that conflict while the later memoirs are written by professional soldiers who have made the regiment their life. In the early memoirs the first two of J. Glenn Gray's list of the attractions of combat are most evident whereas in some of the later memoirs the third element surfaces. This is only to be expected; after all the SAS today consists of soldier killers par excellence.

The Good War

There can be little doubt that an important part of the appeal of the wartime SAS memoirs derived from the fact that here, during an industrialised war fought by mass armies, were men engaged in daring adventures taking on overwhelming odds. Sweeping out of the desert in their jeeps, machine guns blazing, these men fought a wild and exciting war in which individual courage and expertise still made an effective difference to the outcome of operations. In this sort of irregular warfare, the individual still counted, was still identifiable, and his contribution left its mark whether it was in the shape of a blown-up aircraft, a burning lorry or a derailed train.

The SAS were definitely not cannon fodder, not part of an anonymous mass army. For them war was still an adventure.

There was a strong element of self-indulgence in all this. The opening words of John Hislop's memoir, *Anything but a Soldier* capture this: '"The great thing about the 1939–45 war was that everyone did what they liked", Harry d'Avigdor-Goldsmid once remarked to me, and there is truth in his observation.'[2] Some, like Hislop, decided that they wanted to serve in private armies undertaking exciting operations behind enemy lines, and the SAS and a variety of other special forces were there to satisfy this particular inclination. Of course, this particular view of the war, that one did what one liked, was only applicable to officers and even then only to officers with elite backgrounds. Harry Challenor comments in his memoirs on the way the SAS seemed to attract more than its share of aristocrats: 'they seemed to favour the swashbuckling informality of the SAS'.[3] It was a very different experience from that of the great majority of service men and women and this difference was in good part the origin of its fascination for a postwar readership.

Hislop, who was attached to the SAS in early 1944 and served in France, describes the regiment as 'an entertaining organisation' and emphasises that 'all the time I served with the SAS I never quite overcame the impression that I belonged to a species of banditti'.[4] Many other memoirs make a similar point: Fraser McLuskey, chaplain to the SAS in France, felt that they were 'leading this Robin Hood existence' while Derrick Harrison, also serving in France, felt like 'a modern D'Artagnon'.[5]

One of the attractions of this outlaw existence was the close relations that existed between officers and men, the extent to which the barriers of rank and class were relaxed. Roy Farran, on joining the SAS, found 'a pleasant sense of intimacy with the men, who were all of a higher standard than any other ranks I had met in the past two years'.[6] This intimacy operated both ways, with Harry Challenor, a working-class corporal, writing of how he and Farran 'became close friends – a situation only possible in a freebooter outfit such as ours – and we have remained so ever since'.[7]

This intimacy is celebrated in a quite remarkable evocation of wartime masculine camaraderie by Malcolm James Pleydell, medical officer with the SAS in North Africa. He describes the scene in a secret desert encampment behind enemy lines:

> It was our custom to linger over our evening meal; waiting until the red sun had dipped behind the flat rim of the desert; watching the transparent colours as they throbbed and pulsed and died away ... this was the occasion we had been looking forward to with silent longing throughout the heat of the day.

How pleasant to sit round the cook's lorry, or perched on the
escarpment slope nearby ... As a rule we sat talking and telling
stories until somewhere around nine or ten ... But one evening,
I remember we broached an extra jar of rum; soon there was a
party in progress ... A memory such as this remains very clear
... A memory of the atmosphere of men: the deep jumble of
voices; the sound of a laugh that seemed to hang in the air for
a fraction of a second before it was lost in the night; the yellow
flame of a match lighting up a man's bearded face, throwing
the features into sharp relief, sketching in the lines in deep
shadows; the brighter glow of ruby red as he drew on his
cigarette. The men themselves; some hunched forward, talking
eagerly; some joking; some lying back quietly. One huge fellow
bare chested, sitting facing us on the floorboards of the lorry,
with his thick legs dangling over the tailpiece – a self-appointed
master of ceremonies. Another coming round with the jar of
rum ... As it grew darker the men began to sing ... We had formed
a small solitary island of voices; voices which faded and were
caught up by the wilderness. A little cluster of men singing in
the desert. An expression of feeling that defied the vastness of
its surroundings.

Even the three German prisoners-of-war join in the singing! He
might well ask, 'Were any men as happy as these?'

This is a marvellous example of J. Glenn Gray's 'comradeship
as ecstasy'. The deliberate and skilful evocation of what Pleydell
calls 'the atmosphere of men' is a constant concern of his *Born of
the Desert* memoir. The camaraderie of the desert, at risk but safe
behind enemy lines, men without women, bound together by a
shared solidarity that embraces even their prisoners. This is an
experience that he cherishes and can summon up as if it were
yesterday. A time of happiness! He actually opens the book with
a telling quotation from William Morris's *The Dream of John Ball*:
'Forsooth, brothers, fellowship is heaven, and lack of fellowship is
hell: fellowship is life, and lack of fellowship is death: and the
deeds that ye do upon the earth, it is for fellowship's sake that ye
do them.' His book is an overwhelming endorsement of this
proposition.

Despite his enthusiasm for this man's life, Pleydell does actually
present a critique of it in his memoir. He uses the viewpoint of a
female nurse who tells him over a drink what is wrong with men
in the desert. What they lack is 'family life'. Young men without
their families to keep them in line are like 'a lot of overgrown
schoolboys ... only instead of a sports blazer you've got a uniform'.
They are all engaged in an act, something they did not do at home,

and if anyone tried, he 'would soon have it taken out of you if you tried to'. He admits to 'knowing full well she was right'.[8]

The war changed once the Allies returned to Europe. Here the SAS found themselves fighting alongside the resistance, saw at first hand Nazi reprisals against the civilian population and if they were captured were themselves tortured and shot. This was a much grimmer war, imposing a much greater strain on the participants. The use of Benzedrine became routine.

SAS activities in Italy and France inevitably put the civilian population at risk because of the German resort to reprisals. These were often horrifyingly brutal. Ian Wellstead, in his account of France in the summer of 1944, describes how German troops punished the village of Dun-les-Places. They hanged the curé from his own belfry and herded another 20-odd men into the church courtyard where they were shot and mutilated with hand grenades. The bodies were left to lie there under guard for two days as a warning. Johnny Cooper remembered how after a successful ambush, German troops had carried out 'the inevitable reprisals', burning down half the village of Montsauche. They shot the mayor, the curé and eleven others, throwing the bodies into the church before setting fire to it. A number of women were raped. This was a different kind of war from that fought in North Africa.[9]

Sometimes, too rarely, the tables were turned. On one celebrated occasion, Derrick Harrison with two heavily armed jeeps drove into the village of Les Ormes where the SS were in the middle of shooting hostages. They took the Germans completely by surprise, killing or wounding some 60 of them, before escaping with the loss of only one man themselves. Most of the hostages escaped in the confusion. This sort of heroic exploit is, of course, very much the stuff of the SAS legend.[10]

One feature of the SAS memoirs of the European theatre is the respect and admiration for the heroism of the civilian population that they regularly give voice to. Harry Challenor, for example, admits that he had been contemptuous of Italians until he found himself on the run behind the German lines in Italy. He describes an incident where they were hidden and fed by an Italian farmer and his wife. They were 'served up great mounds of steaming spaghetti which we washed down with glasses of wine, before mopping our plates with great chunks of still warm bread'. This was his first experience of the Italian hospitality which he was to meet with time and time again. Ordinary people, without any apparent thought for their own safety, provided food and shelter, risking execution and the destruction of their homes and livelihoods. His opinions underwent what he describes as 'a radical transformation': 'I shall never forget their kindness and the fact that I owe my survival to them.' They were 'incredibly brave' and he puts the poor performance of the Italian army in North Africa down to the fact that their hearts were not really in fascism.[11]

Roy Farran tells a similar story. 'It is impossible', he wrote, 'to explain what risks these poor people took for Allied soldiers.' If they had been caught assisting the Allies their homes would have been destroyed and they risked execution. In his experience, it was the same in Greece, in Italy and in France: 'Always the poor, the very poor, would share their last crumb.'[12]

Sometimes these reminiscences have a poignancy, a sadness, that brings home both the terrible waste of war and the everyday heroism that it gives occasion for. Both John Hislop and Christopher Sykes describe an incident when they were hiding out in the French countryside with German search parties all around. A car full of Gestapo arrived at a nearby house and dragged the occupants, a woman and her two daughters, one only a young girl, out in the pouring rain for questioning. Despite her fear for herself and her children, the woman did not reveal their hiding place. The Germans set fire to the house and left the family standing in the teeming rain. There was nothing they could do for them.[13]

At this point it will perhaps be useful to consider in more detail one particular memoir, Roy Farran's *Winged Dagger*, a minor classic of war literature. By a man with a considerable reputation for personal courage and military prowess, Farran's often self-deprecatory account reveals his own fears, mistakes and inadequacies at the same time as telling a gripping tale of high adventure. The memoir is also interesting because of how it points the way from the concerns of the Second World War to the concerns of the succession of colonial wars that followed.

Farran began the war as a junior officer in the King's Own Hussars, serving as a tank commander in North Africa and in Crete. His account of the German parachute assault on Crete is quite shocking in its honesty. Farran describes a confused and chaotic campaign which seems to have quite overwhelmed him. War, he insists, is 'a bitter evil business having nothing to do with God'. He describes how on one occasion he ordered his gunner to open fire on what he thought was a German coming down the road only to discover that it was a woman civilian: 'She came on and I could hear her screaming ...' On another occasion, he ordered his gunner to shoot three paratroopers who were trying to surrender. Most telling, however, is his account of an attack on the town of Mallarme. According to regulations, the officer's tank should never lead an attack, but Farran habitually ignored this. This time, however, he felt sure the first tank into the town was doomed and so he asked his squadron leader if he could go first knowing he would be refused. Instead Sergeant Skedgewell took his tank in first and was killed together with his crew. Farran is remarkably frank: 'I should have been in the leading tank. Instead there was Skedgewell dead and his pretty wife waiting at home. I felt as if I had murdered him.' His misery was compounded when they came under air attack. His tank was disabled, and he ran for it: 'My terror of aeroplanes had turned me into a frightened, quivering woman.' Although he does not make this point himself, much of his later career seems to have involved redeeming his failure in Crete.

Farran was captured, shipped off to Greece as a prisoner-of-war, escaped and, with the help of the Greek resistance, successfully made it back to North Africa. Here in March 1943 he joined the SAS. The rest of the memoir provides exciting accounts of daring raids and ambushes, narrow escapes and desperate pursuits, behind enemy lines in France and Italy.

Let us look at his description of the attack that he led on the German garrison in the French town of Chatillon at the end of August 1944. His men ambushed a column of German lorries driving into the town:

> The battle was on. Sergeant Vickers, whose jeep was in the middle of the road, allowed them to approach to within twenty yards before he opened fire. The first five trucks, two of which were loaded with ammunition, were brewed up and we were treated to a glorious display of fireworks. A motor cycle combination skidded off the bridge into the river ... All the sounds of war echoed in the streets – the rattle of the Brens, the rasp of the Vickers, the whine of bullets bouncing off the walls, and in the background, the stonk-stonk of the mortars. I got a Bren myself and balancing it on a wall, hosepiped the German column with red tracers.

While all this is going on he sees 'a pretty girl with long black hair and wearing a bright red frock put her head out of a top window and give me the "V" sign'. She smiles at him. When he finally orders the withdrawal, he waves farewell to her.

This is a quite remarkable account of a ferocious battle that lasted some three hours and in which perhaps a hundred German soldiers were killed. Farran's narrative turns it into something approaching a romantic episode, portraying himself very much as the devil-may-care hero, tormenting the enemy and then taking leave of a beautiful woman to make good his escape. The battle is an exciting, exhilarating affair, heightened, as far as Farran is concerned, by the presence of the young woman. It would have been very easy to continue in this romantic vein, but grim reality intrudes. They split up into small groups and try to slip away, but are closely pursued by the Germans. Farran and his companions have a number of narrow escapes that leave them scared and exhausted. At last, under heavy machine gun fire, they crawl across a ploughed field to be picked up by a jeep and driven to safety. He confesses that it was almost too much for him, struggling across the field 'with the bullets kicking up great clods of earth all around'. 'Never', he goes on, 'have I been so frightened and so incapable of helping myself.' Heroism, Farran makes clear, consists not just in the daring ambush, but also in the gruelling pursuit, in withstanding the pressures of being hunted. He goes on to admit to an 'awful feeling of nervousness when hiding'; he was worried that he 'was getting windy ... I hoped and prayed the others would not think that I was scared'. When their area of operations was finally overrun by American forces, they were all overjoyed, safe at last.[14]

Farran continued to drive himself. In December 1944 he took a squadron back to Italy to carry out operations behind enemy lines. Although ordered to remain at headquarters, in March 1945 he parachuted in to command Operation Tombola. His SAS troops fought alongside the Italian resistance, many of them Communists, in the closing stages of the war. In his account of this particular campaign, he describes how once the Germans were finally forced into retreat, the partisans marched openly along the road, singing resistance songs and waving red flags. They were 'as triumphant as men could be'. Farran was recognised and cheered, with the partisans throwing their hats in the air. 'Never had I been so popular among the Communists,' he wrote. As far as the partisans were concerned, he was 'a partisan chief sharing their honour'. The fact that 'the real battle had been won by regular troops, by the guns and the tanks and the aircraft of a set-piece battle' was neither here nor there. The partisans might have only had a nuisance value but they 'were entitled to their share of glory ... the people had risen and won their freedom'. He joined in singing the partisan songs: 'Avanti populo bandiera rossa'.[15]

This enthusiasm for his Communist allies, for the war as a war of liberation, is already being questioned in the pages of *Winged Dagger*. The concerns of empire are already becoming apparent. When Farran writes of the severity with which the French repressed nationalist protest in Morocco, he wonders whether similar methods might not have been appropriate when dealing with the Jews in Palestine after the war. His generosity towards the Italian Communists does not extend towards the Greek Communists. He writes of them with the most incredible venom, obviously in response to the fighting that took place in Athens in December 1944 between British troops and the resistance. Indeed, he expresses his relief that not all the Greeks who had helped him escape in 1941 were Communist sympathisers. Farran goes on to give a brief and uninformative account of his notorious activities in charge of an undercover police unit in Palestine, an account that recent editions of *Winged Dagger* leave out.[16]

One last point about the SAS wartime memoirs: how much importance do they ascribe to their activities? Farran, as we have just seen, considered Operation Tombola, one of their most successful wartime operations, as a burr beneath the German saddle, an irritant, while the decisive battle was fought out between the great mass armies. What of the other accounts?

Pleydell makes clear that his main concern in writing his memoir was 'to show the sort of family life' there was in the SAS, 'to recapture those moments of good fellowship'. He acknowledges that to some, while it might be diverting to read of how they dashed about the desert in jeeps like a crowd of overgrown schoolboys, the question remains, 'what precisely were your results?' He puts his emphasis on the destruction of 400 enemy aircraft 'which probably exerted an influence on the course of the desert war'. Later on in Western Europe, SAS operations 'assisted materially in the rapid advance of the Allied armies'.[17] Certainly they had an effect, an effect disproportionate to their numbers, but their war was always peripheral to the decisive clash of great armies.

Pleydell's view contrasts quite dramatically with that advanced by the artist, John Verney, who served in the SBS in the Mediterranean and took part in Operation Swann, an attack on airfields in Sardinia. He recalls a general at the War Office telling him that none of the private armies had contributed anything to Allied victory. All they did was

> offer a too-easy, because romanticised, form of gallantry to a few anti-social irresponsible individualists who sought a more personal satisfaction from the war than that of standing their chance, like proper soldiers of being bayoneted in a slit-trench or burnt alive in a tank.

He admits: 'I thought he was perfectly right ... so far from being tough little heroes, we were simply escapists'. His disillusion extended to the belief that even the damage Operation Swann had caused to the Germans on Sardinia could have been accomplished in ten seconds by a flight of Spitfires.[18]

Whatever the arguments about the SAS contribution to Allied victory, the fact is that postwar interest in the SAS wartime memoirs that reflected what Verney describes as their romanticised form of gallantry, was a form of escape from the realities of modern industrialised warfare. They were tales of high adventure, where individual heroism made a difference in a war decided by the clash of great armies. What is particularly interesting is that most of these memoirs were to be either republished or published for the first time in the aftermath of the Iranian Embassy siege and the Falklands War. There seems to have developed a taste for tales of daring exploits and military prowess. This was to prompt the publication of a growing number of postwar SAS memoirs culminating (so far) in the tremendous success of Michael Paul Kennedy's *Soldier 'I' SAS*, Andy McNab's *Bravo Two Zero* and *Immediate Action*, Chris Ryan's *The One That Got Away*, Harry McCallion's *Killing Zone*, Peter de la Billière's *Looking for Trouble*, Peter 'Yorky' Crossland's *Victor Two* and Jenny Simpson's *Biting the Bullet: Married to the SAS*.

A Counter-revolutionary Elite

The success of the SAS memoir in the 1980s and 1990s was not an accident. It was very much part of the Thatcher government's encouragement of popular militarism, a spin-off of the Falklands factor. The phenomenon works on two levels: first it demonstrates that a strong, ruthless and determined state is necessary to protect the British people against the threat of terrorism and aggression, both domestic and international and, second, it celebrates a particular warrior masculinity which the British can be seen to excel in. The spectacle of black-clad SAS gunmen storming the Iranian Embassy evoked in many people a perverse national pride. The British had found a way of dealing with the threat of terrorism and people could sleep soundly in their beds. The irony is, of course, that the Conservative governments that encouraged and benefited from this popular militarism at the same time dramatically cut back Britain's military establishment. Consistency has never been a requirement of ideology.

The most senior memoir of the postwar SAS published so far is Peter de la Billière's *Looking for Trouble*. This is very much an 'official' account written by a member of the SAS establishment, a former director no less, although apparently its publication caused serious disquiet in military circles for fear that it would open the floodgates. There seems to have been something in this! After all, what serious objection can be made to the lower ranks selling their stories, when someone as senior as de la Billière had made his fortune out of his own 'shoot-and-tell' revelations?

De la Billière's memoirs are useful from a number of points of view: as an account of his personal odyssey, as a classic instance of special forces' egoism, for the way in which they celebrate warrior masculinity, and for the political agenda they reveal. They are very much the memoirs of a modern professional counter-revolutionary and deserve close scrutiny.

He was born in April 1934, the son of a naval surgeon who was to be killed during the German attack on Crete in 1941. He hardly knew his father and was brought up by his mother and a succession of nannies. His account of his childhood is entitled 'Born Rebel' and tells the story of his resistance to female authority in the home.

He argues that his rebellious tendencies were accentuated by the lack of a father. This rebellion at home consisted of making his mother's life a misery (on one occasion he faked a telephone call to her reporting that he had been hurt in an accident), and driving a succession of nannies into resignation. He describes one incident when he deliberately tried to injure and nearly killed his younger brother by convincing him that he could walk in safety on the plaster floor between the joists in their loft. While he insists that he was a normal exuberant child, the picture he paints is somewhat different, rather disturbing.

He continued his rebellion at preparatory school and later at Harrow public school. In 1950 he painted the slogan VOTE LABOUR on a number of college walls, not out of any adolescent leftism, but because this was the most offensive slogan he could think of! More seriously, he stole a rifle and ammunition from the college armoury, and under cover of darkness, took pot shots at other boys' windows. The only reading he admits to were Second World War adventure stories. While still at school, he became obsessed with the desire to join the SAS.

De la Billière's concern in this account of his early years is to establish his credentials as someone who did not toe the line or obey the rules, as a non-conformist. This is the stuff of which the adventurer, the hero, is made. It is the upper-class misfits who are the best defenders of empire, the real bulwarks of the Establishment. They can be relied on in an emergency, they are not afraid of getting their hands dirty; when desperate measures are called for, it is the rebel who can deliver the goods. His early years of rebellion were an ideal, indeed a necessary, preparation for his years as an officer in the SAS.

He joined the Durham Light Infantry and in April 1953 arrived in Korea. Here the war had become a battle of attrition with both sides dug in, facing each other in apparent stalemate. De la Billière began to learn the art of man-management, of how to get young working-class soldiers willingly to obey orders that might well involve their being killed. The answer was a stern paternalism, looking after your men but without being soft with them. In the troglodyte conditions of trench warfare that obtained in Korea at this time, he came to 'love' his men, they were his life. Of course, not all of them responded to this paternalism and he describes how on one occasion a reluctant corporal had to be forced to go out on night patrol at gun-point.

Not until October 1956 did he achieve his ambition of selection for the SAS. This had one drawback: it meant that he missed the Suez invasion, something he very much regretted. Instead, he was sent to Malaya, to take part in the closing stages of the campaign against the Communist guerrillas. According to de la Billière, the

SAS was the decisive factor in the conflict, with its ability to operate in the deep jungle for long periods of time turning the tide. This is merely the first example of the special forces' egoism that runs through *Looking for Trouble*. In de la Billière's view it was the supermen of the SAS who proved decisive in defeating the Communists. All the evidence available, however, suggests that this was not the case.

De la Billière himself played a part in the last major action in which the SAS participated in Malaya, Operation Sweep, which began in February 1958. This involved driving the small band of guerrillas led by Ah Hoi out of the Telok Anson swamp north west of Kuala Lumpur so that they could be either killed or forced to surrender. He describes the swamp as 'a hellish environment', relentlessly hot. Progress involved sloshing through waist-deep, dark brown liquid or hopping from one mangrove root to the next. The leeches were 'unspeakable'. At night, they had to sleep in hammocks because there was no ground, only water. It was exhausting work, straining to keep alert in case of a contact. After three weeks of slogging through the swamp and never actually sighting a guerrilla, he received a radio message that the operation was over and that Ah Hoi was coming in to surrender. While there can be no doubt as to the courage, fitness or endurance of the SAS when soldiering in these appalling conditions, the fact remains that they played only a minor role in the British victory in Malaya. What de la Billière does in his account is effectively to substitute tales of SAS prowess for any serious consideration of their military effectiveness. The defeat of the Communist guerrillas is portrayed as a triumph of British warrior masculinity rather than as a result of the overwhelmingly superior military-political apparatus that the British had marshalled against them. De la Billière celebrates the SAS ability to master any terrain, no matter how inhospitable, to make it their own and move through it as hunters in search of their prey. It can be argued, however, that the Communist guerrillas who had sustained their revolutionary war against overwhelming odds for more than a decade had demonstrated even greater courage and endurance.

With the Malayan Emergency coming to an end, the SAS faced disbandment. It was saved, as we have already seen, by rebellion in a British client state, the Sultanate of Oman. De la Billière provides a graphic account of the taking of the Jebel Akhdar, a feat accomplished once again in the most testing conditions over the most difficult terrain. It was, he writes, 'an ideal operation for the SAS'. The men were all extraordinarily fit, positively rejoicing at the challenge that climbing the Jebel presented. Here, unlike in Malaya, they saw the enemy every day and 'once we were up in the mountain, pretty well any Arab was fair game'. Morale soared. This is the stuff of *Boy's Own* adventure stories. It does, however, leave out one important dimension of the campaign: the Jebel had been under heavy and sustained air bombardment for some weeks and the SAS received continual and effective close air support. This is not to say that the SAS did not accomplish the taking of the Jebel more efficiently than other infantry could have, but it puts the campaign in a different perspective from that adopted by de la Billière.

He went on to serve in the disastrous Aden campaign in 1964. He took part in the Radfan operation, which saw a patrol from his squadron overrun by rebels and the heads of two of his men put on display across the border in Yemen. He was also involved in the much more successful confrontation with Indonesia in Borneo in 1964–5 and actually sings the praises of Denis Healey, the Labour minister of defence at the time. By 1969 he was second-in-command of 22 SAS and in 1972 took full command. His responsibilities were worldwide with SAS officers and men deployed in 23 different countries. The most important commitment without any doubt was the war in Dhofar. Here de la Billière identifies the battle of Mirbat as the turning point, once again giving the decisive role to the SAS. Finally in 1978 he became director of the SAS, a post he held until 1984. Interestingly, he has very little to say about SAS operations in Northern Ireland. Presumably the subject is still too sensitive. What he does say is quite revealing though. He discusses the Dunloy incident of 11 July 1978 in some detail. His men had found a weapons cache in a graveyard and had staked the site out for several days and nights. One night, according to de la Billière, a man appeared, took a semi-automatic out of the cache and pointed it at the SAS ambush whereupon they killed him. Although only 16, the dead man was clearly IRA. This is a complete travesty. In fact the arms cache was discovered by 16-year-old John Boyle on 10 July. He told his father, who informed the RUC, and the SAS were called in to stake out the cache. The very next day John Boyle returned to the graveyard for another look at the weapons and was shot dead in broad daylight. He quite categorically had no connection with the IRA. For the many readers of de la Billière's bestselling memoirs the killing of John Boyle is just another success in the war against terrorism, a success which republican sympathisers have tried to turn into a *cause celèbre*.[19]

The SAS in which de la Billière rose to prominence was a very different unit from the wartime SAS. Whereas the wartime SAS had often fought alongside popular resistance movements against Nazi tyranny, the postwar SAS was a specialised counter-revolutionary force employed, among other things, to suppress popular resistance movements. The wartime SAS had an outlaw reputation, constituted a kind of banditti, was among the hunted, while the postwar SAS was a professional elite, composed of the ultimate soldier killers, and usually very much among the hunters. De la Billière's memoirs are adequate testimony to this transformation. Before moving on to look at other SAS memoirs, it is worth briefly pausing here to consider the American memoir, *Delta Force*, written by the founder of that unit, Colonel Charles Beckwith. He had arrived in Britain in June 1962 on an exchange from the US Special Forces to spend a year serving with the SAS. The SAS, he notes, already had a reputation as 'the free world's finest counter terrorist unit', but to his initial disappointment he found that it 'resembled no military organisation I had ever known'. The lack of discipline, in particular, appalled him. What he soon discovered, however, was that everything he had been previously taught about soldiering had to be 'turned upside down'. What he had mistaken for lack of discipline, he soon recognised as concealing a degree of dedication and professionalism that he had not encountered before. Beckwith was converted with all the fanaticism of the convert. He became an SAS obsessive, determined to establish a comparable unit in the US Army.

After he returned to the United States, he campaigned for a new elite unit to be established, but found himself ignored. Beckwith went on to serve with the US Special Forces in Vietnam and commanded a detachment at the siege of Plei Mei in October 1965. This battle completely dwarfed the much celebrated Mirbat engagement. The difference was that Plei Mei was only one episode in a much larger-scale war that was lost.

Not until mid-1976 was Beckwith to get any support for his continuing efforts to establish an elite unit comparable to the SAS. The decisive factor for this change was, he argues, that the Pentagon felt it necessary to have a specialist unit that could deal with terrorism. The Mogadishu rescue greatly strengthened his hand. Delta Force was formed soon afterwards as 'part of the free world's counter terrorist community'. It has never managed to rival the SAS. Instead, its reputation has been dogged by the failure of Operation Eagle Eye, the attempted rescue of the American hostages held in Teheran. The aborting of this mission after the disastrous accident at Desert One inside Iran was a blow that the unit never really recovered from, at least as far as popular perception was concerned. Arguably, the failure cost Jimmy Carter his chances of securing re-election to the presidency. Nevertheless it is important to keep things in perspective. While Delta Force has never successfully played the role that the SAS has played in Britain, this should not disguise either the extent or the success of covert US intervention in many countries throughout the world, intervention on a scale that is completely beyond the capabilities of the British state. Indeed, the British have often acted as a client of the United States, two examples being SAS involvement in Colombia and in Cambodia.

Nevertheless, it remains an interesting cultural difference between Britain and the United States that there has been no American equivalent of the remarkable SAS phenomenon that has manifested itself in Britain.[20]

The Soldiers' Tales

While there have been a number of other memoirs written by SAS officers (Johnny Cooper's *One of the Originals* and Tony Jeapes's *SAS Operation Oman*), one of the most interesting features of the recently published postwar memoirs is that so many of them have been written by members of the lower ranks. The first to appear was 'Lofty' Large's *One Man's SAS*, first published in 1987. This provides a view from below that covers much the same ground as the first half of de la Billière's memoirs (Malaya, Oman, Borneo, Aden), but offers an interesting contrast to his officer's perspective. Interest in the book was limited however. There were two reasons for this. First of all, Large was too much his own man, serving up his experiences and opinions very much on a take-it-or-leave-it basis. Second, Large's memoirs were concerned with old-fashioned colonial wars whereas the great concerns of the 1980s and 1990s were the war against terrorism and the Falklands and Gulf wars. Large's memoirs were targeted at the limited but already established readership of military memoirs and war experiences. They were not intended to become a bestseller.[21] From this point of view, the most important of the contemporary memoirs was the ghosted volume written by Michael Paul Kennedy, *Soldier 'I' SAS*, that was first published in 1989. Not only did this make possible and prepare the way for the later books by McNab, Ryan, McCallion and others, as well as Jack Ramsay's 1996 collection of oral accounts, *SAS: The Soldiers' Story*, the book of the Carlton TV series, to both of which Soldier '1' contributed, but it also spawned a series of popular 'factoid' novels, 'Soldier A to Z SAS' which will be looked at later.

Soldier 'I' SAS was marketed as the story of one of the participants in the storming of the Iranian Embassy, indeed the book's jacket photograph shows a heavily armed SAS team going into the Embassy with Soldier '1' picked out by a red arrow. This is the story of someone who was actually there when the terrorist threat was exorcised, who actually took part in killing those responsible, and was prepared to describe how it was done and what it felt like. The result was a bestseller.

Kennedy's book in many ways established the format for later SAS memoirs, with considerable emphasis being placed on selection, on the gruelling process whereby the warrior elite are chosen. The

hell that has to be endured in order to get into the regiment
establishes beyond any doubt that these are men apart, extraordinary
individuals, capable of extraordinary exploits. They are the best.
Soldier 'I' describes having to crawl through a ditch filled with
stagnant water and sheep's entrails, of punishing route marches over
mountainous terrain in appalling weather with heavier and heavier
packs, of disorientation techniques designed to test the character.
Of the 135 candidates who had put themselves forward for selection
when he had, only 17 completed initial selection. This was to be
followed by another five months of training and tests before he was
finally accepted into what he describes as 'the Praetorian Guard'.

His motivation for getting through selection had been the desire
for revenge against the Communists for throwing Britain out of Aden,
a defeat that he had taken as a personal insult. He was engaged in
a crusade against Communism and to his great delight his first
posting was Dhofar. Here, the fate of the West was at stake. If Oman
fell to the Communists, they would be in a position to hold the
West to ransom, threatening to cut off oil supplies through the Straits
of Hormuz. The SAS were there to stop them.

Soldier 'I''s account of the Dhofar war transforms this relatively
minor campaign into one of the decisive episodes of the Cold War.
The turning point was, of course, the battle of Mirbat of July 1972.
As we have already seen some 300 PFLOAG guerrillas raided
down from the Jebel to try and overrun Mirbat, attacking the two
protective forts. Their attack was broken up by fire from the
fortified BATT house where Soldier 'I' was one of the SAS
defenders. He provides a graphic first-hand description of the
battle. First, his state of mind:

> My mind is drilled to precision. The steel shutter has crashed
> to the floor; humanity is locked outside beating its fist on the
> cold, hard surface. No sound, no cry of compassion can
> penetrate within. I am now ruthless and single-minded. It's a
> kind of insanity. You have to be insane to survive. It's me or
> him ... Brutal, efficient killing. We don't even kill them. We
> take them out, we root them out, we blow them away, we pick
> them off, we eliminate them ... The enemy are not human beings.
> They are everything else – a threat, an attack, a movement in
> the rifle sight, a running, lunging, shouting adrenalin-charged
> shape. But they are not human beings ... They are to be
> eliminated, it's as simple as that. That is my duty, my role. At
> this moment my only concern is not to let my mates down. I
> am determined not to be the weak link. In the split second that
> battle is joined, we are together, we are a team, the sum is now
> greater than the parts. We have fire in our eyes, ice in our veins

and metal in our hearts. The highly lubricated precision machine bursts into life.

This is a veritable hymn to the soldier killer. Those to be killed are not human beings, you cannot afford to think of them as real people, as fathers, husbands, sons. It is nothing to do with politics, world affairs or even heroism, instead it is the law of the jungle. It is me or him.

They pour fire into the ranks of the advancing guerrillas. The language is most expressive: tracer and explosive incendiary rounds converge 'in a frenzied dance', it 'rained fire and lead', men were 'falling, twisting, screaming', machine-gun fire scythed 'a lethal harvest', it was 'a nightmare scene', the guerrillas were like 'homicidal zombies', falling down and getting up again, 'the whole battlefield emptied', the 'inferno of fire raged on', the battle 'reached a crescendo', a 'hurricane of fire whirled and roared across Mirbat plain', 'screams of agony filled the air', it was 'an orgy of violence and killing', 'a carnival of carnage' and so on.

This is very much an exercise in the pornography of war, an attempt to thrill and excite the reader, to involve him or her vicariously in the experience of combat with all of its horror and excitement, exhaustion and exhilaration. It is hard to believe that after the veritable holocaust that Soldier 'I' describes, there were only 70-odd men dead, two of them SAS. Of course, for each of these men death was 100 per cent, but nevertheless it has to be insisted that this was a small-scale engagement that has been built up into an incident of epic proportions. Overcoming fearful odds, Britain's warrior elite emerge victorious, bloody, with good friends dead, but still on top.

While Soldier 'I''s description of the battle of Mirbat is an important contribution to the myth of the SAS, the key section of the book is without any doubt the account of the storming of the Iranian Embassy. He provides a blow-by-blow account of the siege, the preparations for the assault and the assault itself. He helped clear the cellars, riddling a dustbin lurking in the shadows by mistake, then on the stairs he was confronted by a terrorist clutching a grenade. He knocked him down with his machine pistol whereupon the man had two magazines emptied into him. The siege was over.

This day, Soldier 'I' argues, will live for ever in regimental history. It had been 'a triumphant day; we had restored the nation's pride and morale'. He felt light-headed, intoxicated, but the best was yet to come. Margaret Thatcher came to offer her personal thanks: 'I stared at her with growing admiration. She certainly had the Nelson touch.'[22]

Before we go on to consider the two bestselling SAS memoirs of the Gulf War let us briefly look at the two accounts of Operation

Fire Magic, the storming of Lufthansa Flight LH181 in Mogadishu in October 1977, written by one of the participants, Barry Davies. The plane had been hijacked by a Popular Front for the Liberation of Palestine (PFLP) team, who were demanding the release of Red Army Faction (RAF) members, including Andreas Baader, held in West Germany. Davies was one of two SAS men sent to advise and assist the West German anti-terrorist unit GSG9. In his book, Fire Magic, first published in 1994, he describes the Mogadishu operation which left three of the hijackers dead, and one, Souhaila Andrawes, seriously wounded. He goes on to make clear that he believes that the subsequent suicides of Andreas Baader, Jan-Karl Raspe, Gudrun Ensslin and Irmgard Moller were staged, that they were in fact killed. If this was indeed the case, he is perfectly happy to go along with it.

Two years later, Davies published another account of these events, Shadow of the Dove, using much of the same material as the earlier volume but incorporating the outcome of meetings he had since had with Souhaila Andrawes, then living in Norway and facing extradition to Germany. These meetings were set up as part of a TV documentary which was shown towards the end of 1996. The result is quite remarkable. Davies remains wholly committed to his time in the SAS, 'an altogether brilliant life', and still endorses what he believes to have been the execution of Baader and his comrades. His views on Palestine and the Palestinians have been dramatically changed however. Whereas the word Palestinian had once been synonymous with terrorist as far as he was concerned, he now recognises Israel's crucial role in provoking conflict and instability in the Middle East. He writes sympathetically of George Habash and Wadi Haddad as men driven to terrorism by Israeli aggression and atrocities. The more he looked into the Arab–Israeli conflict, the clearer Israel's role as aggressor became. He makes a plea for understanding. Of all the SAS memoirs, this is the only one where the author actually begins to question, in however limited a fashion, the politics behind the operations he has been involved in. It is unlikely to be the last.[23]

This brings us to the two rival bestselling Gulf War memoirs, Andy McNab's Bravo Two Zero and Chris Ryan's The One That Got Away. One interesting point about these two books is that they are both accounts of the SAS patrol that went wrong. So far, other than the brief oral testimonies in Jack Ramsay's SAS: The Soldiers' Story and Peter Crossland's Victor Two, no other celebratory first-hand accounts of the more successful heavily armed motorised patrols that operated behind Iraqi lines have appeared. Instead we have these two accounts of men on the run, hunted by a brutal enemy, one escaping and the other being captured, dominating the SAS version of the war. Bravo Two Zero was one of three eight-man patrols that were sent to establish observation posts behind Iraqi lines. The other two patrols were both motorised but Bravo Two Zero took the fateful decision to operate on foot. This decision seems to have been their doom: when things went wrong they had no way to extricate themselves. All three patrols were aborted, but only two got out.

McNab's account is very much a gung-ho story of high adventure. Everybody hopes for a major war once in their life, he writes, and this was his. He had command of a patrol engaged in a classic SAS operation. What more could a man ask for? In fact they found themselves inserted by helicopter into an area without effective cover, with inadequate maps, too much kit (each man was carrying over 200lbs), too close to Iraqi troops, without radio contact, and confronting the worst weather conditions in the area for 30 years. Two members of the patrol were to freeze to death!

Once they were discovered by the Iraqis, they had to make a run for it and McNab provides a graphic and exciting account of their attempt at escape and evasion. This is the story of a bunch of super-tough Brits taking on the might of the Iraqi army in the most appalling conditions ... and nearly getting away with it. It is a no-nonsense tale, recounted with humour and without sentiment, positively reeking of authenticity. This is the case even when events approach the surreal, for example, when McNab and his comrades hijack a vehicle and find themselves crammed into a highly conspicuous 1950s' New York yellow cab. He couldn't believe this was happening himself.

In one passage McNab discusses how to stab an enemy to death. In films, the attacker grabs them around the neck and stabs them in the heart, but this is not the most effective method. What you do is grab your enemy's head, jerk it back and keep on cutting his throat until you've gone through his windpipe and his head has nearly come away in your hands. This passage, in particular, was to inspire two 19-year-old-public-school boys with SAS fantasies, Jamie Petrolini and Richard Elsey. They cut the throat of a chef, Mohamed al-Sayed, in London in 1994. Petrolini claimed that he believed he was carrying out some sort of SAS initiation ritual. This is an extreme demonstration of the power of the SAS myth.

Inevitably McNab and his comrades were captured and subjected to brutal interrogation, beaten and tortured. He had worried before the operation about being raped if captured but decided that if it happened he simply wouldn't tell anyone. More worrying was the prospect of being castrated, and if that happened he had decided to try and provoke his captors into killing him. He was, in fact, subjected to savage beatings, but emerged from the experience alive and unbroken. He describes how a few weeks after their release, he and the other survivors showed less evidence of stress in a psychological test than the psychologist who was administering it. Looking back, McNab did not regret the ordeal he had undergone, was not worried about the rights and wrongs of the war, and in the end concluded that it had been 'very exciting' and that he had 'got high doing it'. Incidentally, he pays tribute to Chris Ryan, describing his escape as one of the most remarkable feats in regimental history.

The tremendous potency of McNab's book is obvious. It is written in a vernacular, down-to-earth style. All this happened to an ordinary bloke. He manages to be both super-tough and one of us. His adventures behind enemy lines, the terrible beatings he endured, all this happened to a working-class Londoner, a common man who had nevertheless proven himself good enough to join the warrior elite. McNab's superiority over his barbaric captors establishes his readership's superiority. This is without any doubt an important part of the book's success. Another reason is the way it contributed to transforming the war from a technological massacre, in which large numbers of Iraqi troops were slaughtered without being able to offer any effective resistance, into an adventure, a chase with the British underdog being pursued and brutalised by a savage inhuman foe. The story of Bravo Two Zero contributed effectively to blocking out the reality of the Gulf War.[24]

The publication of Chris Ryan's *The One That Got Away*, a year after McNab's version of events, to some extent spoiled the Bravo Two Zero story. Ryan made clear that he considered the whole operation to have been misconceived, the preparation inadequate and the leadership poor. He describes McNab as a Cockney Jack-the-Lad with the gift of the gab and is obviously concerned at the way a disaster like Bravo Two Zero had come to be celebrated, turned into an apparent triumph. This was not what the SAS was about. It was his escape that was in the regiment's best traditions, not being captured and tortured, however stoically endured. Without any doubt, Ryan's escape, walking nearly 200 miles through Iraqi territory with hardly any food or water, and successfully avoiding capture, was a remarkable feat of skill and endurance. It is a story straight out of *Boys' Own*. Once again, however, it provides a very different picture of the war to the reality, converting a massacre into an adventure.[25]

The only other SAS memoir of the Gulf War so far, Crossland's *Victor Two*, an account of the half-squadron motorised raiding party, Alpha Two Zero's operations behind Iraqi lines, will be discussed in the next chapter.

Before going on to consider the Northern Ireland memoirs, it is worth looking at one remarkable SAS memoir, Peter Stiff's *See You in November*, which has never been published in Britain (it was published by Galago in Alberton, South Africa, in 1985) and is ignored in all the histories of the regiment. This is rather surprising.

After all, the protagonist, Taffy, served in Borneo and Aden; indeed in Aden he was a member of the disastrous patrol that was nearly overrun by the rebels and had the corpses of two of its number beheaded. Why the neglect? The reason seems likely to be his revelations about his later SAS activities in Thailand and his subsequent service with the Rhodesian Central Intelligence Organisation (CIO). What Taffy reveals here is still sensitive.

He was a member of an SAS team despatched to Thailand by Harold Wilson's Labour government to train Thai special forces. This, it was hoped within the regiment, would be the beginning of a substantial commitment that would end with British troops committed to the war in Vietnam. He worked closely with the US Green Berets stationed in Thailand, carrying out operations against the Ho Chi Minh trail:

> We were given sectors across the border in Laos to work in, and patrols of three or four of us would cross the border, seek out the locals and gather intelligence ... Our major task was reconnaissance, but we were conscious that our prime purpose was to set the pattern for more troops, both British and American, to be committed later ... I was in Thailand for eleven months altogether.

In fact, of course, there was to be no commitment of British troops to the Vietnam War as such. The Thai initiative was stillborn. Nevertheless some British SAS did serve in Vietnam, but with the Australian SAS.

After leaving the SAS, Taffy worked as a mercenary before finally ending up in Rhodesia. In 1973 he was recruited into the CIO by another former British SAS man, Desmond Simpson. He began a career as a terrorist, carrying out a campaign of bombings and assassinations in neighbouring Zambia. Together with Hugh Hind, also ex-SAS, he bombed public buildings in Lusaka including the Central Post Office and the High Court, and assassinated Rhodesian nationalists, among them Herbert Chitepo, blown up by a car bomb. He provides considerable detail of Rhodesian operations in Zambia, including the unsuccessful Rhodesian SAS attack on Joshua Nkomo's house in Lusaka in early 1979.

Assassination, the book argues, is an art that can be taught from a text book, just like it is in the SAS. There are various set terms for the exercise: positive, non-positive, direct and indirect. The most certain way of killing someone is the direct positive method: for example, pressing a gun against them and pulling the trigger. The next most certain way is the direct non-positive. This might involve shooting someone with a rifle from a distance. A direct method but with the possibility of a miss present. The indirect positive might involve planting a bomb in a car. It is positive in that it is guaranteed to kill ('a strictly no-nonsense goodbye') but indirect because it might kill the wrong person if they use the car. He demonstrates the indirect non-positive with the example of poisoning someone's milk left on their front door. They might not drink it. In the end, however, the ultimate failure is to be caught. One other method of assassination he discusses ('an old trick popular with various government security services throughout the world') involves knocking on the victim's door, clubbing them when they answer and, while they are still stunned, throwing them out of a window. Such killings are normally put down as accidents or suicide. Such a candid discussion is unprecedented!

More astonishing, however, is the revelation that during the Lancaster House talks, he and another former SAS member, Angus Monro, were sent to London to assassinate Robert Mugabe. They decided to place a claymore mine concealed in a briefcase in the foyer of the Royal Gardens Hotel. The bomb would be detonated by remote control when Mugabe was going in. The effect would have been devastating, killing and maiming people in the foyer and in the street outside. The policeman at the hotel entrance would certainly have died. Nevertheless, he was quite prepared for all this carnage as long as Mugabe and his entourage were killed.

This admission by a former member of the SAS that he was prepared to bring devastation to central London probably explains why the memoir has been ignored. As it was, the operation was blown and he and Monro returned to Rhodesia. One last point is worth considering here with regard to the involvement of former British SAS personnel in the Rhodesian war. There is no way of knowing the exact numbers, but every likelihood that it was significant. The Rhodesian commander-in-chief, Peter Walls, served in the SAS in Malaya, as had the commander of the notorious Selous Scouts, Ron Reid-Daly. A number of other individual former SAS members can be identified, but neither the British government nor the SAS itself are particularly keen to establish the exact numbers. The same goes for former SAS serving with the South African armed forces. What we do know is that when the Rhodesian SAS finally disbanded at the end of 1980, they received a telegram of commiseration from 22 SAS in Hereford to whom they handed over their mess silver for safekeeping.[26]

The Longest War

There are three memoirs that have the war in Northern Ireland as one of their central concerns: Harry McCallion's *Killing Zone*, Michael Asher's *Shoot to Kill* and Andy McNab's *Immediate Action*, the prequel to his *Bravo Two Zero*. They recount the whole of their authors' military careers, and have much of interest to say about the SAS, the sort of men it recruits and more particularly the conduct of the war in Northern Ireland.

McCallion's memoirs are very much the calculated reminiscences of a soldier killer, written with the apparent intention of shocking his readers. He tells an unvarnished story of violence and brutality, portraying himself all the way through as the hardest of hard men. Without realising it, he provides at least part of the explanation for the protracted nature of the Northern Ireland conflict. He came from a poor working-class background in Glasgow, joining the Parachute Regiment in 1970. This was, he observes, a hard place, with some of the paras making the Waffen SS look like boy scouts. He became more brutal than most. One revealing incident in training tells us a lot about the paras' performance in Northern Ireland: he hesitated over finishing off a 'wounded terrorist' and was kicked so hard in the ribs by an officer that he was bruised for months. The Parachute Regiment mentality is captured in his account of a shooting incident that occurred on 7 August 1971: a van carrying two men backfired and a para shot dead the driver, Harry Thornton. His passenger was beaten up. McCallion reveals that one of the paras managed to get hold of a piece of the dead man's skull which he used as an ashtray. The very idea of these men playing any sort of policing role is, of course, disturbing. There was, it is obvious, a grim inevitability about Bloody Sunday.

After seven years in the Parachute Regiment, McCallion left to join the South African Defence Force, serving in the elite Special Forces Reconnaissance Commando. He took part in operations in Angola, Mozambique, Zambia and the then Rhodesia and boasts of how his unit killed over 2,000 of the enemy while only losing 17 killed themselves. After two years, he returned to Britain and took the SAS Selection. Out of 120 applicants only eight got through. He was one of them and soon found himself back in Northern Ireland.

McCallion categorically denies that the SAS have a carte blanche to kill in Northern Ireland, insisting that they are bound by the yellow card rules like everyone else. This is accompanied by the qualifying remark that they are highly trained and extremely aggressive soldiers, however, and putting them near armed IRA volunteers is 'like putting hungry wolves next to red meat'. The reader draws what conclusion he or she wants from this. In fact, his time in the province was a time of increasing frustration and anger. He started cruising the hardline Catholic areas of West Belfast, armed to the teeth, hoping for a confrontation: 'I just wanted to hit a contact.' At one point he makes clear that the answer in Northern Ireland is the covert elimination of the IRA, but later he rejects this approach on the grounds that it would 'hand them a propaganda

bonanza'. McCallion does not consider the SAS to have been a great
success in Northern Ireland. It was not their sort of war. After six
years with the SAS, he resigned to join the Royal Ulster
Constabulary.[27]

Interestingly, his reservations about SAS effectiveness in Northern
Ireland are also reflected in Soldier '1''s memoirs. The simple
solution 'was to take out the ringleaders', and the SAS could
certainly do that, but if they were required to pick their way through
a minefield of rules and regulations then it was a matter for armed
police not special forces. According to Soldier '1', they thought they
had arrived in the province to take out the opposition, but were
instead told to photograph them.[28]

Michael Asher was another ex-Para and his memoir provides a
powerful account of how that regiment made him into a killer. The
civilian masculinity he brought with him into the Paras was forcibly
and brutally demolished and reconstructed as a warrior masculinity
which celebrated the willingness and ability to commit acts of
violence. Killing replaced the sexual act in the fantasy life of the
new recruits. According to Asher, you spent 18 years learning to
control your violent impulses and then the Parachute Regiment
ordered you to 'let it rip'. He is absolutely explicit with regard to
'the thrill of power' that shooting practice gave him, a thrill that is
described almost as a sexual experience. The Paras made a man
of him.

In Northern Ireland, he began to worry about what sort of man.
He provides a horrific account of para life in Belfast. There were
off-duty 'gunge' contests in which groups of paras tried to out-do
each other in acts of gross obscenity, 'like eating shit and drinking
urine'. He writes of how during house searches some paras smashed
down doors and broke up furniture, beating anyone who resisted
and threatening and insulting the women and kids in the house.
A couple of paras boasted of having dragged a mentally deficient
girl into their observation post and of forcing her to perform oral
sex. According to Asher, the nature of their training combined with
the situation that existed in Northern Ireland, turned them into
savages. They had become 'a hurricane of human brutality ... a caste
of warrior-janizaries who worshipped on the high altar of violence
and wanted nothing more'.

Asher joined the Paras' Intelligence Section and describes an
attempt in February 1973 to take advantage of an IRA 'own goal'.
Two young volunteers, a man and his 17-year-old girlfriend, were
blown up while planting a bomb, and it was decided to try and turn
the dead man's father into an intelligence source. He was known
to be hostile to the IRA and so it was decided to bring him in for
a chat. The intention was to show him photographs of his son's
corpse, burned to a crisp, show him some sympathy, and see if he

could provide any information about the men who had sent his son to his death. The subtleties of intelligence gathering were unfortunately lost on the patrol sent to bring him in. When he arrived in the screening room, his nose was bleeding: 'He moved his hand away and I noticed five distinct human tooth-marks in the flesh.' One of the patrol had been unable to restrain himself! Any chance of using the man as a source was gone. As Asher observes, despite attempts to prevent the Paras assaulting people brought in for questioning, the story of the old man's nose proved so amusing that it started a fashion!

Asher left the army and went to university. It was while he was studying for his degree that he joined the Territorial SAS. This was soldiering a world away from the mindless brutality of the Parachute Regiment. It was a thinking man's army, where strength and endurance were not an end in itself, but were there to serve intelligence, subtlety, skill. The macho values of the Paras were replaced by a philosophy of soldiering where the head had uses other than head-butting. His eulogy of the SAS is in striking contrast to his distaste for the Parachute Regiment. Those days are long gone, however, the SAS having been colonised by the Paras in the course of the 1980s.[29]

McNab's memoirs tell of his early life in Bermondsey in London, coming from a poor working-class background, where the army seemed a good alternative to a life of petty crime and prison. He joined the Royal Green Jackets, served in Northern Ireland, but, after missing the Falklands, determined to join the SAS where he was guaranteed to see action. It became a 'pathological fixation'. He failed his first selection but passed the second time. Once again considerable emphasis is put on selection as the initiation into a warrior elite. Only a special breed of men make it. And then back to Northern Ireland.

He describes a conversation with Tiny, the regiment's armourer, where the idea of a shoot-to-kill policy is ridiculed as totally counter-productive: 'It's little things like that that bring down governments.' Of course, Tiny makes clear, there can't be a shoot-to-wound policy either. His own account of SAS activity in the province hardly inspires confidence. An attempt to ambush IRA gunmen attacking an off-duty UDR man leads to a wild car chase which ends with the IRA making good their getaway and an innocent bystander dead. He gives the impression of a bunch of cowboys at work rather than the cool, ruthless professionals of legend.

McNab enthuses about the Killing House and close-quarter battle training. The SAS, he proudly tells his readers, fires more rounds in the Killing House than the rest of the British Army put together. It is one of the tourist attractions at Hereford with visiting VIPs, among them Princess Diana, being given demonstrations of

SAS firepower. And as for Margaret Thatcher, she visited Hereford so often she might as well have had a bed there. She was, he insists, as tough as any man when it came to the crunch. Part of their training involved how to be terrorists and, predictably, they were the best: 'With our skills and knowledge we could bring down governments in months.'

McNab was detached for two years to serve in the 14th Intelligence Unit that specialised in covert surveillance in Northern Ireland, and by general agreement performed more effectively than the SAS. He provides a racy, humorous, exciting account of his adventures in Derry, breaking into buildings, shadowing suspects, mounting surveillance, planting bugs, in constant fear of discovery and having to shoot his way out of danger. On one occasion he was involved in a Friday night stakeout of a bus depot in the Bogside in the expectation that after closing time buses were to be hijacked, set on fire and used in barricades. It was a typical Friday night scene with the boys busy trying to chat up the 'fat slags' who were more interested in eating pizza. Two women came over the scrubland towards where they were hiding and then virtually standing over them 'squatted and opened fire'. McNab had a great time in Northern Ireland. Among the other deployments that he admits to are anti-drug operations in Colombia and an aborted operation to rescue Terry Waite in Lebanon, cancelled because of lack of intelligence. This was a life of adventure, shared with good mates, and in the knowledge that they were the elite. It was a great life.

How does McNab sum up his time in the SAS? Having spent most of the book pushing the regiment as an action-man elite, in the last few pages he changes tack to claim that elitism is in fact alien to the traditions of the SAS. They are merely more professional than the average soldier, men with aptitude rather than attitude. By the end of his career, he claims that he got more of a kick from stopping death than from killing people.[30] Certainly his account is a world away from either McCallion or Asher's brutal and violent odysseys. What all three memoirs demonstrate pretty effectively, however, is the extent to which the SAS and the British Army more generally have been part of the problem in Northern Ireland rather than part of the solution.

One other book requires consideration with regard to Northern Ireland: Paul Bruce's *The Nemesis File*, subtitled *The True Story of an SAS Execution Squad*, published in 1995. In this bestselling book, the pseudonymous Bruce tells the story of his participation in an SAS squad that carried out random sectarian attacks and summarily executed some 20-odd republicans, secretly disposing of their bodies in 1971–2. This account was always suspect. Not because the British Army does not do such things. Covert plain clothes units had operated in Cyprus and Aden and certainly operated in Northern Ireland in the period to which Bruce refers. They carried out sectarian attacks and assassinated people. Moreover in Kenya during the Mau Mau rebellion in the 1950s British pseudo-gangs (mixed units of ex-Mau Mau under British command) had tortured and killed on a scale exceeding anything Bruce has to tell. And, of course, there were plenty of individuals in the security forces who actually favoured such methods. What made his story implausible, however, was the fact that no one else noticed these 'disappearances', not even the IRA. Faced with such an operation, the IRA would have taken counter-measures and would have publicised what was going on in order to score a propaganda victory. We would have heard about the operation long before Paul Bruce's conscience had finally got the better of him. In the circumstances, it seems reasonably safe to assume that the book was an unsavoury publishing stunt, a cynical and disreputable attempt to cash in on the SAS boom and the Northern Ireland conflict. The arrest of Paul Inman, the book's author, at his Somerset home at the end of July 1996 by seven RUC officers seemed momentarily to indicate that there might be something in his story. Far from arresting him for his part in multiple murders, they in fact threatened him with prosecution for wasting police time. It seems clear that *The Nemesis File* is fiction, a shabby hoax.[31]

The Wife's Tale

For all the differences between these various memoirs, they nevertheless have one thing in common: they are all men's tales, stories told by men to other men and boys. There is really no place for women in the experiences they recount other than as wives, girlfriends or casual sexual partners with strictly walk-on parts. Women play no active role in the stories these men tell – with the exception of Margaret Thatcher! What we have instead is the celebration of warrior masculinity and the brotherhood of soldiers.

Such has been the level of interest in the SAS, however, that a memoir by an SAS wife has been published, Jenny Simpson's *Biting the Bullet: Married to the SAS*. This is in many ways a much more revealing account than those written by the men. Her husband, Ian, served in the Falklands, in Northern Ireland and in the Gulf and her story provides an interesting insight into 'the psychological strain, and even damage, that a life in the SAS causes'. Despite the fact that both she and her husband were patriots and royalists and fully supported what the British Army and the SAS do, she gives voice to complaints, worries and fears. In the Falklands, for example, Ian was involved in the final SAS attack at the end of the war that was intended to make them the first British soldiers into Port Stanley. This was, he considered, 'an unacceptable risk mission' undertaken for prestige reasons after pressure from above. The attack was driven off. He returned from the Falklands having lost his religious faith and with his nights disturbed by nightmares – 'vague swirling visions of Argentinian soldiers, blizzards and helicopters'.

In Northern Ireland, Ian was bitterly frustrated at the fact that the SAS were not simply allowed to eliminate known terrorists. The politicians 'did not have the courage to let the lads sort it out'. Sometimes his frustration at this lack of political will absolutely 'consumed' him. Ironically, perhaps, he was the SAS medic who saved Bernadette McAliskey's life when she was the victim of an assassination attempt. He phoned his wife telling her to watch the news that night and when the McAliskey shootings were reported, her first thought was that it was Ian who had shot her! Northern Ireland was a terrible strain, 'a particularly damaging place emotionally, for both of us'. He had recurring nightmares in which he was captured by the IRA, hooded, placed on the floor of a car and driven off. Each night the dream progressed further to its resolution. She admits that 'Ian's demons' led to them physically attacking each other and almost wrecked their marriage. The situation was not helped by the fact that Ian was not prepared to admit any problems. Any suggestion that he was having difficulty coping was taboo. This was not just macho pride, but fear of being returned to unit. Things were not helped by the petty jealousies, backbiting, selfishness and bloody-mindedness that were a constant feature of life in the regiment. While Ian was in Northern Ireland, she began pistol shooting herself, courtesy of the regiment. She became 'quickly addicted ... intoxicated'. It was, she writes, 'the most exciting thing I had ever experienced in my life'. Something to share with her husband, although he was appalled at this trespass onto men's territory.

Ian served in the Gulf, spending 46 days behind Iraqi lines with Delta One Six patrol. He was mentioned-in-despatches for his part in the destruction of what was believed to be an Iraqi Scud convoy. Once again though, he came home with terrible nightmares, continually reliving the shooting of some Iraqi soldiers who turned out to be 'scared old men who should have been taken prisoner'. He had killed people many times before, she writes, but the image of these men lying dead on the ground would remain with him forever.

Her account is certainly the most revealing as far as the psychological strain of life in the SAS is concerned. A respected veteran, 'a key player' in Andy McNab's words, he nevertheless continued to have problems coping throughout his career. What of his wife? There were the continual worries that he might be killed or injured, the way his 'job' affected his personality and her distaste for aspects of regimental life. Nevertheless, this is the story of a woman proud of having stood by her man. She reveals more of the strain they were under than any man's account does, but remains wholeheartedly behind what they do.[32]

War Memoirs and British Society

There has always been a readership for war literature. What is remarkable is that this readership has been large enough to make a number of the recent postwar memoirs massive bestsellers. The resurgence of popular militarism in the 1980s and 1990s has seen this memoir literature both helping to sustain the phenomenon and benefiting from it.

One aspect of this popular militarism is without any doubt an enthusiasm for the tough, no-nonsense ruthlessness of the SAS. These men have become the symbol of a Britain that can no longer be pushed around. They are the best in the world. The SAS memoirs provide an 'alternative history' of the postwar period where Britain is still on top. All this is pure delusion, fantasy. The last major war fought singlehanded by Britain was the confrontation with Indonesia. Victory was achieved without publicity and without any of the celebration and chauvinistic excess that accompanied and followed the Falklands. All this shows is that the popular militarism of the Thatcher era had considerably less to do with war and international politics than it had to do with domestic politics and keeping the Conservatives in power. How important it was in helping achieve this is difficult to say and one must not exaggerate. Nevertheless the popular militarism of this period is a fact that we cannot afford to ignore.

One last point worth mentioning is the official disquiet these memoirs have occasioned. While the memoirs written by officers did not cause too many worries, those by NCOs and other ranks were another matter. The regiment has taken steps to stop the flood of memoirs, first by making serving officers and men sign contracts with a 'gagging' clause, and second by barring the authors of already published memoirs from regimental premises and regimental functions. This ban extends even to the likes of Peter de la Billière. The SAS is apparently to return somewhat belatedly to the shadows. While many on the left will welcome a curb on these celebrations of British military prowess and masculine endeavour, the fact is that we urgently require more information about what the SAS has been up to in the past and will be getting up to in the future. Whether it concerns SAS activities in Northern Ireland, Cambodia or Colombia, or covert links with mercenary outfits such as Executive Outcomes, we need to know more.[33] The return to clandestinity that the regiment and the British Ministry of Defence seek is intended to allow this particular arm of the British state to continue its counter-revolutionary activities unhindered. We need more disclosure about the SAS, not less.

CHAPTER 3

Celebrating the SAS

In this chapter we shall examine the way in which the SAS has been publicised and celebrated in a number of media: in books of military history, both 'serious' and 'popular', in a variety of popular war and combat magazines, in one particular spin-off, the SAS survival handbook and SAS personal trainer, on TV and in film and video. Let us begin by looking at the development and consolidation of the SAS's reputation in the many histories and studies of the regiment that have been published since it was first re-formed in 1950.

The SAS as History

The first important account of the SAS was Virginia Cowles's *The Phantom Major*, originally published in 1958, but reprinted in 1985. This was an enthusiastic celebration of David Stirling's genius and the SAS's exploits up until his capture in January 1943. Here, Stirling is the object of quite unashamed hero-worship. He was, Cowles tells us, 'almost a legend to the men who served him', not served with him, but served him! They felt that he 'led a charmed life; that there was no trap from which he could not fight his way, no occasion on which he could not outwit the enemy'. Back in Cairo, he seemed something of a Sir Percy Blakeney, 'vague, soft-spoken, aristocratic and a bit of a dandy', but in the desert he became 'a blackbearded giant with inexhaustible energy and a loving and extensive knowledge of explosives'. She provides an exciting blow-by-blow account of the regiment's daring exploits behind enemy lines, emphasising the disproportionate damage they inflicted on the Afrika Korps and the high regard in which they were held by friend and foe alike.[1]

This early volume, together with the various SAS wartime memoirs published in the late 1940s and 1950s, were merely part of a large body of books that were published celebrating British special forces and operations during the Second World War. The Chindits, the Special Operations Executive, the Commandos and the SAS were all highlighted at this time as examples of the British way in irregular warfare. Their exploits were held up as having something to say about British national character. They showed a brave underdog hitting back against superior forces, they showed

71

skill, daring and endurance overcoming impossible odds. At this time, the SAS was only one among a number of examples of this particular aspect of the British at War and certainly not the most important. It was to be the reincarnated regiment's later activities that were to focus attention on its wartime exploits at the expense of those of other British special forces.

Little was written about the regiment in the 1960s and 1970s because at the time its activities in Britain's colonial wars remained secret. A notable exception was Philip Warner's *The Special Air Service*, first published in 1971 and reprinted many times since. This was an 'official' history written at the regiment's request and with its cooperation, by an established military historian with a popular and accessible style. Most of the book is concerned with the Second World War, detailing operations in Western Europe as well as in North Africa, but something like a quarter of its 273 pages was taken up with the postwar activities of the re-formed regiment. Somewhat predictably, Mike Calvert 'was already a legend' when he re-formed the regiment in Malaya. He was, we are told, 'an idealist who believed in the Commonwealth as a means of spreading justice, faith and honesty'. This tribute reflected the consensus of the time and would certainly not figure as anything worth extolling in any contemporary account informed by present-day harshness. As well as an unlikely humanitarian, Calvert was 'a great guerrilla fighter' and 'a creative thinker', one of the architects of the celebrated Briggs Plan. While he did not think the SAS could win the war against the Communist insurgents in Malaya on their own, 'he did think they could have a considerable influence on it'. How does Warner square this with the fact that of the 6,398 guerrillas killed during the Emergency, only 108 were killed by the SAS? He emphasises the importance of their deep penetration patrols and of their efforts at severing Communist links with the aboriginal Orang Asli peoples, tasks that other troops were not trained to undertake. In reality, however, these were mopping-up operations and the SAS contribution to British victory in Malaya was marginal. He goes on to provide brief accounts of SAS operations in Oman, in Borneo and in Aden, before concluding with a eulogy to 'the SAS today'.

You do not, he writes, have to be a millionaire or a peer, a public-school boy or even a great athlete to join the SAS. You just need the right attitude and enough determination. The SAS soldier is, he insists, 'the finest in the world'. He is at the peak of physical fitness, surrounded by hand-picked men he can trust with his life. He excels at everything he attempts, indeed 'the world is his oyster'. At Hereford you will find him reading the quality papers, *The Times*, the *Telegraph* and *The Economist*, not the *Mirror* or the *Sun*. He wants 'the facts', not cheesecake. He is trained to kill, but so are all soldiers. The difference is that the SAS soldier will 'be quicker and more efficient at it'. This is not to say he is a psychopath. There are, for example, SAS soldiers who are opposed to blood sports! But when in combat the SAS soldier will 'be so swift and ruthless that he will appear to be like a machine'. To Warner goes the credit for creating the image of the SAS as being made up of thinking man's soldiers, philosopher soldiers. This view was always a gross exaggeration but in the course of the 1980s it was to become completely untenable.[2]

Without any doubt the most important and influential history of the SAS was, and still is, Tony Geraghty's *Who Dares Wins*, first published in 1980 and updated and reprinted many times since. Geraghty, a former sergeant in the Parachute Brigade, was *Sunday Times* defence correspondent at the time the book was first published and, as a reserve officer in the RAF, was actually to serve as a liaison officer with the Americans in the Gulf War. He was someone wholly committed to the British armed forces. His *Who Dares Wins* very definitely caught the tide. He provided a racy, well-informed and not uncritical account of SAS operations since 1950, culminating in the Iranian Embassy siege that had occurred only months before the book's publication. The book was significantly different from what had come before. Whereas Philip Warner in 1971 was still writing of the SAS as part of the regular army, a specialist elite unit certainly, but one that made a particular contribution to the efforts of conventional forces, Geraghty added a whole new dimension of immense potency: the war against terrorism.

The 'moral panic' about the threat posed by the IRA, various Middle Eastern terrorist groups, and by their supposed Soviet sponsors, was to become a central theme with both the rightwing press and the Thatcher government. Geraghty, a contributor to the influential volume, *Ten Years of Terrorism*, was well placed to launch the celebration of the SAS as the antidote to this poison that threatened Western civilisation.[3] While SAS operations against the IRA had not, as of yet, ended the war in Northern Ireland, their storming of the Iranian Embassy on 6 May 1980, was, in his words, 'of incalculable help in propagating the unfashionable idea that democracy could defend itself from terrorism if it had to'. 'It had', he went on, 'been a good day for the SAS, and an even better day for Britain.' One fortuitous consequence of this very public success was that it 'shattered the anonymity with which the SAS had masked itself for thirty years'. *Who Dares Wins* was very much the benefactor. The importance of the war against international terrorism in raising the regiment's profile cannot be underestimated. They were not just engaged in distant colonial wars of little real interest to the great majority of the British people but were actually protecting them from the bomber and the gunman here and now.

The regiment served a vital purpose in validating the Thatcher's government's pose as the sworn enemy of international terrorism. Geraghty's book made its own modest contribution to this. Since 1980, *Who Dares Wins* has been reprinted many times and substantially revised twice, most recently in 1993 to incorporate accounts of the Gibraltar shootings and of the Gulf War. It is arguably the most successful regimental history ever written, preparing the way for a host of other celebratory accounts, and for one or two more critical.[4]

Even before Geraghty's book appeared, John Strawson, a former major general and established military historian, had been approached by the regiment to write an authorised history. He could not, he wrote, have written its 'official' history because so many of the SAS's activities were unofficial. The outcome was the publication in 1984 of *A History of the SAS Regiment*. This volume covered the history of the regiment from its founding in 1941 by David Stirling through to the Falklands War although without any discussion of SAS activities in Northern Ireland! Strawson's *History* is quite uncritical, absolutely carried away with enthusiasm for these military exemplars, these veritable supermen. He exaggerates the SAS contribution to every campaign it has been involved in. With regards to the Falklands, for example, he argues that SAS operations behind Argentinian lines gave the British a crucial psychological and military domination over their opponents. Huge military dividends were extracted from the proper use of the SAS in this campaign. Indeed, in Strawson's account the rest of the British invasion force seems to have had little more than a walk-on role, mopping up after the supermen of the SAS had done their work. There is no mention of the aborted suicide attack on the Rio Grande air base and the unprecedented dissension it caused within the regiment. He ends his account of the Falklands War with an almost embarrassing eulogy: 'They had dared, they had excelled, they had won!' If only the Argentinians had realised beforehand 'that it would be men like these they would be required to face in battle for the Falkland Islands, it may be doubted whether they would ever have undertaken so unpromising an enterprise'.

In his concluding chapter, 'Daring to Excel', Strawson asks what it is about the SAS 'which makes us admire them so?' He positively gushes with an almost schoolboy enthusiasm:

> There is something bewitching and awe-inspiring about their speed, their professionalism, their elusiveness, their single-minded dedication, their almost insolent certainty about being on top of the job, which endears them to us, which excites our imagination and fixes our wonder. There is, after all, despite the clinical efficiency with which they set about certain aspects

of their business, something of the romantic image ... about them. Their panache, their physical toughness, their stealth and ingenuity, their unpredictability, their extraordinary coalition of perseverance and dash, their matchless record of raising and leading irregular troops from far-off countries, their fearlessness ...

This is the language of unashamed, indeed positively embarrassing, hero-worship. The SAS has, according to Strawson, 'the quality of glamour'.[5]

The number of histories and studies of the SAS has been increasing, year by year, ever since Geraghty's crucial volume. In 1983 Peter Dickens published his *SAS: The Jungle Frontier*, an account of the regiment's part in the confrontation with Indonesia; in 1985 Robin Hunter published his *True Stories of the SAS* and William Seymour his *British Special Forces*; in 1986 James Ladd published his *SAS Operations*; in 1988 James Adams published his *Secret Armies* and that same year, together with Robin Morgan and Anthony Bambridge, *Ambush: The War between the SAS and the IRA*; in 1989 Eric Morris published his *Guerrillas in Uniform*; in 1990 Father Raymond Murray published his *The SAS in Ireland*, an exhaustive indictment virtually ignored in Britain; in 1991 Anthony Kemp published the first volume of his history of the SAS, *The SAS at War 1941–1945* to be followed in 1994 by volume two, *The SAS: Savage Wars of Peace*; in 1992 Mark Urban published his *Big Boys' Rules*, arguably the best study of the SAS so far; in 1994 Alan Hoe and Eric Morris published their *Re-enter the SAS*, a history of the SAS in Malaya; and in 1996 Paul McCue published his *Operation Bulbasket*, a study of one SAS operation in France in 1944, and Charles Whiting his *Death on a Distant Frontier*. There have also been biographies of David Stirling (Alan Hoe's *David Stirling*, published in 1992) and of Paddy Mayne (Patrick Marrinan's *Colonel Paddy*, published in 1960 and Roy Bradford and Martin Dillon's *Rogue Warrior of the SAS*, published in 1987). The list is certain to get longer.[6]

Let us look briefly at four of these volumes: the two by James Adams and those by Father Raymond Murray and by Mark Urban. James Adams was *Sunday Times* defence correspondent at the time *Secret Armies* was published. It was very much a Cold War book, warning against the Soviet peril and urging preparedness for the waging of clandestine war. *Secret Armies* examined the historical development of special forces, not just in Britain, but in the United States and the Soviet Union as well. Conventional wars were, Adams suggests, probably a thing of the past. Instead, the future of modern warfare lay with the special forces (the SAS, Delta Force and the Spetsnaz). There is 'a new secret battlefield ... where special operations forces act out their deadly games in a clandestine

environment that is only rarely visible to the public'. Adams is one
of those privileged individuals able to lift the veil on this secret war
for world domination that is taking place all around us. Much of
the book is taken up with celebrating the prowess of the SAS,
lamenting American failure in the field of clandestine operations
and warning of the magnitude of the Soviet threat. While he does
provide some interesting detail, his political perspective is so
damagingly flawed as to render the book worthless. First of all, his
account of the SAS grossly exaggerates their contribution to the
various postwar counter-insurgency campaigns that Britain has
waged since 1945. In Malaya, for example, we are seriously told
that the war 'was largely dictated by the SAS' with the conventional
forces 'there in a supporting role'. He goes on to celebrate the wars
in Borneo and Oman, where once again 'the SAS were successful',
and to lament defeat in Aden, where SAS tactics were a success
but there was a lack of political will to win. All this is a complete
travesty. With regard to the United States, his focus on the failure
of US special forces in Vietnam, on the troubled performance of
Delta Force and on the US military establishment's hostility to special
forces, seriously distorts the picture. The United States has, since
the Second World War, carried out covert operations worldwide
and with considerable success, overthrowing or contributing to the
overthrow of numerous governments, from Mussadiq in Iran to
Arbenz in Guatemala, from Sukarno in Indonesia to Allende in Chile.
Adams mentions none of this. His agenda involves presenting the
United States as responding defensively to Soviet aggression and
so these very successful and extremely bloody US interventions go
unnoticed. By the same token, he wildly exaggerates the effectiveness
of Soviet Spetsnaz troops and the threat they supposedly posed to
Western security. The collapse of the Soviet Union so soon after
the book's publication provided dramatic evidence of this.[7]

Adams's other book, *Ambush: The War between the SAS and the
IRA*, was co-authored by Robin Cook and Anthony Bambridge,
also *Sunday Times* journalists. This book was very much a response
to the furore over the Gibraltar shootings of March 1988, a rush
job to put the record straight! It celebrated SAS prowess (they are
'the most proficient of the world's special forces') and trumpeted
their crucial part in the war with the IRA. According to Adams,
Cook and Bambridge, the Loughall ambush of May 1987, that saw
eight IRA volunteers killed, together with other security force
successes, saw IRA frontline strength reduced to 'perhaps no more
than 30 men with 150 in reserve'. The Gibraltar operation was the
IRA's attempt to regain the initiative. It ended with 'three of the
IRA's most ruthless operatives ... dead. Could anyone complain
of that?' The Thames TV award-winning documentary 'Death on
the Rock' did complain and the book continues the *Sunday Times*'

attack on the programme. Once the critics were silenced, the SAS could get on with the job of defeating the IRA. Adams *et al.* warn that we are going to see even more bloody conflict in Northern Ireland with what has gone before, in their words, paling into insignificance! The security forces, we are told, 'are bracing themselves for a new campaign of unrivalled ferocity ... the IRA is on the brink of a new and particularly savage campaign in Europe and Northern Ireland'. It is perhaps somewhat predictable that these dire warnings should have prefaced the republican initiatives that were to culminate in the IRA ceasefire which even since its formal ending, has not (as yet) seen a return to war on any significant scale.[8]

Father Raymond Murray's *The SAS in Ireland*, published in Ireland in 1990, was virtually ignored in Britain despite the immense interest in anything to do with the SAS. The reason for this is immediately apparent. The book is a detailed and comprehensive indictment of British security policy in Northern Ireland in general and of the SAS in particular. This is not to say that Murray is any friend to the IRA, indeed his hostility to their military activities is uncompromising. What he indicts is the way in which the SAS have killed IRA volunteers and on occasion innocent bystanders when they could have arrested them. He accuses the SAS of carrying out what amount to summary executions, of implementing a no-prisoners, shoot-to-kill policy. He does this by means of a painstaking discussion of the rival accounts of dozens of fatal incidents involving the SAS. Murray takes seriously the version of events given by members of the local community, a version that often differs radically from that of the security forces, and is pretty systematically ignored by the British media for whom 'our boys' can do no wrong. Let us look at one incident out of many: the shooting in Strabane on 23 February 1985 of three IRA volunteers, Charles Breslin and two brothers, Michael and David Devine. They were coming back from an aborted ambush, returning weapons to a secret arms dump, when they were themselves ambushed, shot from behind and all three killed. Murray reports local witnesses to the effect that the three men were cut down in a hail of gunfire without any warning and that this was followed by three single shots as they were finished off. The SAS version was that the three men had levelled their guns at the soldiers who had opened fire in fear of their lives. All three men had been shot at close range, Michael Devine 28 times, Charles Brulin 13 times and David Devine 5 times. At the very least Murray establishes quite conclusively that the inquest system works to protect members of the security forces from the legal consequences of their actions and to deny justice to the families of those they have killed. Both the legal establishment in Northern Ireland and the political establishment in Britain have effectively condoned the SAS acting as judge, jury and executioner.[9]

This brings us to Mark Urban's important study, *Big Boys'*
Rules, an outstanding account of the undercover war in Northern
Ireland and of the part played in it by the SAS. Urban was formerly
defence correspondent with the *Independent* before joining the
BBC and had already written a study of Russian intervention in
Afghanistan, *War in Afghanistan*. In *Big Boys' Rules*, he provides a
critical but still sympathetic discussion of the security forces'
undercover operations in Northern Ireland. It is quite clear that
he is not a supporter of Irish republicanism but nevertheless he
proceeds to criticise with considerable vigour aspects of the attitudes
and activities of the security forces, including the SAS. The book
is, he claims, the first in which the SAS, intelligence officers and
senior decision-makers speak frankly about their attitudes towards
the conduct of the undercover war. It certainly makes for fascinating
reading.

For the purposes of this discussion, the most interesting issues
raised by Urban concern changes in SAS operating procedures. He
makes the point that from 1976 to 1978 the SAS killed ten people
in Northern Ireland, seven IRA and three innocent bystanders. Even
those senior officers who were prepared to endorse a no-prisoners
approach – the application of big boys' rules – were perturbed by
this propensity to kill civilians. In fact the SAS had a better record
in this respect than the rest of the army. Nevertheless, he argues
that they were reined in. Between December 1978 and December
1983, the SAS did not kill anyone in Northern Ireland. This
restraint came to an end in December 1983 and in the next 15
months the SAS were to kill ten more IRA volunteers. As Urban
puts it, if we are to believe the official version then from December
1983 onwards IRA members suddenly began making threatening
hand movements when challenged, whether or not they were
armed. There had obviously been a change in British security
policy although Urban argues that this took place at an operational
rather than at a political level. It seems certain, however, that the
prevailing political climate would have inevitably influenced
operational decision-making, even assuming he is right on this.

He provides an interesting account of the Strabane ambush that
left the three IRA volunteers, Charles Breslin, Michael and David
Devine dead, an account that is even more damning than that of
the unrelentingly hostile Father Murray. As he points out, none of
the three IRA men fired their weapon and two of them still had
their safety catches on. The SAS men carried on shooting at them,
even after they had been hit and had fallen to the ground, changing
magazines to do so. Most damagingly of all, he reveals that all three
men had at least one shot in the head, but that their balaclavas had
no bullet holes in them. The Crown argued at the inquest that the
bullets could have gone through the eyeholes.

Leaving aside morality and legality for the moment, what of the effectiveness of the SAS? As Urban points out, between 1976 and late 1987 conventional army units killed nine IRA and two INLA members, while in the same period the SAS and 14th Intelligence killed thirty IRA and two INLA. What contribution has this made to ending the conflict however? His conclusion, that involved a change of mind on his part, is that SAS ambushes and shoot-outs had not, in fact, contributed to lowering the level of violence, that the undercover war had fed on itself. This conclusion starkly contradicts the usual portrayal of the SAS as the only effective protection against terrorism.

One last point worth noticing here is that Urban argues that there was a change in the character of the SAS brought about by an influx of members of the Parachute Regiment after the Falklands War. According to one of his informants, by the mid-1980s just over half of the SAS were ex-Paras. This has led to an increased emphasis on endurance, hardness and violence over intelligence, skill and initiative. Certainly the evidence provided by the memoirs of ex-Paras such as Harry McCallion would seem to bear this proposition out.[10]

The Illustrated SAS

As well as these 'serious' histories and studies of the SAS, there have also been a number of more popular, profusely illustrated volumes celebrating the regiment's exploits published over recent years. Geraghty once more led the way with his *This is the SAS* but there have been many more: Peter Macdonald's *The SAS in Action*, Steve Crawford's two volumes, *The SAS at Close Quarters* and *The SAS Encyclopaedia*, Mike Robinson's *Fighting Skills of the SAS*, Peter Darman's two volumes, *SAS: The World's Best* and *A – Z of the SAS*, Craig Philip and Alex Taylor's *Inside the SAS*, Barry Davies's *SAS: The Illustrated History* and others. Steve Crawford has also written an account of the SAS in the Gulf War to a similar text and illustration format: *SAS: Gulf Warriors*.[11] These volumes are all explicitly celebratory, not just recounting SAS operations and experiences in print, but arguably more importantly, providing portfolios of photographic images for the generally young male reader to fantasise about and admire. If it were a written account of the regiment that these readers were after, then Geraghty's volume, those by Anthony Kemp or even by Mark Urban would do. There is a substantial readership, however, for whom the visual image of the warrior hero is essential. Let us look at some of these volumes in more detail.

All of them offer a combination of pictures and text with the page-after-page of colour photographs that they feature making a major contribution to their attraction. Steve Crawford's *The SAS at Close Quarters* contains 91 photographs, many of them covering more than one page, along with a number of drawings and diagrams; Peter Macdonald's *The SAS in Action* has 149 photographs, once again with many covering more than one page; Mike Robinson's *Fighting Skills of the SAS* has only 76 photographs but over 100 line drawings; Peter Darman's *SAS: The World's Best* contains 110 photographs; Barry Davies's *SAS: The Illustrated History* has 267 photographs; and Steve Crawford's *SAS: Gulf Warriors* has 107 photographs, many covering more than one page. Whatever the intentions of the authors, the attraction of these books could be described as pornographic, but instead of the pornography of sex, what is on offer here is the pornography of war. The page-after-page of photographs are, in fact, pin-ups, but instead of pictures of young women, naked or partially clothed, they are pictures of soldiers and their weapons and equipment, of warriors 'on the job' so to speak. Whereas the traditional pin-up celebrates and endorses hetero-sexuality, these soldier pin-ups celebrate a particular notion of masculinity, a tough warrior masculinity that effectively excludes women, and validates the ready resort to violence. As war pornography goes, these books must be considered 'soft-core' because, by and large, they avoid the portrayal of the dead and wounded, of the damage and destruction that combat inevitably involves. One particular feature worth noticing is the very dramatic nature of the photographs of the SAS in their black anti-terrorist garb together with hood and gas mask. While obviously designed for practical reasons, this particular ensemble has become a kind of fetish-wear. Photographs of SAS men encased head to toe in these menacing and mysterious outfits are the most popular illustrations and figure prominently in all these books.

To what extent are these photographs homoerotic? Obviously there is an element of this to their attraction, but for most readers this is very much subordinated to other concerns. Sex is what men do with women, war is what men do with other men. These books satisfy warrior fantasies that have a sexual component but this should not be exaggerated.

Steve Crawford's *The SAS at Close Quarters* has a colour photograph of black-clad, hooded and gas-masked SAS men on the balcony of the Iranian Embassy on its dustcover. They are preparing to make their explosive entry. Beneath this image, the book promises 'unpublished accounts by SAS soldiers of their great actions'. The promised combination of action photographs and text telling it like it really was is meant to be irresistible. Inside, the book covers the early history of the regiment up to the Dhofar campaign in 44 pages with the remaining 131 pages covering selection and the regiment's exploits in the 1980s and 1990s. The book celebrates the fitness and skill of the SAS, their toughness and determination, the fact that each man who gets through selection is 'an elite operative' engaged in a 'never-ending pursuit of excellence'. It barely glances at the Second World War and Malaya, but does devote 16 pages to the battle of Mirbat. This in itself is quite significant. The book is not really concerned with a serious discussion of the effectiveness of the SAS, with evaluating their contribution to any particular campaign; instead it concentrates on describing the SAS in action, recounting their combat experiences and celebrating their skill and prowess. The outcome at Mirbat was predictably 'a great victory'. While Crawford actually ascribes the final victory in Dhofar to the SAS's hearts-and-minds policy rather than to military action, nevertheless he knows what his readers want: graphic descriptions of combat.

The chapter on the storming of the Iranian Embassy is illustrated by a number of full-page photographs of SAS men in full anti-terrorist garb and a handy diagram of the Embassy showing where each terrorist was killed. There are graphic first-hand accounts of the operation. According to one of the participants, who now works in the security industry, 'Princes Gate was a turning point that showed the powers that be what the regiment could do and what an asset it was to the country.' It led, he goes on, to the regiment and its territorial reserve being overwhelmed with applicants and to an ever increasing number of men actually claiming to have taken part. He reckons to have interviewed around 700 men for security jobs who claim to have been there! Accounts of the Falklands War, of Northern Ireland (focusing on the Loughall ambush which is illustrated by a two-page diagram, a two-page aerial photograph of the scene and a one-page photograph of the bullet-riddled van in which the IRA had hoped to make their getaway), of the Gibraltar shootings (once again with a two-page diagram of the operation) and the Gulf War follow. Crawford ends by emphasising the regiment's continuing role in the war against terrorism and a new role in the war against drugs. They are a small hard-pressed band of elite soldiers facing multiplying dangers in an unsafe world, but all is not lost, because they are the best.[12]

Peter Macdonald's *The SAS in Action* is very much the same. The dustjacket is a photograph of a SAS man in full anti-terrorist kit including gas mask and hood against a background of smoke. He is portrayed poised for action, aiming his weapon at the camera. Once again the book is dominated by the photographs which in this case include pictures of death and destruction: there are photographs of dead terrorists at Mogadishu and in the Iranian Embassy in London, and of the charred remains of a US marine, killed during Delta Force's abortive operation to rescue American hostages in Teheran. As the title suggests, this book is action-oriented. The text is, of course, 100 per cent behind 'our boys', but it does acknowledge some mistakes and tragedies such as the shooting of innocent bystanders in Northern Ireland. Nevertheless the book is inevitably a celebration of the SAS's skill, courage and effectiveness in combat: 'there is no doubt that the Regiment offers the ultimate in soldiering', Macdonald, a former British and Rhodesian army veteran, assures his readers.[13]

Even more action-oriented is *Fighting Skills of the SAS* written by the pseudonymous Mike Robinson. Here we are offered, among other things, chapters entitled 'Weapon Skills', 'Explosives and Sabotage', 'Counter-Terrorist Tactics', 'Silent Killing Skills', 'Civil Disorder Control', 'Staying Hidden' and 'Booby Traps'. This book, it can be said without any equivocation, is aimed at men who want to know in some detail how the SAS kill people. The chapter entitled 'Counter Terrorist Tactics', for example, reveals that the SAS are taught not to take chances with terrorists: the old-fashioned 'double-tap', two quick shots to the body, is no longer considered adequate to put down a terrorist. Nowadays a whole magazine will be emptied into the target. Where possible the shots are fired into the trunk which contains the vital organs – heart, liver and lungs. Head shots are too difficult. Different kinds of ammunition are used. Mairead Farrell in Gibraltar was, we are told, shot three times in the back with standard 9mm rounds which all passed through her chest and exited at the front. For hostage situations, special bullets are used which are designed not to exit the body, for example, various kinds of Accelerated Energy Transfer round which cause massive tissue damage and are considered superb specialist bullets. This discussion is accompanied by accounts of the Killing House, of the storming of the Iranian Embassy and of the Loughall ambush in Northern Ireland.

The chapter entitled 'Silent Killing Skills' is especially interesting. We are told that the

> human body has numerous vulnerable organs and areas, which if destroyed, will result in death. These include the heart, lungs, liver, neck and the central nervous system. For silent killing techniques the neck and heart are perhaps the most accessible targets. The neck contains the spinal column and the jugular vein. Break it with a martial arts blow or hold, or with a strike from a weapon or blunt instrument, and the victim dies without uttering a sound. Cut the jugular and the victim drowns in his own blood, the only sound uttered being a low gurgle (though care must be taken as his body may go into spasms and start thrashing around).

The chapter goes on to advocate the use of crossbows and compound bows, spears, silenced firearms, knives, machetes, blackjacks, sharpened stakes and the garrotte. A machete cannot be guaranteed to kill with a single blow, but a well-aimed blow to the neck can in theory decapitate an opponent. While it is believed that a severed head remains conscious for up to 20 seconds, SAS personnel we are assured need not worry as there are no records of a severed head ever calling out. Garrotting is perhaps the simplest method and almost any type of wire or cord can be used, 'though the connoisseur will employ a length of razor wire'.

Once again this book is profusely illustrated with both photographs and line drawings that are intended to attract a young male readership. It discusses in a sometimes flippant way the various methods which can be used to kill and wound people without any concern with regard to the consequences.[14]

Peter Darman's *SAS: The World's Best* offers a comparison of the SAS with other special forces ranging from the US Navy Seals to the Soviet Spetsnaz, from the German GSG9 to the Green Berets, from the French Foreign Legion to Delta Force. It looks at selection, weapons skills, adaptability and combat effectiveness in conventional war and in counter-insurgency and anti-terrorist operations. Predictably, the conclusion is that the SAS is 'the most elite military unit'.[15] Which brings us to *SAS: Gulf Warriors*, another book by Steve Crawford that claims on its dustcover to tell the story behind Bravo Two Zero. Once again, the book is profusely illustrated, including many posed photographs of SAS patrols operating behind Iraqi lines. The book celebrates the SAS contribution to victory, focusing on intelligence gathering, raids and the hunt for Scud missile launchers. There is a chapter on the weapons they used in the war. What is completely missing is any awareness of the fact that the war involved a massive technological assault on an opponent that was to all intents and purposes incapable of hitting back. The reality of the war as a technological massacre is replaced by celebration of the prowess, heroism and endurance of the SAS, of small groups of men raiding behind enemy lines, lying concealed close by unsuspecting Iraqi troops, and, of course, in the case of Bravo Two Zero, enduring capture and torture. This is likely to be the enduring British memory of the war, another instance of British pluck overcoming a brutal foe.[16]

The most recent of these illustrated accounts of the SAS is Barry Davies's *SAS: The Illustrated History*. This is, in fact, an album of photographs taken over the years by members of the regiment, including Davies himself. It boasts many photographs that have never been seen before, all accompanied with captions that recount the particular circumstances in which they were taken or their special significance. The volume is handsomely produced to a standard

normally reserved for coffee-table art books. It contains a brief section
on the early years that covers the Second World War, Malaya and
Aden, but then goes on to give considerably more attention to
selection and training, combat survival, troop training, counter-
terrorism and counter-revolutionary warfare, and to the more
recent conflicts in Oman, Northern Ireland, the Falklands and the
Gulf. Once again we have photograph after photograph of uniformed
men on patrol in a variety of settings, firing their weapons, engaged
in various training exercises, cooking and making camp, parachuting,
skiing, rock climbing and so on. Inevitably the book contains a series
of particularly striking photographs of 'the men in black', heavily-
armed SAS taking on the menace of international terrorism.

The chapter on counter-terrorism has some 20 photographs of
hooded men in gas masks, body armour and black overalls, heavily
armed, practising storming buildings, coaches, trains and aircraft.
These are the book's most 'sexy' photographs with full-page shots
of mysterious, threatening, masculine figures, weapons in their
hands, emerging from the smoke, set against the backdrop of the
flare of a stun grenade or emerging from the sea. There are also
photographs of Prince Charles, Princess Diana and Princess Anne
taking part in hostage-rescue simulations and of the corpses of
terrorists killed in the storming of Lufthansa 737 and of the Iranian
Embassy. The SAS, a caption assures us, are 'the best anti-terrorist
team in the world' and their skills and expertise have been exported
to many other countries. In the chapters on the more recent
campaigns fought by the regiment, Davies provides a number of
hardcore photographs of dead and mutilated enemies. He recounts
how in Oman a group of rebels were killed by a mortar bomb, leaving
four dead bodies and a spare arm. The book contains a half-page
colour photograph of the detached, mutilated arm lying in a mess
of gore. On the facing page is the colour photograph of three dead
rebels with *rigor mortis* clearly set in. This sort of pornography is
difficult to justify. It is not a case of showing what war is really like,
but more of exhibiting trophies, in this case gory and macabre
trophies, but still just that. It is interesting to speculate on the reaction
in Britain to the publication of a book elsewhere containing
comparable photographs of dead and mutilated British soldiers.
Nevertheless, the publishers know their readers, and Davies's *SAS:
The Illustrated History* is merely the most recent attempt to satisfy
an apparently insatiable market. One last point worth noticing is
that Davies, one of the most prolific of the new SAS authors, is
somewhat on the defensive in this volume. In his 'Introduction',
he notes that many people dismiss the SAS as 'a bunch of highly
trained killers'. He accepts that they are highly trained, but argues
that when all else fails, Britain needs these men. They are, he

insists, just ordinary men, sons and brothers, husbands and fathers, good, just men 'of whom we should be proud'.[17]

The Monthly SAS

The SAS have also figured prominently in various magazine publications. Most notable of these was *The Elite*, published in weekly parts by Orbis in 1985. The first issue opened with an article on 'SAS Siege Breakers', yet another heavily illustrated, celebratory account of the storming of the Iranian Embassy. This was the operation that 'gripped the nation's imagination' and 'thanks to television, everyone in the country had a grandstand view of the unfolding drama'. It was carried out with 'almost surgical precision' and the anti-terrorist techniques developed by the SAS 'were shown to be second to none'. The article also provided some background on the SAS and discussion of their weaponry. We learn, for example, that the 9mm Heckler and Koch MP SA3 'was perhaps the most effective part of the SAS arsenal deployed at Princes Gate'. This can fire 650 rounds per minute or 'if need be, single shots to take out individual targets'. There are 13 photographs or illustrations in a seven-page article.

In the same issue of *The Elite* there are also articles on 2 Para in the Falklands and quite incredibly on the murderous Rhodesian Selous Scouts, celebrated here as 'the most experienced anti-terrorist unit in the world'. The first issue was accompanied by a large full-colour poster of heavily armed Royal Marines on a training exercise. The second issue had articles on the Royal Marines in the Falklands, the 'Hitlerjugend' SS Panzer Division and the US 1st Air Cavalry. Later issues carried articles on the SAS and the battle of Mirbat, on GSG9 and the Mogadishu hijacking, on the French Foreign Legion and the battle of Dien Bien Phu, on the US Marines in Khe Sanh and Hue, on Mike Hoare and his European mercenaries in the Congo, on the Gurkhas in the Falklands and on the Dambusters Squadron. All of these articles introduced the magazine's young male readership to these 'elite units', crack fighting men and their weapons, to their battles against impossible odds with soldiers recounting their own combat experiences. Every article was profusely illustrated with colour photographs and diagrams.

The same publisher, Orbis, had also published the earlier *War in Peace* magazine series, that first appeared in 1983, following the success of an illustrated book of the same title. Once again this was a heavily illustrated product with each issue combining a quite exhaustive ongoing history of war since 1945 with regular features on 'Key Weapons' and 'The Fighting Men'. The magazines were full of photographs of explosions, weapons and soldiers, including in virtually every issue at least one of some unfortunate being tortured, executed or otherwise killed. While the SAS makes an appearance in this series, it is not central to it.

These magazines and others like them can be usefully considered as another example of the pornography of war. What is interesting is that whereas the pornography of sex is relegated to the top shelves of W.H. Smith and Menzies, the pornography of war is acceptable on the open shelves at easy access level. It is perfectly acceptable reading for juveniles and young men. To be fair, these magazines are softcore pornography, a sort of cross between fan and pin-up magazines, but nevertheless they provide interesting testimony with regard to the acceptability and domestication of popular militarism. The war fantasies of juveniles and young men are perfectly legitimate, an acceptable part of growing up and becoming a man.

There are other magazines targeted at an older audience, most notably *Combat and Survival*. This particular magazine is ostensibly written for men with a service background but can be bought at newsagents throughout the country. Once again it is profusely illustrated and carries articles on elite units, weapons and military hardware, battle training, on the military situation throughout the world and on particular conflicts and crises. Let us look at a few recent issues in more detail. The February 1996 issue has articles on the US Marines, on the Israeli *Merkava* battle tank, on the Battle Courses at the Infantry Training Centre in Wales, on the activities of the Executive Outcomes mercenaries in Sierra Leone and lastly an article on 'How To Pass Your Annual Personal Weapon Test'. This issue was accompanied by a special supplement on the SAS which the magazine promised would become a regular feature. This first 'SAS File' contains a report on SAS activities in Bosnia, a feature on the weapons and equipment of the SAS Hostage Rescue Team and an account of a 'Key SAS Skill'. The October 1996 issue opens with a report on the UN peacekeeping force in the Lebanon, an article on the Chindits, an article on how to succeed on the SAS endurance march, a feature on 'Purple Star', a joint British-US training exercise, a guide to looking after your combat boots and lastly an article on battlegroup tactics. All of the articles and features are accompanied by photographs, most in colour, of weapons, equipment and of soldiers ready for action.

What is also interesting about *Combat and Survival* is the advertising it carries. There are adverts for all kinds of military equipment ranging from boots, smocks and bergens to bullet-proof vests, an incredible variety of knives, night sights, batons and blank firing or deactivated firearms. For £3,500 it is possible to buy a deactivated British Field Gun with guaranteed overnight delivery. One particular advert, 'Big Bang', offered 17 different blank firing handguns, ranging from £122 for a Beretta Automatic to a mere £34 for a Magnum Revolver. Another £14.95 would purchase a leather shoulder holster. Commando, stiletto, throwing, bowie and hunting knives are all available on mail order. One company actually offers to provide the full SAS Hostage Rescue outfit. The magazine also carries regular advertisements for bodyguard training. And somewhat inevitably there are also advertisements for guides on 'How to Pick Up Girls', 'How to Meet Women' and 'How to Win with Women'. All these are 'guaranteed' to work. One cannot help feeling that the typical *Combat and Survival* reader is a man in his twenties, walking the streets in combat fatigues, carrying a concealed blank firing pistol, and trying to work up the nerve to speak to a woman! Clearly though, as far as this magazine is concerned, fantasy is beginning to overlap with real life. What is interesting from our point of view is the extent to which the SAS are acknowledged to be the elite, the role-models, for this particular subculture. They are the men most admired, most to be emulated.

The SAS as Lifestyle

One of the spin-offs from the profitable SAS industry that has developed to exploit the regiment's reputation is the SAS handbook or manual. A number of volumes by various hands offering the SAS as a guide to civilian life have appeared in recent years. So far we have John Wiseman's *The SAS Personal Trainer* and *The SAS Survival Handbook*, Barry Davies's *The SAS Escape, Evasion and Survival Manual* and Andrew Kain and Neil Hanson's *SAS Security Handbook*. They range from little more than attaching the SAS label to an advanced fitness manual to a proposed militarisation of personal life in a violent and dangerous world. They once again bear testimony to the cultural impact of the SAS.

Wiseman's *The SAS Personal Trainer* is in many ways a conventional keep-fit book. The blurb claims that with this book 'you too can acquire the unique range of skills taught to members of the Special Air Service'. Nevertheless, despite the fact that it was written by someone with over 20 years' service in the SAS, the bulk of the book is concerned with commonplace fitness issues. Some chapters, those on 'strength training', 'running', 'swimming', 'cycling' and 'injuries' do little more than pay lip-service to the SAS connection and the book is remarkably free of photographs of soldiers. What separates out the average fitness practitioner from the hardcore, however, is, according to Wiseman, the Complete Fitness Programme supposedly modelled on the 'Professional SAS Programme'. This is presented in typical gung-ho fashion: the

SAS training programme 'is tough but only the best get to wear
the sand-coloured beret and the winged sword. "Who Dares Wins".
Do you dare to win? Do you dare to take on this fitness programme?'
It proposes an intensive seven-week programme involving lengthy
training sessions three times a day.[18]

Inevitably, there is a chapter on 'self-defence' or 'close quarter
battle'. This advocates walking away from trouble ('it takes courage
– and confidence – to walk away'). If this is not an option, never
threaten, just explode into action. Wiseman recommends attacking
your assailant's eyes, nose, throat, solar plexus, groin or knee. It
is possible, he remarks, to kill someone by a sharp blow to the throat
or a powerful kick to the testicles. This is reported absolutely
matter-of-fact rather than as any sort of precautionary warning. He
goes on to discuss the elbow strike, the head butt, the knee strike,
the kick and the combination strike. The recommended combination
strike involves first poking your assailant in the eyes, then driving
your palm into his chin, followed by an elbow in the face and a
knee to the groin. This needs to be practised so as to develop a
flowing rhythm. The SAS, he insists, believe in five-second fights.
Any longer and you risk injury to yourself.

Wiseman offers his thoughts on 'positive thinking', adopting
the pose of the guru communicating the secret of life to his disciples.
Positive thinking, he pontificates, is the key to success. Life in a
competitive world is hard and in order to survive it is necessary to
identify our own weaknesses and to take steps to eliminate them.
Much of the advice on offer is almost comically trite: a sense of
humour is vital, always try to look on the bright side, count your
blessings, remember there are many people worse off than you are,
and so on. The SAS are offered as a positive inspiration and role
model with the SAS training programme as the way to succeed.
'Use your SAS training programme', he urges, 'to help attain your
goals and develop that wonderful sense of achievement.
Achievement, fulfilment and inner happiness are the well-spring
of confidence.' This is the extent to which Wiseman embraces
competitive individualism to the absolute neglect of any collective
or team effort. It is in stark contrast to the SAS experience which
is all to do with team work, with a collective response to situations;
its celebration of competitive individualism makes it very much a
book of our times.

The last chapter, 'Facing Danger', instructs the reader on how
to survive in a world full of menace and danger. It combines both
the fantasy of SAS activity and the fear of social breakdown in a
paranoid account of how to negotiate the mean streets of
contemporary Britain. When you leave home to go to work or to
the shops, scan the ground ahead keeping a look-out for anything
unusual whether it be an open door, kids loitering on a street

corner or drunks sitting on a bench. Always check your back. Just as an SAS patrol on active service has the last man check for danger in its rear, so you have to be continually aware of what is happening behind you if you are to proceed in safety. Be prepared to take evasive action in order to avoid danger and to work out an escape route. Avoid areas where you can be 'easily ambushed' (his words) and if possible always mingle with crowds ('other people provide camouflage, concealment'). Always walk with your head up, avoid eye contact with strangers, never carry a bag unless it is absolutely necessary (it makes you a target for muggers), carry an old wallet stuffed with paper cut to bank-note size, and wear stout but comfortable shoes to facilitate either flight or a powerful kick. The very last words of the book emphasise that in the event of confrontation you have to be ready 'to launch a powerful kick if necessary'. This paranoid view of the streets of contemporary Britain as a war zone in which you need SAS skills to get home safe with the shopping is, of course, a very political view. It implicitly embraces a rightwing law-and-order agenda traditionally associated with the British Conservative Party but increasingly laid claim to by New Labour.[19]

What of Wiseman's *The SAS Survival Handbook*? This book is intended to turn its readers into survivors, to provide them with the knowledge and techniques necessary to survive in desert, jungle or arctic wastes. It offers a vast area of advice hardly anyone is ever likely to need from never eating the liver of a polar bear you have killed (it might contain lethal quantities of vitamin A) to never urinating whilst immersed in the waters of the Amazon (an Amazonian *candriu* catfish might swim up your urethra). There are sections on edible plants worldwide, on trapping, hunting and fishing, on building shelters, on first aid, and on how to survive disasters from avalanche to nuclear explosion. This is essential holiday reading for paranoid tourists, but really it tries to cover too much ground to be really useful. It is more of a fantasy volume for armchair explorers content to imagine themselves confronting nature red in tooth and claw. An exotic coffee-table book.[20]

Barry Davies's *The SAS Escape, Evasion and Survival Manual* comes with a dustjacket recommendation as 'an essential book for all who enjoy the wild, and for all-weather city or country dwellers – whose lifestyle may bring them face to face with prolonged isolation and danger'. With this insistence on the book's relevance in mind, it is somewhat surprising that the first chapter deals with 'capture', with being taken prisoner by enemy forces! Chapters on how to escape from captivity and on how to evade recapture follow. The 'Escape' chapter includes handy sections on tunnelling to freedom and on how to pick locks, including advice on how to make the necessary equipment. Just in case the reader should get too

excited about all this, the lock-picking section actually carries a
warning that possession of the necessary equipment, which we have
just been assured is 'fairly easy to improvise', is actually illegal. The
lock-picking advice should only be made use of by prisoners-of-
war! The 'Evasion' chapter contains useful hints on how to lose
tracker dogs, scare them off or even kill them. It is really quite difficult
to see what practical value these first three chapters might have for
anyone other than the aspiring criminal.

What follows is a manual for survival in the world similar to that
provided by Wiseman's somewhat better produced *The SAS
Survival Handbook*. There is advice on first aid, locating water,
constructing shelter, lighting fires, what plants to eat, hunting and
fishing, navigation and so on. The last chapter is concerned with
'self-defence'. This advocates avoiding trouble, if at all possible,
by flight if necessary, but if you have to fight make sure you win
no matter what it takes. Recommended target areas include your
assailant's hair, eyes, nose, ears, temple, throat, stomach, crutch,
thigh, knee and feet. Davies is alone in recommending that you bite
('sink your teeth into them') your opponent's testicles! [21]

The *SAS Security Handbook* was written by Andrew Kain, a
former SAS man and Falklands War veteran and Neil Hanson, a
professional author. Two other SAS veterans, Ken Connor and Paul
Brown, also assisted with the project. The handbook is a 360-page
loose-leaf affair in a yellow ring-binder and comes with Andy
McNab's advice not to wait to become a victim of crime, but to
do yourself a favour and 'read this book'. What this handbook, in
fact, proposes amounts to the militarisation of everyday life in
order to survive in a world where crime has run wild. 'There is',
the authors write, 'probably no one in the Western world who does
not know someone who has been attacked, had their car stolen,
their house burgled or their property vandalised.' Crime has
increased tenfold in Britain since 1950 and the police have been
overwhelmed. The *SAS Security Handbook* can fill the gap. What
it has to say 'is relevant to every single family in the UK'.

The handbook does contain some useful advice on house security
and on safety within the home, but this is effectively marginalised
by the paranoid militarism that predominates. Everything is
demonstrated with examples and analogies from SAS combat
experience. Protecting oneself and one's property against crime is
treated as a counter-insurgency operation! In a modest section on
house security, headed 'Garden Obstacles', the authors write of how
in a military context the enemy can be denied the use of ground
by mines and booby traps. This is not possible for the householder
who will have to make do with fences, shrubs and garden furniture
positioned so as to make access difficult. Deep gravel is a useful
deterrent because of the crunching noise it makes. Just as one

prepares an SAS observation post, the householder is putting things in place to give an early warning of anyone approaching. 'Instead of the noise of a Claymore mine going off, however,' they inform the presumably disappointed householder 'you'll have to be content with the crunch of gravel.'

Their discussion of Neighbour Watch and Response schemes is indicative. Predictably they advocate the active Response to the passive Watch. They compare such schemes to the SAS hearts-and-minds strategy in Borneo and Dhofar, enlisting the local people against the enemy. Advice that any Response scheme should be careful not to take on too much is supported by more lore drawn from the SAS experience of counter-insurgency warfare. It is pointed out that when the regiment was in Malaya they only rounded up 25 suspects a month because they only had the resources for that number of in-depth interrogations. When internment was introduced in Northern Ireland, however, 350 suspects were rounded up in one night. There were not enough skilled interrogators to handle this number with the consequent loss of much potentially useful information. Moreover, having untrained personnel interrogating suspects (the handbook uses the word 'interview') led to allegations of ill-treatment. Leaving aside the tendentious and inaccurate account of what went wrong with internment in Northern Ireland, what exactly are the members of neighbourhood response schemes to make of this?

Three responses in the event of an incident are recommended: two or three strong guys head for the house from which the alarm has come while others drive cars across the end of the street to block it off. If there are not enough of you to make a citizen's arrest then they recommend that you 'throw rocks and bottles from a safe distance, to drive the criminal off, or keep him penned up until the police arrive'. The third suggestion is even more astonishing: that the watch should emulate the people of the Falls Road and the Bogside and get everyone out on the street. 'A lot of women out doing a lot of shouting is frightening', they point out, 'and will deter anyone.' It has successfully forced the withdrawal of the police and the army in Northern Ireland and will drive off criminals! This is pretty amazing stuff. What they are proposing amounts, despite their claims to the contrary, to a kind of militarised vigilantism and this is leaving aside the question of the actual legality of stoning suspected criminals and blocking off public roadways! The *SAS Security Handbook* has broken dangerous new ground in this respect.

The section entitled 'Security in the Street' starts out by warning that the perception of crime is always greater than the reality and that it is important not to become paranoid. It then proceeds to stoke up that paranoia for page after page. The very next paragraph goes on to advise that, like an SAS sniper, 'you have to learn to look beyond the edge of the cover ... to look through cover and shadows, rather than just looking at them.' In the street this apparently means looking past those people nearest to you because a mugger might be using them as cover, as camouflage. Try to pick out people who might pose a threat and places where you might be vulnerable. The handbook goes on to advise the wearing of one's own protective camouflage when venturing out, that is, dress down with nothing flashy that might attract attention. This is compared to the SAS 'Keeni-Meeni' operations in Aden, patrolling the streets disguised as Arabs. Continued vigilance and preparedness is necessary, treating a visit to the shops or the journey to work as if it were an operation behind enemy lines. If you think a mugger is stalking you, check by looking in the reflection in shop windows. You can try 'looping the track' to throw them off: circle back on yourself to ambush them. In 1965 an SAS patrol pursued by Arab guerrillas did this twice, wiping out their pursuers. You can do the same, 'obviously without the deaths', by going into a shop and then turning round to take a good look at the face of the person following you. This attention should be enough to scare them off in a public place. Whenever you walk down the street always identify safe havens, places that you can flee to in case of attack. This is the advocacy of paranoia and is more likely to contribute to worsening the crime situation than to improving it.

With regard to dealing with street violence, they quite correctly advise avoiding injury by running away, but go on to discuss what to do if confrontation is unavoidable. Speed, aggression and surprise are recommended:

> You must focus all your energy on the short but ferocious assault. Drag up your most primeval instincts from deep within you, focus your hatred on the person trying to harm you, then unleash one violent attack, *the most violence that you can produce* [my emphasis]. If there's enough hatred behind it, it will succeed.

The emphasis put on hatred here is because of the need for most people, both men and women, to overcome their inhibitions with regard to violence, their reluctance to hurt someone seriously.

They recommend targeting your attacker's eyes, nose, mouth, ears, throat, groin, knees, shins and the arches of the feet. There is a handy photograph with these features carefully identified and labelled! It is important not to hesitate but to launch an all-out attack. This handbook suggests the SAS men storming the Iranian Embassy as an example to emulate: they reacted instantly, killing the terrorists. For you to hesitate in a confrontation with a mugger could be as dangerous as it would be for an SAS man to hesitate in shooting a terrorist! Absolutely crucial, however, is to focus your hatred!

There are other sections on car security, security abroad, business security, VIP and executive protection and on working in 'hostile regions'. This last section deals with survival in active war zones and is ostensibly advice for journalists and others working in such dangerous areas. What is most significant about the handbook, however, are its domestic sections with their proposed militarisation of everyday life. The message here is that you should conduct your life as if operating behind enemy lines, taking inspiration and guidance from the military experiences of the SAS. This is the most pernicious feature of the handbook: that despite its occasional disclaimers, its overwhelming effect is to foster a paranoid fear of crime and to encourage people to regard everyday life as a war, and society as a battlefield.[22]

The SAS as Documentary

There have been a number of documentary films made about the SAS for the video market. They are part of a growing number of documentary videos dealing with war and combat. These are quite specialist items that people, almost invariably men, interested in the SAS, have to go out of their way to find. More significant was the prestige seven-part documentary series that Carlton put out on television at peak viewing time in May and June 1996. This was heavily advertised, both on television and in the press, and attracted a mass audience. Let us look first of all at a selection of the videos that have appeared in the shops.

In 1995 Castle Vision brought out a 65-minute video, *The Story of the SAS*. This joined other Castle Vision videos about elite units (*Paras: The Official Story* and *Gurkhas: The Official Story*), a large number of battles and various military leaders and commanders. Given the significant niche market for this sort of video, the SAS was an obvious choice of subject.

The Story of the SAS, directed by John Doukas, is clearly an 'official story' although the phrase does not appear in the title. It is very much the SAS establishment's view of the unit with Peter de la Billière providing an introduction and a number of senior officers and senior NCOs putting in an appearance. Reg Seekings, Bob Bennett, Johnny Cooper, Tony Dean-Drummond, Tony Jeapes and de la Billière himself, all tried and trusted veterans, tell it like it was, or at least, like it was supposed to be. The video recounts the history of the SAS, narrated by Joss Acland, and illustrates the story with rare archive film. It is a celebratory account, presenting a quite uncritical view of the unit's performance and effectiveness. According to this account, the SAS made decisive contributions in the Western Desert, Malaya and Borneo. In Dhofar, the heroic SAS stand at

Mirbat broke 'the enemy's will to fight' so that the war was 'effectively over'. News to those still fighting there two years later. The SAS contribution in both the Falklands and the Gulf wars demonstrated their vital importance in conventional wars. As for their counter-terrorist role, they are, de la Billière tells us, 'the very best ... in the world'. With the storming of the Iranian Embassy, the SAS had 'burst onto the world stage'. This crucial operation was 'the pinnacle of years of training, planning and seemingly endless reappraisal, and the world was watching ... it made great television'. There is no gloating over the dead terrorists, the emphasis here is on highly trained men capable of making milli-second life and death judgements. The SAS is a national asset, a regiment to be proud of, 'the world's premier elite unit'.[23]

For devotees of the military and combat documentary there is the Aviation and Military Video Club that is run by DD Video. This distributes a wide range of material, most of it concerned with aviation, but also including videos on the First World War, the Second World War and the Vietnam War. A recent catalogue also offered members audio tapes of 'Military Music of Adolf Hitler's Liebstandarte SS' and three volumes of 'Military Music of Adolf Hitler's Third Reich'. More important for our discussion is the DD video series 'Elite Fighting Forces'. This features documentaries on the Gurkhas, the Spetsnaz, the Royal Marines, the US Navy Seals, the French Foreign Legion, and, of course, their bestselling title, *The SAS*.

The production quality of this video is inferior to that of Castle Vision's *The Story of the SAS*, compensating with a much more gung-ho tone. Much the same ground is covered (although here the war in Rhodesia is treated as if it were a British war) but the celebration of the SAS is cruder. We are told quite candidly, for example, that in Malaya the aim of the SAS 'was to terrorise the terrorists', and that this was 'instrumental in achieving victory'. As for the storming of the Iranian Embassy, here we are shown still photographs of the dead terrorists with a voice-over commentary that points out that all 'but one of them were killed with machine-like precision. One terrorist alone was hit with 82 bullets. The entire operation took just eleven minutes to execute'. In Northern Ireland, the SAS has been responsible for killing some 30 IRA members, indeed their effectiveness has been so great that so far as the IRA is concerned, SAS stands for 'Special Assassination Squad'. This account of the SAS's exploits in Northern Ireland is accompanied by footage of IRA funerals. The video's message is summed up by Bob Bennett, the veteran SAS NCO when he pontificates that 'you've got so many weak people now, in the courts, the judges, everything else, you've got so many weak people, but thank God, you've got an SAS because without SAS the country's finished'.[24]

The Carlton TV series, *SAS: The Soldiers' Story* was radically different from anything that had appeared before. It was a prestige production, heavily advertised both on TV and in the press (a succession of full-page ads) and was accompanied by the publication of a bestselling companion book, Jack Ramsay's *SAS: The Soldiers' Story*. The official version of the SAS as tough, brave, dedicated and highly trained professionals engaged in the clinical neutralisation and taking out of the enemies of state and society was replaced by an altogether more visceral celebration of violence and mayhem. What the Carlton series revealed was a collection of masked, pseudonymous men who positively revelled in their macho warrior masculinity, actually enjoyed combat and seemed to derive satisfaction if not pleasure from killing. And all for queen and country. It celebrated the SAS as a band of one-dimensional killers, ill-adjusted psychos and all at peak-time viewing. Presumably editorial decisions were taken to emphasise the 'macho killer' aspect of the SAS in order to guarantee high viewing figures. The result was as much a caricature as the official version. As far as the regiment's reputation was concerned, the series was a disaster.

Episode 1 inevitably dealt with the storming of the Iranian Embassy. This, the voiceover tells us 'was the SAS calling card to the world'. It goes on to promise that in this hour-long film the viewer will be taken beyond the newsreels to see events, not through the eyes of the politicians, but 'through the eyes of the men who took part ... us'. The film shows the SAS in training, with footage of Killing House exercises, taking up position once the Embassy had been seized (they waited six days in full-kit with bullets ready in the chamber for the word 'go'), and then moving in to storm the building. The terrorists, an SAS soldier tells us, thought 'the British had gone soft, they thought they were in for a good day out, they just hadn't heard of the SAS'. There is only one way to deal with terrorists: 'you go in hard and kill them'. And the SAS are just the men to do the job. We are told that once 'the leash is pulled, the shutters go up, you can get to grips with the enemy, you know you can kill them'. The choice of words is interesting: these men apparently regard themselves as trained killers who have to be kept leashed and hooded until someone has to be killed. There is no nonsense about making arrests, taking prisoners, or limited force.

The film combines news footage of the SAS breaking into the Embassy with a dramatic reconstruction of the hunting down of the terrorists inside. Once again in the words of one of the SAS soldiers: 'we were not part of society at that moment in time, we had created our own society within No. 16, the law of the jungle, kill or be killed. For that moment in time we could have been on a different planet.' He somewhat disturbingly laughs to himself in the middle of this little speech.

The men in black, hoods, gas masks, body armour, black overalls and boots, machine pistols, mysterious, threatening, potent, go through flame and smoke in pursuit of their enemy, the international terrorist. What we are shown on the screen is men being killed, riddled with bullets, fired at close range with the camera lovingly moving in on machine gun muzzles spitting flame. When the hostages are being manhandled down the Embassy stairs by the rescue team, they realise that one of the terrorists has slipped in among them. He is knocked down the stairs and shot dead while sprawled on the floor. This is the climactic moment of the film. The killing of this terrorist is luxuriated over, shown from different viewpoints, once in colour and once in sepia, with slow motion and freeze frame effects to heighten and intensify the impact. Once again we see machine gun muzzles spitting flame. The result is straight-forwardly pornographic. The SAS soldier's voiceover tells us that two or three magazines 'were emptied into him and the sound was deafening and he twitched and vomited his life on the carpet'. It took two point something seconds 'and there's something like eighty rounds in him'. To some this overkill might seem to indicate that they had momentarily lost it, but here it is presented as a tribute to their prowess. Only the SAS can shoot someone so many times in so little time. Over still photographs of the dead terrorists, we are told that the SAS 'proved to the world that if you go in hard against terrorists, they fall like a pack of cards'. The film reduces all the political considerations and complexities inherent in this sort of episode to the question of unleashing the SAS. It is more to do with unburdening the national psyche and making the terrorists pay for past national humiliations, both real and imaginary, than it is to do with resolving a crisis. The Thatcher government had found a cost-effective way of creating the feel-good factor. The contrast with the two video documentaries considered earlier and their coverage of the Embassy siege could not be starker.

Other episodes (only half an hour in length) looked at the battle of Mirbat in Dhofar, at operations in the Gulf, the Falklands and in Colombia. The Mirbat episode opened with an AK47 being cocked and an SAS voiceover saying, 'the guy who owned this AK47 was trying to kill me with it at Mirbat. Now I own it, and he's dead.' The fourth episode focused on selection and training and the sort of men who were good enough for the SAS. It emphasised endurance over intelligence, toughness over skill, and quite perversely focused on the brutalities of the mock interrogation that candidates undergo. The film featured a long graphic sequence of men being brutalised (once again this was presumably what it was felt the audience wanted!). It has been known, we are told, for hard men to be physically broken by this particular ordeal, reduced 'to sobbing wrecks'. The SAS do not so much have a selection process as a rejection process that is designed to get rid of 'the weaklings'.

The Gulf War episode follows the exploits of a heavily armed motorised SAS patrol, Alpha Three Zero, half-squadron in strength, that raided deep behind Iraqi lines. It provides graphic reconstructions of the killing of the first Iraqi soldiers in the ground war ('the first kill, white-eyed and up close') and of a night attack on an Iraqi microwave installation. The attitude adopted is resolutely gung-ho: 'the advantage we had was that we had the bottle' – 'every mobile column achieved their aim' – 'SAS soldiers had probably stopped the Israelis' entry into the war.' Since the series went out on the air, the SAS soldier from whose point of view the Gulf episode is told has published his own memoir, *Victor Two*, under the name Peter Crossland. His published account provides an interesting contrast with the approach taken by the TV series. First, he reveals that the half-squadron's Officer Commanding (OC) 'lost it' once they were behind Iraqi lines and had to be replaced. His account of the first kill is predictably more obscenely realistic than anything that can be shown on TV. They pull a dying Iraqi out of the vehicle they have just shot up and his blood sprays in a large arc for two or three metres. He lies on the ground choking on his own blood with his eyes rolling. His bodily functions 'were letting go, and steam and stench started to rise as the mortally wounded soldier slipped rapidly and painfully into oblivion'. Crossland will never forget this man's face. As for the man he had personally killed, he found himself continually replaying the episode in his mind in increasing detail. He calls this 'first kill syndrome'. The new OC is described in most uncomplimentary terms as only getting into the SAS because of a shortage of officers while the sergeant major actually running the patrol was universally hated and despised. The attack on the microwave installation, codenamed 'Victor Two' is described as a protracted cock-up rather than the precision exercise shown on TV. Once the shooting started the sergeant major 'fucked off ... leaving the rest of us behind'. He got the Distinguished Conduct Medal and has since been commissioned. Crossland even reports the suspicion that the operation was militarily unnecessary, that air power could have destroyed the installation, but it was staged to 'blood' the troops.

One incident particularly stands out in the film. When they are approaching the microwave installation there is a noise from a vehicle parked in the vicinity. The door is pulled open and an Iraqi soldier is discovered inside. The film shows an SAS soldier standing by the vehicle's door firing round after round into the cab. You never see the Iraqi soldier, just his hand gesturing as he dies. In his memoir, 'Crossland' reveals that the Iraqi soldier was a boy not more than sixteen years old, 'scared shitless', whom he has nevertheless to shoot. Their eyes met and the boy 'registered my decision to kill him'. As the bullets hit, the boy's head was still 'shaking and pleading'. The reason we are not shown the Iraqi in the vehicle's cab in the TV series becomes obvious. Crossland returned to Britain after the Gulf War to a broken marriage, a much-loved son dying of muscular dystrophy, and regular nightmares of killing the Iraqi boy soldier but now with his son's face. In his memoir, he is not a superman, but someone overwhelmed by life's catastrophes, very critical of the regiment to which he was devoted, desperately trying to cope. This 'soldier's story' is very different from that told by the TV series, more human, more convincing.[25]

The seventh episode of the series, on SAS exploits in Northern Ireland, has never been televised, presumably because it was considered too provocative in view of the ending of the IRA ceasefire. It apparently had the shooting of three IRA members at Drumnakilly, County Tyrone on 30 August 1988 as its centrepiece. Interestingly enough, the series scrupulously avoided the Gibraltar shootings, presumably because of embarrassment at the three IRA volunteers killed on that occasion being unarmed. What is particularly interesting about the other episodes is that these graphic portrayals of violence, killing and brutality that went out at peak viewing time over six weeks attracted hardly any criticism. No 'fictional' drama would have got away with such images of violence and killing, but this series seemed above and beyond criticism. Only in the *Observer* was the series castigated by Peter Beaumont, the newspaper's defence correspondent, as 'sadistic and salacious'. Even he was more concerned to call for a return to the SAS code of silence rather than to ponder the significance of the fact that a number of SAS veterans were prepared to glory in this portrayal. Official dissatisfaction with the series was later shown when a number of members of the Territorial SAS involved in making it were either asked to resign or thrown out.[26]

A five-volume edition of the series has since been made available on video. The Northern Ireland episode remains unavailable.[27]

The SAS as Film

The contemporary potency of the SAS myth receives powerful testimony from the 1996 American feature film, *The Rock*, directed by Michael Bay and starring Sean Connery and Nicholas Cage. In this 'action' movie, Connery plays an ageing SAS captain, John Patrick Mason, who has been held without trial in the United States for thirty years. His crime: stealing FBI microfilm secrets. When rogue US Marines commanded by General Francis X. Hummel occupy Alcatraz and aim missiles armed with UX gas warheads at San Francisco, demanding a $100 million ransom, the US authorities are forced to turn to Mason for help. He is the only man to have ever escaped from 'the Rock', although he was soon recaptured, and now they want him to show them the way in. He has to lead a crack team of US Navy Seals together with bomb disposal specialist Stanley Goodspeed (played by Cage) back to Alcatraz to foil the threat. Everything goes wrong. The Seals are massacred and Mason, the SAS veteran, has singlehandedly to defeat the Marines, making it possible for Goodspeed to save San Francisco.[28]

There is immense symbolic significance in an American film having US Marines go murderously rogue, the Navy Seals blunder into a trap that none of them survive, and the day being saved by the SAS, even if it is in the familiar shape of Sean Connery. The symbolism is further heightened by the way that Connery, the former James Bond star, has abandoned the British secret service for the new undercover elite, the SAS. The film is a remarkable testimony to the international reputation of the SAS, although whether it presages a fashion for SAS films remains to be seen. What is perhaps surprising is how little impact the SAS has actually had in film, whether made for television or for the big screen. We shall examine the nature of that impact here.

A number of films about British special forces were made even before the SAS came to prominence in the 1980s. In 1958 there was Guy Green's *Sea of Sand*, in 1967 Arthur Hiller's *Tobruk* and in 1969 Andre de Toth's *Play Dirty*. These three films, all set in the Western Desert during the Second World War, dealt with motorised raiding parties operating behind German lines. They were made at a time when the SAS was still just one of a number of such units and not necessarily the best known. There was certainly no compulsion to identify these films as SAS films. Today it seems certain that any similar films would inevitably embrace the SAS, taking advantage of the regiment's high profile. Arguably these three films actually benefited from not having to carry the weighty baggage of the SAS myth.

Both *Sea of Sand*, starring Richard Attenborough and John Gregson, and *Play Dirty*, starring Michael Caine, Nigel Davenport and Nigel Green (with a script co-written by Melvyn Bragg), are solid craftsmanlike films that take war seriously. *Sea of Sand* is the more self-consciously heroic but even here the costs of heroism are confronted. A serious attempt is made to portray the various members of the Long Range Desert Group patrol, whose exploits the film follows, as ordinary men engaged in a real war, rather than as cardboard heroes whose antics are primarily intended to carry the narrative from explosion to explosion. An attempt is made to suggest that they have a real life off the screen and that their deaths will actually leave wives widowed and children fatherless. *Play Dirty* also treats war seriously, but is a far more cynical exercise. A seriously underrated film, its anti-heroism was fashionable in 1969, but would not be so acceptable today. The shooting of the survivors of this raiding party by their own side is one of the ironies that identifies *Play Dirty* as very much a film of the Vietnam War era.

Much less successful was *Tobruk*, starring Rock Hudson, George Peppard and Nigel Green. This film was based on an actual wartime operation: the September 1942 attack on Tobruk by John Haselden's Special Services Regiment. Haselden's intention was to penetrate German defences by having his men pose as prisoners-of-war, guarded by members of the Special Identification Group (SIG), a unit of German-speaking Palestinian Jews, disguised as German soldiers. The Tobruk attack was part of a larger operation, Operation Agreement, that included an SAS attack on Benghazi. The real life operation was a costly disaster. Predictably, in the film victory was snatched from the jaws of defeat. *Tobruk* is resolutely mediocre, relying on its very average action sequences to carry the day, the characters are cardboard and the final turning of the tables on the Germans is most unconvincing. Despite the laudable intention of giving the little-known wartime SIG some limelight, the film's attempt to turn a defeat into a victory was seriously misguided.[29]

What is surprising is that the emergence of the SAS as a significant cultural phenomenon in the 1980s has not prompted a spate of films celebrating either their wartime or their postwar exploits. All we have had so far is *Who Dares Wins*, directed by Ian Sharp and going on general release in 1982. This reflects the weakness of the British film industry, a weakness that is particularly apparent with regard to action films. Even so, it is still surprising that there have not been more SAS films. Perhaps the poor quality and lack of commercial success of *Who Dares Wins* contributed to this.

Who Dares Wins was a particularly crude attempt to make money while grinding a political axe. It attempted to exploit the SAS's storming of the Iranian Embassy, to champion Thatcherite politics and to inflict political damage on the left, in particular on the British Campaign for Nuclear Disarmament (CND). It succeeded in none of these things. The story concerns a ruthless terrorist cell that is using a CND-type organisation, the People's Lobby, as a front. The terrorists are being financed by a Andrei Malik, the agent of a mysterious Middle Eastern power that is engaged in stirring up trouble throughout the world. In Britain, they are planning some sort of dramatic coup that will force the West to abandon nuclear weapons and leave it open to blackmail and conquest. The British security services know that something is going on but the agent they had on the inside has been killed. They turn to the SAS!

The hero of the film is Peter Skellen, played by Lewis Collins of the popular TV action series, *The Professionals*. He poses as an embittered ex-SAS officer, thrown out of the regiment and determined to strike back at the Establishment. It is not his military credentials that get him on the inside, however, but his sexual credentials. Skellen's masculinity proves to be the terrorists' undoing. His good looks, his being tall, athletic, handsome and arrogant, and his being smartly dressed in blazer, slacks and polished shoes, and his short hair, might well have made him somewhat obtrusive in peace movement circles and a most unlikely choice for undercover work. What *Who Dares Wins* is concerned with, however, is not the unsavoury realities of spying on radical and protest movements, but with the potency of a particular heterosexual masculinity. Skellen is very much a down-market James Bond, combining violence with sexual charisma. He effortlessly seduces one of the terrorist leaders, the beautiful Frankie Lee, an American activist, successfully penetrating the conspiracy in more ways than one. She finds him irresistible and falls in love with him. Frankie is an idealist and a fanatic, a misguided do-gooder, hoping to save the world through violence. A proper relationship with a real man might have saved her, won her away from political extremism to a woman's proper role, turned her into a wife and mother. Skellen has arrived too late on the scene, however, and is already married! This is the nearest the film gets to subtlety. The terrorists pose a threat not just to the nuclear deterrent, but to the nuclear family as well. When they discover that Skellen is still in the SAS, they take his wife and child hostage. They are held prisoner by the fanatical Helga, a sour, butch lesbian killer, played by Ingrid Pitt, best known for her classic portrayals of female vampires! Helga is the conservative heterosexual male's feminist nightmare. Skellen's wife fights with this monstrous woman for her child, for her family, for all families everywhere. Helga recovers her gun after their brawl and is just about to shoot mother and child when the SAS burst through the wall and clinically take her out with the two shot 'double-tap'. In this respect, the film is considerably more restrained than 'real life' where she would be more likely to be shot anywhere between a dozen and eighty times!

The terrorists plan to seize the US ambassador's country residence when he is hosting a dinner for the visiting US secretary of state and British foreign secretary. Once they have taken their hostages, they demand that the British fire a nuclear missile at the Holy Loch nuclear submarine base, 'in the name of peace'. They believe that a demonstration of the devastation nuclear weapons are capable of will turn public opinion against them and force the West to disarm. The SAS come to the rescue, mounting an Iranian Embassy-type assault on the residence, killing all the terrorists and saving the day, with a little help from Skellen.

Who Dares Wins is ludicrous in every respect, a pernicious and grotesque exercise in political witch-hunting, that fails because of its very excess. It is a rabid rightwing fantasy let loose on the big screen, a Thatcherite rant against a host of imagined enemies who are all conveniently lumped together as part of the Soviet menace. Pacifist, liberal and leftwing peace campaigners are shown as so many dupes, unwittingly enlisted in a covert terrorist campaign to disarm and bring down the West. There is a particularly savage portrayal of a pacifist bishop, weak, sanctimonious and foolish, being manipulated by forces he could not even begin to understand. Such people have to be protected from themselves. The film ends with a senior Labour politician expressing private sympathy for the terrorists and walking arm in arm with the Mephistophelian Andrei Malik through Westminster. Malik promises him many more such incidents while the 'Red Flag' is played in the background. This crass McCarthyism was too much for British audiences even in 1982.[30]

While *Who Dares Wins* is the only SAS feature film made in Britain, in 1979 a feature film about the Australian SAS, *The Odd Angry Shot*, went on release in Australia. This received a video release in Britain in 1993. Directed by Tom Jeffrey and starring Graham Kennedy, John Hargreaves and others, *The Odd Angry Shot* is a grim anti-heroic Vietnam War film. It follows an SAS squad through their tour of duty in Vietnam, fighting a small-scale, low-key war against an elusive, unseen enemy. In this film when men are wounded they scream in agony, bodies are mutilated, feet are blown off, and all for nothing. The war is shown as sheer waste, a waste of time and a waste of lives, that the soldiers endure with humour, stoicism and increasing bitterness. When the two survivors from the squad arrive back home and are having a drink in a bar, they both deny having been to Vietnam! Theirs is not a popular war. What is interesting about *The Odd Angry Shot* is that the elite character of the SAS is actually played down. They are portrayed as just 'poor bloody infantrymen', engaged in a particularly unrewarding war, without anything really to distinguish them from any other foot soldiers. In this respect, the film starkly contradicts the 'official' history of the Australian SAS in Vietnam, which is a story of success and heroism against overwhelming odds. In the film the SAS lose more men killed in the first half hour than the regiment admits to losing in the entire war.[31]

At this point, it is worth considering briefly how successful Hollywood was in its treatment of special forces prior to the release of *The Rock*. Defeat in Vietnam and the Desert One fiasco together prevented the various US special forces, the Green Berets, the Navy

Seals and Delta Force, from achieving the popularity, status and profile of the British SAS. This failure has been reflected in the US film industry's response. *The Green Berets*, directed by and starring John Wayne, that came out in 1968, was not only crude propaganda, although it has to be said that it appears sophisticated compared with *Who Dares Wins*, but more important it was about a war effort that was becoming increasingly discredited and was to end in defeat and national humiliation. Much more successful was the Rambo trilogy *First Blood* (1982), *Rambo II* (1985) and *Rambo III* (1988) that shows special warfare specialist, John Rambo, inarticulately waging war across America, Vietnam and Afghanistan. Further sequels were planned, but *Rambo III*'s commercial failure happily killed the project. These appalling films have to be seen, as Gilbert Adair insists, as 'a veritable archive of Reaganite attitudes and aspirations'.[32] They are, without any doubt, of considerable importance as a cultural phenomenon. Nevertheless, they celebrate the warrior as loner, as solitary hero, rather than celebrate a particular military unit. Hollywood films celebrating Delta Force and the Navy Seals have been much less successful. There has been no American equivalent of the SAS phenomenon.

While the British film industry barely responded to the cultural impact of the SAS, British TV companies have made a belated effort to climb aboard the bandwagon. We have already looked at the Carlton documentary series, *SAS: The Soldiers' Story*, but there has also been a TV film made of Chris Ryan's Gulf War memoir, *The One That Got Away* by LWT. The BBC are also reputed to be making a TV film of Andy McNab's *Bravo Two Zero*, but this has not, at the time of writing, appeared. Both, of course, deal with the fate of the same SAS patrol, cut off behind Iraqi lines. The showing of *The One That Got Away* in February 1996 provoked considerable controversy.

The One That Got Away, written and directed by Paul Greengrass and starring Paul McGann and David Morrissey, was a prestige production, expensive and well made. Its showing brought widespread condemnation from other surviving members of the patrol, from the relatives of the men who died, from the British Ministry of Defence and unprecedentedly from the Colonel Commandant of the SAS, David Lyon, in a letter to *The Times* (19 February 1996). What was it that excited such hostility? The film told the story of Bravo Two Zero from Chris Ryan's point of view. It celebrated the military prowess of the SAS and Ryan's own courage and endurance but at the same time condemned glory-seeking heroics, showed the British military effort as an incompetent shambles and a number of patrol members as just not being up to the demands made of them. Vince Phillips, who died of exposure, is shown as having 'lost it', while Andy McNab is portrayed as a glory-seeking bullshitter, unfit to be in command. These remarkably unsympathetic portrayals have reputedly cost Ryan many friends. More serious perhaps is the way that the film aggrandises his own role. It claims to tell 'the true story' of Bravo Two Zero but admits that some scenes, dialogue and characters 'have been created for the purpose of dramatisation'. One such scene occurs towards the end of the film and was obviously regarded as a necessary climax: he singlehandedly confronts two Iraqi vehicles. He destroys one vehicle with a rocket launcher, stops the other with a grenade and shoots the terrified Iraqis crammed into the back. One lone survivor makes a break for it and Ryan chases him, pulls him down and stabs him to death. This is all very exciting, very dramatic. The aftermath of what is a veritable massacre is sad, plaintive rather than exultant, with Ryan staring into the face of the man he has stabbed to death. The director, Paul Greengrass, manages to have it both ways here: exciting dramatic violence and regret at the need for it. This hypocrisy is compounded by the fact that the episode is fictional. The contrast between Ryan's 'authentic' heroism and McNab's 'pseudo' heroism is highlighted by a scene of the latter in Iraqi hands, still bullshitting, pathetic rather than defiant. While it is easy to see how the film managed to annoy so many people, the fact is that this controversy has more of the character of a family quarrel than anything more serious. The film wholeheartedly endorses the SAS myth, which Ryan is shown as living up to, while the SAS itself and many of his former comrades-in-arms fall short.

CHAPTER 4

The SAS as Fiction

The storming of the Iranian Embassy and the Falklands War were the key events in the emergence of SAS fiction, in the writing and publishing of a growing number of novels either about the SAS or in which former or serving SAS soldiers played an important role. The SAS became, as we have already seen, 'a metaphor for efficient violence' and this metaphor has since been worked out, extended and elaborated on in numerous works of fiction, both war novels and thrillers. In the years since the Falklands, many thriller writers (Frederick Forsyth, Gerald Seymour, Gavin Lyall, James Follett, Terence Strong, Alexander Fullerton, Jack Higgins, Stephen Leather and others) have produced SAS novels; two series of SAS novels ('The Fighting Saga of the SAS' and 'Soldier A to Z') have appeared; a number of former SAS soldiers have written SAS novels; and there have even been a few critical treatments of the regiment and its soldiers. Overwhelmingly, however, the SAS novel has celebrated a warrior masculinity, militarism and a reactionary politics. It is a significant presence within popular fiction today.

The rise of the SAS novel has intersected with a transition phase in the development of the political thriller, a period of transition from the certainties of the Cold War to the increasing importance of international terrorism. International terrorism, a threat that is able to incorporate the IRA, Islamic fundamentalist groups and a variety of other organisations, has become the new 'fear' that thriller writers have sought to exploit. The opening words of Gavin Lyall's *Uncle Target* (1988) are classic in this regard: 'Since terrorism had become normal ...'.[1] This obsession with terrorism very much fits in with the concerns of Conservative politicians and the rightwing press. The shadowy figure of the terrorist, coward, psychopath, sadist, has emerged to threaten the very existence of Western society. They hide in the dark, are impossible to identify, strike without warning, with an arsenal of terrifying weaponry, and leave a trail of dead and mutilated humanity behind them. When the terrorists are women, the threat takes on a whole new dimension, with motherhood, domesticity and the family all violated. Only the death of these monstrous females can restore the patriarchal order. Conventional police and soldiers are helpless against such a diabolic menace; only the men of the SAS can save us. Of course, the actual threat that terrorism poses to Western societies is in practice minimal, but the terrorist has become a convenient lightning conductor, focusing, carrying away and earthing wider social and political tensions. The SAS novel has both responded to and amplified fear of terrorism.

What we shall do in this chapter is first of all look at the SAS novels produced by a number of thriller writers, next we shall examine the SAS series, in particular 'Soldier A to Z' and lastly we shall consider the handful of novels that can be considered as being in some way or other critical, in particular, Derek Robinson's outstanding war novel, *A Good Clean Fight* (1993).

The SAS Thriller

Let us look first at James Follett's *The Tiptoe Boys* (1982), the novel of the SAS film, *Who Dares Wins*. The book can be seen as a quite straightforward exercise in Thatcherite political paranoia that goes even further in exhibiting its reactionary prejudices than the film was able to. Here the SAS are the thin red line confronting a whole array of enemies determined to bring the country down. The actual terrorists are only the most extreme members of this far more widespread conspiracy. The object of the novel's hatred is the anti-nuclear weapons campaign, the People's Lobby, led by Horace Wilberforce Crick, the bishop of Camden Town. This organisation involves 'all the familiar faces': the revolutionary actress, the Troops Out MP, the Trotskyist journalist, the pro-PLO TV commentator and three trade union leaders who had called over a million of their members out on strike in support of a man justifiably sacked for breaking a foreman's nose. The novel's prejudices extend predictably enough to include homosexuals and social workers, especially those who fit both categories. All in all, it provides a fairly exhaustive round-up of *Daily Telegraph* prejudices which Follett adds up to find the country in the grip of social and political decay. Festering within this decay is a small group of ruthless terrorists, cruel, heartless fanatics, mad dogs that need to be put down.

Women play an important part in Follett's terrorist organisation: one of the leaders, Frankie, is the daughter of a multi-millionaire, a young, beautiful liberated woman who has been completely drained of conscience and pity by her devotion to the revolutionary cause. She is a sexually liberated Lady Macbeth. In this respect, the novel differs from the film where Frankie actually falls in love with Skellen, the SAS hero, and is shown capable of human feelings. Here, she is an abomination and cannot be allowed to live. At the end of the novel, Skellen shoots her in cold blood, while in the film, they look sadly at each other, both hesitating, and another SAS man steps in to gun her down. The novel manages to be more coarse in its one-dimensional prejudices than the film, a pretty remarkable feat. Another woman terrorist is Helga, a lesbian who delights in killing and who holds Skellen's family hostage. The involvement of women in terrorism is portrayed as the most unnatural political perversion that he can think of. It stands as an indictment not just of terrorism but of women's liberation for making such things possible. The lesbian terrorist holding a man's family hostage is a particularly potent threat to all that *Daily Telegraph* readers hold dear. Only the SAS can exorcise these demons.[2]

With Terence Strong's *Whisper Who Dares* (1982), the scene shifts to Northern Ireland and we are confronted with a novel that works on a different level from Follett's. Whereas *The Tiptoe Boys* indulges its political prejudices quite openly, Strong successfully blends his into the narrative and has written a much darker and more powerful novel.

Strong deals with the heroic efforts of a four-man SAS team, commanded by Captain Jack Ducane, which is engaged in preventing the IRA establishing their own elite unit, modelled on the SAS and trained by ex-Green Beret mercenaries. The Irish are incapable of combating the SAS themselves, and with defeat staring them in the face in 1976 they call in professional help in the form of an American psychopath, McClatcher. The IRA are portrayed as third-rate gangsters, good enough to murder defenceless women and children, but no match for the hard men of the SAS. The Army Council is shown as a bunch of self-important incompetents, small-minded bigots dealing out death and destruction for their own self-aggrandisement and petty gratification. McClatcher threatens to change all this, turning the rather pathetic IRA volunteers into real fighting men. He has to be stopped.

To do this, Ducane and his team raid an IRA training camp deep in the Republic and, after various setbacks, succeed in wiping out the elite unit before it can go into action. Ducane's men slaughter some 45 handpicked IRA men, the best the Provisionals have to offer, and suffer only one fatality themselves (predictably inflicted by McClatcher). They daub the scene with UVF slogans and slip away.

All of the IRA's best efforts are brought to nothing by what Strong calls the 'Paddy Factor', that is, the supposed congenital stupidity of the Irish, their inability to get anything right. This causes problems, because if the IRA are to be portrayed as a gang of incompetents without any popular support, how does one account for the failure of the British Army and the RUC to defeat them and the need for SAS involvement? Strong overcomes this difficulty by showing the British Army as a well-meaning but blundering military machine neither trained nor equipped to combat a guerrilla challenge, even of the sort posed by the IRA. The SAS, however, turn the IRA's own methods against them, with greater success.

Whisper Who Dares draws its strength from its powerful graphic descriptions of acts of violence. Early on in the book, Ducane's men ambush a carload of Provos and in the shooting, one of them has his head literally shot off. The man's last few heartbeats project a fountain of blood up onto the inside roof of the car. Later on, a young woman, Roisin McGuire, is kneecapped by the IRA and Strong provides a graphic description of the drill biting into her and spewing up blood and gristle flecked with chips of bone. He gives this particular assault the appearance of a sexual act as the unfortunate victim thrusts her pelvis forward in a grotesque imitation of orgasm. Of course, this can be justified on the grounds of realism, as being no more than the brutal truth; after all two high velocity bullets in the neck would tear someone's head off and blood would spray all over the place, and kneecapping is a bloody brutal affair, but Strong's writing has the effect not so much of horrifying as of thrilling and exciting his readers.

What place is there for women in this world of ambushes, gunfire and smouldering corpses? They are the fighting man's Achilles' heel. Ducane himself is betrayed by his wife, Trish, and another British officer, working undercover, Lieutenant Harrington, is betrayed by Roisin McGuire. Both women are, in the course of the novel, raped, Trish by McClatcher and Roisin by a member of the Army Council, but the frailty of women is such that they both enjoy the experience and participate in it. The novel plumbs the murky depths of masculine insecurity here, but retribution is at hand. Both women are punished for their betrayals: Trish is murdered and Roisin is, as we have already seen, crippled. The attitude towards women in *The Tiptoe Boys* seems almost progressive in comparison.

Whereas *The Tiptoe Boys* deals in the politics of the *Daily Telegraph*, *Whisper Who Dares'* universe is a much more libidinous affair, a universe where killing, torture, mutilation and bloodshed seem to be the only reality. The book ends with McClatcher still at large and the hunt for him just getting underway. The killing goes on. In this charnel house of a universe we can only sleep easy in our beds because the SAS is there to protect us.[3]

Since the success of *Whisper Who Dares*, Strong has published another nine novels, six of them either about the SAS or involving former members of the SAS. *Whisper Who Dares* was followed by *The Fifth Hostage* (1983), the fast-moving story of an SAS hostage-rescue operation into Iran in 1980, a blood and thunder tale in which the British supermen show the Americans how it should have been done. In this novel, however, Strong abandoned the grim, blood-soaked, sexually-charged landscape of the earlier book in favour of a more conventional thriller formula which he has since stuck with. In 1985 he published *Conflict of Lions* which saw an SAS advisory team despatched to the African state of Free Guinea.

Here they find the government facing a serious challenge from a Russian-sponsored revolutionary movement. The government is too discredited by corruption and brutality to survive, but the day is saved when the SAS pull off the most far fetched hearts-and-minds operation ever. Corporal Lionel Wilcher is captured by the rebels, but uses his imprisonment as an opportunity to win their leader away from the Communists and over to democracy! The quite ludicrous notion of some sort of SAS commitment to democratic government in the Third World is merely one of a number of quite outrageous fictional extravagances present in this novel. *The Last Mountain* was published in 1989. Here an SAS Arctic Warfare team are involved in spiriting a Russian defector out of Sweden with the Russian Spetsnaz commanded by the beautiful Captain Valia Mikhailovitch in pursuit. This is a routine spy story with an SAS motif imposed upon it. The following year, he published *The Sons of Heaven*, which pitted Rob D'Arcy, a former SAS officer now running his own up-market security firm against fanatical Islamic terrorists financed by the Iranians. The Sons of Heaven are distinctive in that their leader, Sabbah, secures the absolute loyalty and obedience of his acolytes by giving them a taste of the heaven they will ascend to if they die in his service. In fact heaven is a drugged sexual experience with a prostitute, but who's to know! And in 1992 he published *This Angry Land*. This was a somewhat unusual novel to come from Strong's pen. Mike Branagh, a former SAS sergeant, racked by guilt and living in drunken obscurity in Mozambique, finds himself drawn into the war with the South African-backed Renamo guerrillas. The novel adopts a sympathetic stance to the Frelimo regime and quite correctly portrays Renamo, a byword for brutality and murder, as the Khmer Rouge of Africa. This does not indicate any sudden move to the left on Strong's part, however. Instead, it reflects British government policy at the time which was resolutely hostile to Renamo; indeed the British unofficially provided military advisers for Frelimo, including former SAS members. There is an Irish dimension to the novel, with Branagh being hunted by an IRA hitwoman for what he did in Northern Ireland 14 years before.[4]

These are all rather routine thrillers, purporting to offer some insight into great power politics (the blurb in a number of the novels makes a point of emphasising Strong's 'keen interest in international politics'), but in fact viewing the world with a *Boys' Own* simplicity. Let us look at his most recent SAS thriller, *Stalking Horse* (1993) in a little more detail.

Stalking Horse is the untold story of how close Saddam Hussein came to winning the Gulf War. Strong's hero, Max Avery, is a disillusioned ex-SAS soldier (the author presents an uncharacteristically critical view of the regiment's Falklands performance with men's lives being put at risk by glory-seeking senior officers: 'Mistakes were brushed beneath a convenient carpet of ecstatic media coverage. No lessons were learned, no souls searched. He realised then that the Regiment had changed, probably forever. It was time for him to go'). Since leaving the regiment, Max has been working undercover for MI5. This began only by chance when he became involved with Maggie O'Malley, an Irish nurse with republican connections. Max is deeply in love with Maggie and they have a child, but he is persuaded to use her to penetrate the IRA, eventually becoming quarter-master for their British and European operations. The irony is that Maggie has long since broken with republicanism, getting involved in trade union activity at work, in animal rights, and joining the Green Party. By now, Max wants out, but MI5 blackmail him into one last operation: using the IRA to uncover any plans Saddam might have for international terrorist attacks in the event of war in the Gulf. He is backed up by a joint SAS-Delta Force team.

Strong, as one might expect, provides an extremely hostile portrait of the IRA. The war in Northern Ireland has long since lost any dubious political validity it might once have had. It is only being prolonged so that the IRA leadership can continue to 'feather their own nest'. The terrorist hierarchy are using the war to get rich, channelling the funds raised by extortion and robbery into their legitimate businesses. They are ruthless gangsters, thriving on the profits of terrorism, while their followers lay down their lives like so many 'sacrificial lambs on the altar of Irish history'. Young men are being recruited in the Catholic slums, where republicanism offers some meaning to their 'stark and desolate lives', only to be cynically used by men without conscience or scruple, whose only concern is to enrich themselves. This is a pretty straightforward reproduction of the British propaganda view of the IRA and its leadership. Strong takes it much further however.

In *Stalking Horse*, Con Moylan, an IRA leader, is prepared to put the organisation's terrorist capability at Saddam Hussein's disposal in return for the modest sum of two billion dollars. This money will allow him to start his own terrorist outfit, independent of the IRA. All Saddam wants in return is for the IRA to carry out chemical and germ warfare attacks on American and British targets. First there is to be a warning attack on US bases at Souda Bay in Crete, and then, if this does not break Allied resolve, major attacks in London and Washington. The London attack will involve releasing anthrax spores in the capital with an estimated half a million casualties. This will surely bring the Allies to heel and force them to leave Saddam in control of Kuwait. The monstrous nature of this plan provides a useful fictional justification for the Allied bombardment of Iraq during the Gulf War.

While the preparations for the attack on the West unfold, Strong develops a significant sub-plot involving Maggie, Max's wife. Her republican past is revealed: she had been Con Moylan's sex slave, physically abused by him, and handed over to be gang-raped by his IRA unit. Despite this, she remained under his domination, even killing for him. Eventually, she broke away from her past and made a new life with Max, but now her past returns to haunt her and she finds herself coming under Moylan's influence once again. This process is completed when he exposes Max as a British agent. Moylan rapes her. He

> had buggered her as he always had. Drawing her back in time, into the dark excitement of her forbidden world. Swooning in the warmth and fulfilment of being plugged and stoppered, as if a stake had been driven into the very core of her sexual being. Wallowing in the blessed relief of her total subjugation ...

Moylan is not only unmoved by the prospective slaughter of half a million Londoners but he can also give women what they secretly desire, abuse and subjugation. He is a villain conceived on a grand scale, although Strong's limited literary abilities let him down in the execution. What of Maggie and her dark secret? While she desperately wants to be faithful to Max and to her son, Moylan appeals to a hidden, suppressed side of her personality. He offers her an excitement that she cannot get from her conventional relationship and family life with Max. Once again Strong is playing to male insecurity, returning to the sexual themes of *Whisper Who Dares*. Whether intentionally or not, this succeeds in giving the book a reactionary ideological charge that his other novels lack. Maggie has, of course, to be punished for her transgressions. She partially redeems herself by shooting Moylan, but this is not enough to save her, and she is herself shot down.

Needless to say Saddam's plot fails with the joint SAS-Delta Force team playing a key role. Max's earlier disillusionment with the SAS is forgotten when he takes part in a daring raid on an Iraqi prison bunker in Baghdad itself. The way is clear for the Allied victory in the Gulf War.

The politics of *Stalking Horse* are reactionary through and through, demonising the enemies of the British state, portraying them as genocidal mass murderers against whom any 'defensive' measures are justifiable. His portrayal of the IRA is straightforward propaganda. This is all compounded by the novel's sexual politics, its prescribed role for women, with death as the punishment for transgression. Certainly a remarkable work of popular fiction.[5]

This was not the only SAS operation that made victory possible in the Gulf. Max Avery and his comrades were lucky not to bump into Captain Mike Martin of the SAS, busy hunting down Saddam's supergun in Frederick Forsyth's thriller, *The Fist of God* (1994). Forsyth, one of the most overrated of contemporary thriller writers, is perhaps best known as author of *The Day of the Jackal* and for being one of Margaret Thatcher's favourites. He had long been fascinated by the SAS, and now published his 600-page plus celebration of their exploits. The novel is dressed up in his usual camouflage of supposed technical expertise and insider knowledge, revealing to the world for the first time that Saddam Hussein had actually built one of Gerald Bull's superguns, the so-called Fist of God. The weapon, 180 metres long, with a range of 1,000 kilometres, is carefully hidden. All the 3,000 Vietnamese labourers involved in construction were subsequently massacred together with their guards! The supergun is ready to destroy the Allied forces assembling in Saudi Arabia with a surprise nuclear strike.

The hero of the hour is Major Mike Martin of the SAS, a man who can speak street Arabic fluently and pass convincingly as a bedouin. He is sent into occupied Kuwait on a 'Lawrence of Arabia' mission, to conduct a one-man guerrilla war against the Iraqi army and start up a Kuwaiti resistance movement. His incredible military skills are only equalled by the Iraqis' brutal incompetence. So far the novel is a fairly unexceptional war story with its main protagonist apparently blessed with invisibility, invulnerability, telepathy and various other superhuman attributes. His far-fetched war is so successful that one might almost believe he is well on the way to driving the Iraqis out of Kuwait singlehanded. The novel's lack of distinction is compounded by the fact that Forsyth's literary abilities do not extend to characterisation so that his protagonists remain empty shells, men who do, but who never feel or reflect. He relies on technical detail to make up this deficit. What is more interesting is the way Forsyth shows the British and Americans assessing their intelligence sources and coming to the reluctant conclusion that Saddam has an unpleasant surprise in store for them. Martin is ordered to give up his one-man war in Kuwait and with Russian assistance (a nice touch!), establishes himself in Baghdad. Here he successfully reactivates an Israeli intelligence contact, 'Jericho', and eventually locates the site of the supergun. Inevitably, it is Martin who leads the SAS team that is inserted to guide the US warplanes onto the target. It is successfully destroyed and they fight their way to safety. That same evening, General Schwarzkopf is given the order to begin his ground attack. The SAS have foiled Saddam and made victory possible.

Towards the end of the novel, Forsyth waxes lyrical over the SAS. There is, he tells us, 'no graveyard' for these heroes, 'no cemetery collects their dead'. Instead, they lie on 'fifty battlefields whose very names are unknown to most'. Once the Gulf War is over, a simple ceremony is held in the rain at Hereford to commemorate the five

SAS killed fighting Saddam. Mike Martin is there, a secretive man, glad that no one will ever know of his adventures in Kuwait and Iraq! Some chance.

Two other features of *The Fist of God* are worth noticing. First of all, the almost complete absence of women. Indeed, there are only two women characters of any importance, both making only brief appearances: the Lebanese prostitute, Leila Al-Hilla and the Swiss spinster, Elizabeth Hardenburg. The former is raped and beaten to death, while the latter hangs herself after her cynical seduction by an Israeli agent. *The Fist of God* is a story about men, without the complications and distractions that women create, indeed the exclusion of women from the novel almost amounts to misogyny. They have no place in Forsyth's fantasy with its intrepid, asexual hero. One other aspect of the novel is that Forsyth goes out of his way to condemn those in the West who supplied the Iraqis with modern weapons and advanced technology. With remarkable restraint he manages to avoid implicating the former Conservative government in this.[6]

From Afghanistan to Heathrow

In this section we will consider a number of miscellaneous SAS novels written by two established thriller writers, Gerald Seymour and Gordon Stevens, by Shaun Clarke, a regular contributor to the 'Soldier A to Z' series, by the prolific former SAS soldier, Barry Davies, and by the explorer and writer, Ranulph Fiennes. Their novels range in locale from Afghanistan to Guatemala, from Bosnia to Dhofar, from Northern Ireland to Heathrow. The SAS fighting man can go where he pleases, the last vestige of Britain's imperial reach. Let us look first of all at Gerald Seymour's two SAS novels, *In Honour Bound* (1984) and *The Fighting Man* (1993).

Seymour, a former ITN newsman from 1963 to 1978, published his first thriller, the remarkably successful *Harry's Game*, in 1975. This told the story of an undercover soldier, a veteran of the Aden conflict, who is sent into Belfast to hunt down an IRA assassin. Such a novel written today would almost certainly have as its protagonist an SAS soldier, but in 1975, before the regiment went public, Harry Brown, Seymour's angst-ridden hero, is given no affiliation. Since this success, Seymour has written over a dozen more thrillers, all characterised by their tormented British heroes trying to do what is right, trying to retain their integrity in a world without honour. What is in many ways one of his most remarkable novels, *Archangel* (1982), has its unjustly imprisoned British hero, Michael Holly, lead a revolt in the Russian gulag, sacrificing his life in protest against the inhumanity of the Soviet system. Not that

Seymour is some sort of one-dimensional Cold Warrior: his later novel *Song In The Morning* (1986) has its protagonist, another British hero, taking on the Apartheid police state in South Africa. What is true of all his novels is that the main protagonist is always a tortured, self-doubting Briton, let down by those in authority, looking for a woman who can understand him and fighting against oppression whether it takes the form of terrorism, a brutal police regime or an occupying army.[7] His two SAS thrillers are no different.

In Honour Bound has Captain Barney Crispin of the SAS (his very name is redolent of Henry V and Agincourt) sent to Pakistan to train mujahidin guerrilla fighters in the use of the obsolete US 'Redeye' ground-to-air missile. They are to be sent on a secret mission into war-torn Afghanistan to shoot down a Russian M1-24 'Hind' helicopter gunship, strip out its electronics and bring them back for British intelligence. The order for the operation has come from the very top, from the Foreign Secretary himself, not out of any sympathy for the Afghan rebels or even because vital Russian military secrets are at stake. Instead, the Foreign Secretary is acting out of pique, hoping to gain an advantage over the Americans. For this, men, fighting men, are to die.

The mujahidin are sent in before they are ready, only half-trained, and are predictably massacred by the heavily armed and armoured Russian helicopters. Only the boy, Gul Bahdur, returns. Outraged by this squandering of men's lives, Barney defies his instructions and returns to Afghanistan with the boy and a stock of missiles, determined to complete the mission. What is his motivation? He has no particular love for the Afghan people – indeed his own grandfather had been killed during the 1919 British invasion of the country, his eyes gouged out and his testicles hacked off. He is not an ideologically motivated Cold Warrior like the American soldier-of-fortune, Maxie Schumack, whom he finds serving with the mujahidin. Schumack, a former Green Beret and Delta Force veteran, wants revenge for Vietnam and the Desert One fiasco. Barney on the other hand is motivated by his sense of honour. He is obligated to the men who were sent to their deaths and will keep faith with them. He is honour bound by the integrity of the warrior, something that politicians and bureaucrats cannot even begin to understand. He stays on to fight even after he has sent the Hind's electronic systems back, using up his stock of missiles for the sake of the mujahidin.

This quite incredible romanticising of the warrior and of the warrior ethic is a recurring theme of Seymour's fiction. In this particular novel, it provides a bridge between Barney and his Russian rival, the helicopter squadron's commander, Pyotr Medev, a fellow professional. The exciting chronicle of his cat-and-mouse battle with the Russian is the very heart of the book. But what about this warrior's relationship with women? At one point in the book, Gul Bahdur asks Barney if he has a woman back home. He replies that he has never had anything to give a woman:

> No woman would want the things I know of. I know how to break a man's neck with the edge of my hand. I know how to lie in bracken and watch the back door of a farmhouse for three days without moving, in my own country. I know how to walk twenty miles with sixty pounds on my back and then take an assault course. I know how to put down mortar fire so that six have gone before the first lands. I know how to administer morphine and fit a saline drip when a man's in shock with his guts in the mud. I have nothing to give a woman, not any woman I have ever met.

He does meet such a woman in Afghanistan. The Italian nurse, Mia Fiori, who is sharing the suffering of the Afghan people, is a very special woman. She has given up everything to help the mujahidin and is looking for a man like Barney, for a warrior with his sense of honour, his self-sacrificing integrity. They make love on the battlefields of Afghanistan.[8]

Seymour's *The Fighting Man* is an even more remarkable novel than *In Honour Bound* with its SAS hero, Gordon 'Gord' Brown, taking service with Guatemalan rebels and leading a revolutionary war against a murderous military dictatorship that has American backing. Gord enlists as the revolutionary movement's military leader not for cash but because in the aftermath of the Gulf War he was ordered to abandon the Shia population of Karbala in Iraq to Saddam Hussein's vengeance. The Allies had encouraged them to revolt and had then left them to their fate. Gord, an SAS captain at the time, has never forgiven himself for obeying his orders, for sacrificing honour to expediency. The Guatemalan revolutionary leader, Jorge Ramirez, appeals to Gord's sense of fairness, detailing the appalling exploitation and oppression in his country. Despite its Cuban backing, the revolution has nothing to do with Communism, it is about justice. Seymour's distaste for the Guatemalan military is made absolutely clear on numerous occasions throughout the novel.

The tiny band of revolutionaries, driven on by their fighting man, inflict a succession of defeats on the Guatemalan military, rallying support as they go. All those who have suffered under the regime are given hope by the news that a revolutionary army is marching on Guatemala City. A man of flames, 'Gaspar', is bringing vengeance and the Guatemalan elite are already packing for their flight to Florida. Seymour successfully captures the excitement of the revolution, an unusual achievement for a British thriller writer.

Crucial to the rebel army's success is Gord's own use of a flame thrower before which the Guatemalan troops break and run. He is a man possessed, unleashing a fiery vengeance on the oppressors. The rebels infiltrate the town of Santa Cruz de Quiché and successfully overwhelm its defences, taking the garrison by surprise. Gord is exhilarated by the fighting, 'lifted by the drug of killing and the narcotic of going forward'. The men consumed in the flames are not men, but 'objectives', 'targets'. This is the turning point, however. Gord urges that they press on without delay for Guatemala City, before their way is blocked and the weather breaks. The speed of their advance is their only hope of success against trained, well-armed troops. Jorge, the revolutionary leader, has grown over-confident, however, and insists on giving his tired army a brief respite before continuing the advance. The Guatemalan army blocks the way and the weather breaks, leaving the rebels vulnerable to air attack. The rebels are forced to retreat and their army melts away as quickly as it formed. Gord's last service is to ensure that Jorge escapes to keep alive the spirit of revolt, remaining in the jungle to cover the rebel leadership's evacuation by a Cuban plane.

Although the book is a remarkably sympathetic account of an attempted revolution in Guatemala, not the usual subject matter for a British thriller, Gord is very much the typical Seymour hero. The tortured fighting man, driven by his personal code of honour, regardless of political expediency, out of place in normal society. He is typical even to the extent that just as Barney Crispin found a woman who could love him in Afghanistan, so he too finds a woman in the jungles of Guatemala. The civil rights worker, Alex Pitt, a strong opponent of revolutionary violence, is actually saved from rape and a terrible death at the hands of the military, by the rebels. Despite her initial hostility, she is one of those special women who can understand what drives a fighting man and she falls in love with him. They make love in the mud at Santa Cruz de Quiché.[9]

What is clear with regard to Seymour's two SAS thrillers is that they could just as easily have been written without their heroes having any SAS affiliation. Barney Crispin and Gordon Brown could have been members of any regiment or undercover outfit, but Seymour chooses to pay ritual tribute to the potency of the SAS myth. The contemporary thriller writer has little choice in the matter, a very different situation from when Harry's Game first appeared in 1975.

What of his particular brand of hero? It is first of all worth noticing Seymour's regular habit of placing British men of action at the centre of other people's struggles whether it is in the Soviet gulag, South Africa, Afghanistan or Guatemala. Whether intentional or not, there is a clear implication that the British are able to do whatever the situation requires better than any foreigners even though it concerns them more directly. Even when it comes to the revolution in Guatemala, Gord Brown is the driving force and it is the failure to follow his advice that results in the movement's defeat. This might well flatter the sensibilities of a British readership but at the expense of seriously distorting any understanding of political and social conflict in other countries. What of his heroes' habitual tortured idealism, their sense of honour and readiness for self-sacrifice? One suspects that Seymour, a very experienced reporter who covered numerous wars for ITN, must at some time or other have met a man or men who approximated to his particular brand of hero. What he has done, however, is to make this hero part of a formula, something which seriously limits his fiction. What we have in Seymour's novels is much the same character being placed in a variety of different conflicts. In the end, these are novels that exaggerate Britain's role in the world and celebrate the British fighting man's ability to intervene outside his own country.

Another thriller writer to acknowledge the potency of the SAS myth is Gordon Stevens, the author of half a dozen successful novels. His *Provo* (1993), the story of an IRA plot to kidnap Princess Diana and Prince William, has an important SAS presence, but it is not central to the narrative.[10] Two of his other novels, *Kennedy's Ghost* (1994) and the more recent *Kara's Game* (1996) are more straightforward tributes. *Kennedy's Ghost* features ex-SAS man Dave Haslam in a political thriller where a candidate for the American Presidency risks assassination. Can Haslam protect him? Of course.[11]

Let us look more closely at *Kara's Game*. In this novel Islamic fundamentalist terrorists have hijacked Lufthansa Flight 3216 and are bringing it into Heathrow. The terrorist leader is a young Bosnian Muslim woman, Kara. Waiting at Heathrow to kill her and her comrades is an SAS team led by Finn. They have met before under shellfire in Maglaj in Bosnia. On that occasion, Kara saved two of Finn's men from death. What has happened to put them on opposite sides now? Back in Maglaj, Kara had asked Finn how the Muslims could win the war and he had told her that they had no chance. Why won't the West help like they helped Kuwait? Finn replies that the Gulf War wasn't about democracy or freedom, it was about oil. He goes on: 'People like me win because we have power, because of who we are and what we do. So people are afraid of us. Therefore we can win.' His regiment has a motto, he tells her: 'Who Dares Wins'. Later, after her husband and son are killed by Serbian shelling of a hospital, she remembers this conversation. Kara is recruited by an Islamic fundamentalist terror network, financed by Iran. Bosnian Serbs are particularly prized as recruits because they are Europeans and attract less attention than Arabs. She is transformed into a ruthless killer. Somewhat perversely her initiation into the organisation seems to involve her having group sex with a number of men, not something one normally associates with Islamic fundamentalism, but this is a thriller after all.

The terrorists are planning an offensive, but their intentions are discovered and foiled by simultaneous operations in London, Brussels and Istanbul and an SAS attack on their training camp in Afghanistan. Only Kara's attack, the hijacking of Lufthansa Flight 3216, goes ahead as planned. She is not committed to the revolutionary cause, however. She has been using them just as they have been using her. Kara has no intention of killing the hostages on the plane and instead uses the hijacking as an opportunity to call for peace in Bosnia. Finn knows she is on the plane and when his team storm it, they kill the other three terrorists but spare Kara. She is smuggled out alive, the debt is repaid.

In many ways this is just another routine rehearsal of the international terrorist threat theme. What is distinctive, however, is the way it shows the situation in Bosnia as creating the conditions where people might be driven to turn to terrorism out of despair and desperation. There are dark forces out there waiting to take advantage of this, recruiting the desperate and despairing into the terrorist international that threatens the West. This certainly reflects a fear in some security circles that the Bosnian Muslims might become the Palestinians of the next decade. Finn's decision to spare Kara is, of course, the sort of thing you only find in novels.[12]

This brings us to Shaun Clarke, the author of a number of volumes in the 'Soldier A to Z' series that we shall look at separately. Obviously these earlier novels were only an apprenticeship for his massive 700-page novel, *The Exit Club*, subtitled *The Ultimate Novel of the SAS* (1996). This huge, ponderous book tells the story of Marty Butler, one of the originals who was with Stirling when he formed the SAS back in 1941. Butler takes part in virtually every SAS campaign up to and including the Falklands War. Assuming he was 18 in 1941 (he was already a veteran of the Long Range Desert Group), this would make him 59 (and already the victim of a heart attack) at the time of the Falklands! Clearly this is absolutely ludicrous. Such considerations are of no account to Clarke because what the novel provides is a succession of colourful accounts of armed combat, all wildly exaggerated and over the top. Marty's adventures in Malaya, for example, bear no relation whatsoever to the actual Emergency. They are a comic-book account of John Wayne style heroics that owe more to Vietnam than they do to Malaya. The result is all pretty appalling and in a way the book probably is 'the Ultimate' although not quite as the publisher intended.

While Clarke is clearly aware that what his readers want is action, and more action, he does at least try to give the book some political edge. Marty is shown becoming increasingly disillusioned with the road the regiment is going down and with the sort of country Britain is becoming. He regards the war in Northern Ireland, where he predictably takes out an IRA unit in a pitched battle, as 'a filthy immoral job'. The regiment he loves is being used 'in shitty ways'. His disillusion leads to his founding a secret ex-SAS vigilante association that begins assassinating international arms dealers and the like. Marty even decides that Margaret Thatcher is next in line for the chop for involving the regiment with the Khmer Rouge and forever besmirching its honour. Despite this political excursion, Clarke's huge book is likely to be remembered only as an indication of just how bad SAS thrillers can be. It reads as if it were written by a lobotomised Tolstoy doomed to write *War and More War* rather than his more familiar masterpiece.[13]

The last two novels we shall look at in this section are both by former SAS soldiers. The first, *Going Hostile* (1995), is by Barry Davies, whom we have already met as the author of a number of SAS books and handbooks; the second, *The Feather Men* (1991), is by Ranulph Fiennes, the explorer and writer. Fiennes was briefly an officer in the SAS before being returned to unit for blowing up the set of the film *Doctor Doolittle*, served with the Sultan of Oman's armed forces and was a member of the Territorial SAS from 1971 to 1984. First, *Going Hostile*.

Davies's novel is a pretty straightforward adaptation of his auto-biographical volume, *Fire Magic*, that came out in 1994. The most important changes to the account it provides concern the terrorist leader, Mahmud al Dhuhoori, and the Northern Ireland dimension it adds to the story. In the novel, the Baader-Meinhof group are replaced by the IRA. *Going Hostile* brings together the lives of two enemies, both fighting men: the Dhofari revolutionary, Mahmud, and the SAS soldier, Karl Leathers. They first clash at the battle for the Shershitti caves in the closing stages of the Dhofar war. Karl is wounded by a mortar bomb and Mahmud is preparing to finish him off, but his AK47 jams. Karl manages to shoot and wound his enemy, but Mahmud escapes. With the war in Dhofar over, Mahmud throws in his lot with Wadi Haddad's terrorist organisation. He takes part in the international conference of terrorist organisations held in Aden in the summer of 1976 where 'the power barons of the terrorist hierarchy' plan a campaign 'of death and destruction which would breathe new life into international terrorism'. This notion of a secret underground terrorist international with its tentacles extending throughout the world is a powerful, if completely spurious, invention that continually features in contemporary thrillers. It has arguably replaced the Soviet Union and the Cold War as the dominant motif in this particular genre.

While Mahmud is establishing himself as an international terrorist, Karl Leathers is serving in Northern Ireland before returning to England to join the undercover surveillance unit, E4. While on a training exercise in London, following a republican sympathiser, he actually sees the man meeting up with Mahmud in a pub. A terrorist attack of some kind is being planned. Mahmud leads the hijacking of British Airways Flight 120, demanding that the British government frees IRA prisoners and hands over US$15 million. The last confrontation between the two men takes place when Karl leads the storming of the plane, a fictional recreation of the storming of Lufthansa Flight 181 at Mogadishu in 1977 in which Davies took part. Even the name of the terrorist leader, Mahmud, is the same. On this occasion, however, all the terrorists are killed in the attack except Mahmud. He promises that the fight will go on whereupon Karl finishes him off with a headshot. Put simply, this novel seems to be a pretty straightforward attempt to cash in on the SAS publishing boom. Altogether, *Going Hostile* is a pretty poor effort that is likely to be one of the books that finally contributes to the demise of the boom in SAS fiction. Not only is it badly written, but Davies makes too much use of his own experiences which have already featured in two previous books. This recycling of material can only go so far.[14]

In its own way, just as unsatisfactory is Ranulph Fiennes' *The Feather Men*, which purports to be a true story. Fiennes introduces his readers to the activities of the Feathermen, a secret organisation established by David Stirling to look after the interests of former SAS soldiers. Occasionally it has resorted to vigilante action and he gives as an example the torture of a Bristol drug dealer. He first came into contact with the organisation when they saved him from an assassination attempt in October 1990. They chose him to tell their story! The contract on Fiennes was the last of four taken out by a multi-millionaire Dhofari Sheikh Amr bin Issa, whose sons had been killed fighting for the rebels in the Dhofar war. He wants the men responsible killed and hires a team of professional assassins to carry out the killings. The victims have to be told why they are being killed, the killings have to look like accidents and it all has to be recorded on film. This vendetta extends over a 14-year period starting with John Billing in 1977, then Mike Kealy in 1979, followed by Michael Marman in 1986, and lastly Corporal 'Mac' in 1987. Fiennes is the last target, but the Feathermen, who have been patiently tracking the assassins over the years, arrive just in time!

What we have here seems to be an attempt to turn a below-average thriller into a bestseller by claiming that it is a true story. This involves Fiennes in some dubious procedures, because while he claims to have changed the names of some of the individuals involved, he does use some real names (among them Barry Davies!), most controversially those of the men supposedly murdered. Mike Kealy, for example, is extremely well known, having commanded the SAS team at the battle of Mirbat. He died of hypothermia on an exercise in the Brecon Beacons in February 1979. Here Fiennes has him murdered. He is told the reason for his execution by his killers who then film his death from hypothermia which is brought on by an insulin injection. This Fiennes insists is the true story of Mike Kealy's death. What, one wonders, do Mike Kealy's family and friends make of this? The ethics of the whole enterprise seem highly suspect. It has certainly earned Fiennes considerable criticism, made him some enemies and contributed nothing to his reputation.[15]

The War in Northern Ireland

Inevitably a significant number of SAS thrillers have Northern Ireland and the war with the IRA as their subject matter. This reflects the protracted nature of the conflict (Britain's longest war), the IRA's proven ability to strike in Britain and a popular fascination with the struggle carried on between the IRA and various British undercover units, most notably the SAS. Episodes such as the Loughall ambush and the Gibraltar shootings have sustained popular interest, with the SAS appearing as the men who actually know how to deal with the IRA if only the politicians would let them off the leash. Of course, one of the problems that the SAS myth confronts with regard to war in Northern Ireland is actually explaining how it is that Britain with the best anti-terrorist troops in the world has failed after 25 years to defeat the cowards, sadists, drugpushers and gangsters of the IRA. More recently, the prospect of a settlement in Northern Ireland has begun to surface in the fiction of the conflict. How has this affected the SAS thriller? Since 1990 more than a dozen SAS novels, with the Northern Ireland conflict at the centre of their narrative, have appeared. We have already considered Terence Strong's *Stalking Horse* in some detail. Here we will look at a number of others, starting with Chris Ryan's recent *Stand By, Stand By* (1996).

Ryan was, of course, a member of the Bravo Two Zero patrol in Iraq, the man who escaped, and subsequently published his own account in *The One That Got Away*. Now he has turned novelist, publishing what is almost certainly only the first volume of the trials of SAS Sergeant Geordie Sharp. The novel opens with Geordie having returned from the Gulf War where he was captured, tortured and imprisoned by the Iraqis. He has psychological problems that are threatening to wreck his marriage so his wife returns to her parents in Northern Ireland for a temporary separation while he tries to sort himself out. Just when he feels up to getting together again, she is killed by an IRA bomb. Geordie becomes obsessed with the desire for vengeance. When he is posted to Northern Ireland, he goes determined to find the man responsible for his wife's death and to kill him. The novel follows Geordie's pursuit of IRA leader Declan Farrell from Northern Ireland to the jungles of Colombia.

Stand By, Stand By is a fast-paced thriller with plenty of action that strives to make up with authenticity what it lacks in style. Ryan very deliberately brings to it the authority of a former SAS soldier. He sets out to put straight some misconceptions. For example, a lot of outsiders misunderstand the role of officers in the SAS. Rank does not automatically entitle its holder to respect; it has to be earned. That is not to say that officers are looked down on: 'Far from it – there are plenty of first class Ruperts. Unfortunately there are also plenty of pricks.' This is the authentic voice of the SAS soldier.

Ryan describes the ambush of two IRA volunteers when they attack a Unionist MP's house. They are both shot down, riddled with bullets. One of them is still alive, so Geordie finishes him off with 'a quick double-tap to the head'. Neither body looked very pretty:

> One had the skull split down the middle, over the cranium. The armour-piercing rounds had opened up his head like a melon. Grey brain was showing through the gap, and the scalp had slid over to one side, crumpling the face into folds. The eyeballs were bulging out of their sockets. Brain and blood were spattered over the wall behind. Both were very young.

A case can be made, of course, that this sort of graphic description is justified because this is what bullets actually do to the human body. The reader should be exposed to the full horror of this sort of episode rather than have a sanitised version that actually conceals the consequences of violence. The problem is, however, that the description does not so much appal as excite. It has a pornographic appeal. It is more exciting than those accounts of shoot-outs that do not describe the nature of the wounds inflicted. This is a very different effect from any notion that the realistic representation of violence will necessarily turn readers against violence.

The IRA, in Ryan's novel, are sadists and gangsters. Declan Farrell, the man behind the bombing that killed Geordie's wife, is one of the worst. He positively enjoys knee-capping joyriders, preferring to use a hand drill rather than an electric drill because it gives him more pleasure. On one occasion, he and his men raped a woman informer before beating her with hammers, stamping on her and finishing her off by dropping a breeze block on her head. Incidentally, this sort of killing is very much the hallmark of the

Protestant paramilitaries rather than of the IRA. Farrell is also the man in charge of the IRA's trafficking in hard drugs. Nevertheless, he is well educated with a degree in mechanical engineering. He is a formidable opponent. In Ryan's novel even the rank-and-file volunteers possess cunning and, while the 'Paddy Factory' is very much present, it operates in their favour. He describes how two volunteers set out on an operation which had been betrayed to the RUC. They stopped off for a drink on the way, got completely pissed and so missed the ambush that had been arranged for them. Once again this story is told with the confidence of someone who has been there.

Geordie fails to get his revenge in Northern Ireland. His next mission is in Colombia, training the local police for the war on drugs. He spots Farrell in Bogota. The Irishman is leading an IRA team who are training the drug cartel's gunmen in terrorism! Just when you thought everything derogatory about the IRA had already been said, Ryan comes up with a new fantasy: the IRA as narcoterrorists. This is straightforward propaganda. Geordie leads an SAS assault on a jungle drugs factory and at last has Farrell at his mercy. He takes him prisoner. When he returns to Hereford, however, he finds that his girlfriend and his son have been kidnapped by the IRA, preparing the way for the inevitable sequel.[16]

The war in Northern Ireland has also occupied much of the attention of a major new thriller writer, Stephen Leather. In his novel *Hungry Ghost* (1991) he provided a remarkably sympathetic treatment of a psychopathic former SBS man on the loose in Hong Kong,[17] but more relevant here are his three linked novels: *The Chinaman* (1992), *The Long Shot* (1994) and *The Double Tap* (1996). The link is provided by the SAS soldier, Mike 'Joker' Cramer and his continuing war with the IRA. In *The Chinaman*, Joker only makes a brief appearance towards the end of the novel, which is in the main concerned with the efforts of the Vietnamese refugee, Nguyen Ngoc Minh, the 'Chinaman', to find those responsible for the death of his wife and daughter in an IRA bombing in London. Nguyen is a Vietcong veteran, who defected to the Americans and fought with their special forces until the US evacuation. He travels to Belfast to persuade Sinn Fein leader, Liam Hennessy, to tell him the names of those responsible or he will be forced to kill him. Hennessy's problem is that he is committed to ending the armed struggle, and the bombing campaign in London is the work of dissident elements opposed to his policy. He does not know who they are or where they are, but their bombing campaign is being carried out without warnings to kill the maximum number of people. It is a serious threat to his ambitions for the movement, indeed the British indicate that if the campaign does not end, then the gloves are going to come off. Unknown to

Hennessy, his own wife, Mary, is working with the dissidents, who are, perhaps predictably, being financed by Saddam Hussein. The arrival of Nguyen complicates his life even further.

Leather is a skilful and effective thriller writer, capable of careful plot construction and of creating sympathetic characters. His portrayal of Liam Hennessy is one of the few sympathetic portrayals that an Irish republican has ever had in a British thriller. Eventually, he discovers his wife's betrayal, gets Nguyen off his back, locates the bombers and secretly informs the British. At this point Joker Cramer and his SAS team put in an appearance. They are sent in to eliminate the bombers. One of them, the actual bomb maker, Maggie MacDermott, is only wounded. Cramer finishes her off himself. She dies snarling defiance. They are too late, however. Maggie has already had her last bomb unwittingly carried on board an airliner by a luckless stooge she seduced for this very purpose. The plane is destroyed, with over 100 people, including women and children, killed. In reprisal, the British government orders a 'shoot to kill operation'. A list of 25 leading republicans, who are all to be killed, is drawn up. Hennessy is on the list. What is interesting about this novel is that it is dissident republicans who are the villains with those prepared to negotiate already undergoing a partial rehabilitation!

At this point in the sequence there seems to be a novel missing: the story of the actual 'shoot to kill operation' that sees Hennessy and other republican leaders killed, propels his wife Mary into a psychopathic quest for vengeance and sees the unfortunate Joker Cramer fall into her hands. He is forced to watch while she horrifically tortures and then castrates another SAS captive before it is his turn. A rescue team arrives, cutting short her pleasure, so she guts him instead and makes good her escape, leaving him for dead. Joker survives, but scarred both inside and outside. The details of these events are provided in flashbacks in Leather's next novel, *The Long Shot*, but clearly there is a missing novel here. There is a gap in the sequence where a novel dealing with a British government-ordered campaign of assassination carried out by the SAS should be. Leather either never wrote or never published this novel. Either way, the refusal is interesting.

In *The Long Shot*, Cramer, who has by now left the army, is sent on an undercover mission to the United States to track down an IRA gunman, Matthew Bailey. The SAS captain who had the mission before him was found dead, skinned alive and castrated. Clearly the work of Cramer's old antagonist, Mary Hennessy. What he stumbles into is an Iraqi-sponsored conspiracy to get revenge for the Gulf War defeat by the assassination of both the US president and the British prime minister. Mary Hennessy has joined up with Illich Ramirez Sanchez, better known as 'Carlos the

Jackal'. They have put together a team of snipers to shoot the two men when they make a joint appearance at the Baltimore baseball ground for the first game of the season. This will be 'the long shot'. The book has considerable technical detail with regard to long-range shooting and elements of a police procedural as the FBI are shown unravelling the conspiracy. Without doubt, however, the most powerful element of the book concerns Leather's portrayal of the monstrous female, the women terrorists, Mary Hennessy and Dina Rashid. Mary is, of course, unbalanced by the deaths of her husband and her lover at the hands of the SAS. She positively relishes torturing and killing, with SAS men a speciality. She has already left her mark on Cramer and he has the misfortune to fall into her hands once again. She cuts one of his nipples off with some shears before handing him over to the even more perverse Dina Rashid, a Lebanese terrorist associate of Carlos's. Dina's speciality is the simultaneous rape and murder of her victims. While she is riding them, she makes them suck her gun and shoots them the moment they orgasm. This increases their convulsions and her own pleasure. She has already killed a number of American hostages in this manner in Beirut and Joker is next in line. This sort of fantasy tells us considerably more about the thriller and its readership than it does about Middle Eastern terrorists. As we have already seen the monstrous female is a potent element of the contemporary thriller. These women are abominations, violations of nature (Dina Rashid even has hairy nipples), who cannot be allowed to live. When Dina comes to kill him, Joker knocks her to the ground and stamps her to death. This is described in graphic detail. Mary Hennessy is later shot dead by the FBI at the baseball ground. Needless to say, the assassination attempt fails with Joker actually taking the bullet that was meant for British Prime Minister John Major! His body armour saves him.

By the time of the last novel in the series, *The Double Tap*, Joker, who it is by now apparent is one of the most seriously misnamed characters in popular fiction, is an embittered drunk, dying of cancer. He is still being hunted by dissident IRA members out for revenge. There is one last job for him: to act as bait for a professional assassin who has had the temerity to kill, among other people, a British MP and friend of the Prime Minister. The volume is undistinguished with Leather having run out of steam. There is an interesting discussion of serial killers with Joker himself fitting the bill as a classic 'organised serial killer'. Luckily he was able to find a job where he could make a career out of his disposition. This is a book too far in a competently written series that successfully touches upon many contemporary concerns.[18]

Another ex-serviceman to venture onto the terrain of the SAS thriller is the former Welsh Guardsman, Simon Weston, who

suffered terrible injuries in the Falklands that left him seriously
disfigured. He has published two accounts of these events and how
he came to terms with them: *Walking Tall* (1989) and *Going Back*
(1992). Now, with *Cause of Death* (1995), and some help from
journalist Patrick Hill, he has written an SAS thriller. The book
opens with the loss of a helicopter carrying leading figures in the
war against terrorism in Northern Ireland. Such a disaster did
actually take place on 2 June 1994, but in Weston's novel it is no
accident. Here the helicopter is shot down by 'a third force' that
is intent on derailing the peace process and restarting the war. It
is merely one of a growing number of attacks, attributable to
neither Protestant nor Catholic paramilitaries, but intended to set
them at each other's throats. The British government is seriously
concerned and MI6 send in an agent to track down those responsible.
He is Jim Scala, a former SAS sergeant, only recently returned from
Bosnia where he saw just how appalling ethnic conflict can be. Scala
is sent to Belfast posing as a drugs dealer, as a man with ready access
to large quantities of Ecstasy and other drugs. This will enable him
to penetrate the Protestant paramilitaries, who, along with the
IRA, are heavily into drug trafficking.

Unknown to Scala, the third force that is wreaking havoc in the
Province is being run by an old friend, another former SAS man,
Mick Naylor, who has turned mercenary. He has been hired by
wealthy and influential Unionists, to put together a private army
'whose only common denominator was that they enjoyed killing
Catholics'. Among Naylor's schemes is the flooding of Catholic areas
with heroin, with infant schools as particular targets. There is, of
course, a certain novelty in showing hardline Unionists as the men
trying to plunge Northern Ireland into war again. Inevitably, Scala
uncovers the plot and removes his former friend from the scene,
finishing him off with the customary double tap.

While not particularly well written and rather unpleasant in
places, *Cause of Death* was evidently successful enough for a sequel,
once again featuring Jim Scala. In *Phoenix*, he investigates the
activities of neo-Nazis inside the British Army, a topic that has already
drawn criticism from some rightwing quarters.[19]

A much more powerful and accomplished novel is Conor Cregan's
SAS thriller, *With Extreme Prejudice* (1994). This is a well written,
carefully plotted novel with strongly defined characters and a clear
moral centre. It offers an absolutely bleak and hopeless view of the
Northern Ireland conflict. The novel focuses on three main
characters: Tim McLennan, an Ulster Protestant and SAS sergeant,
John Cusack, a Catholic, born in the North but raised in the
United States where he served in the Marines, and Maggie O'Neill,
an IRA hitwoman. They are brought together by a planned attack

on an Army checkpoint that has been betrayed to the security forces. Both sides make ready for the confrontation.

Cregan makes some attempt at exploring his characters' motivations. Maggie O'Neill, for example, the IRA's prized sniper, has an unhappy marriage and is worried about her 15-year-old daughter getting pregnant. One day the news carries details of a soldier she has killed. He had a wife and a two-year-old child. She does not recognise him as the man she shot. When she shoots soldiers, she doesn't shoot human beings, she shoots uniforms:

> The uniform, it was the uniform, always the uniform. He was a victim of the uniform. It killed him. Everything it stood for killed him.
>
> She was hitting back. For all the mess of being born a working class Taig in Belfast. Every shot said fuck you to them. Fuck you and your fucking army and your fucking police and your fucking system ... Screw the politics ... Just to hit back. To feel them suffer like we suffered.

Once though, years ago, before the war began, Maggie had made love to a Protestant boy by a river. She never even knew his name. It could have happened in another life so hateful are relations between the two communities now.

Tim McLennan, the SAS sergeant, has no time for Catholics. He is a bigot, prejudiced and contemptuous, but completely opposed to the Protestant paramilitaries. What he wants is to be able to eliminate the IRA once and for all. He knows what the IRA have done to his community, to his own friends and family, and while some might be able to forgive, he never will. He is worried that the British might be going to sell the Protestants out, but remains loyal, at least for the time being. While McLennan longs for a decisive blow against the IRA, his superiors, who regard the Protestants as almost as big a problem as the Catholics, are waging a war of attrition, wearing the IRA down so as to bring them to terms. McLennan is a pawn in this war. Many years ago, he made love to a Catholic girl by a river and never even knew her name. This coincidence could have been just a sentimental cliché, but Cregan manages to give it a genuinely tragic character, reflecting the fate of two communities. The point is not laboured. It just serves to exemplify the tragedy of war.

While the novel takes a definite moral stance on the war, it perhaps inevitably contains passages of pornographic violence. In one incident, McLennan's squad ambush three IRA men visiting an arms dump. They open fire without warning. One of the volunteers has his spine broken and his heart and lungs ruptured by the high velocity rounds that seem to nail him to the door of the dump. Another goes into 'a comic frenzy' as 'Armalite kisses smothered him'. One of the three is still alive at the end of the firefight although badly injured. McLennan offers to get medical assistance in return for information but is told to fuck off. He finishes the man off. They fire the pistol of one of the dead men to make it look as if they were fired on first. He would have wanted it that way, they joke. This is 'big boys' games, big boys' rules'.

When the novel ends, McLennan is dead and Maggie O'Neill and John Cusack are part of an IRA unit carrying out bombing attacks in London. The last sentence reads: 'It was the eight hundred and twenty second year of the war'. A particularly grim view of the conflict by an accomplished thriller writer.[20]

The last novels we shall examine in this section are the three SAS thrillers written by Eddy Shah: *Ring of Red Roses* (1991), *The Lucy Ghosts* (1992) and *Fallen Angels* (1994). Only the last of these is concerned with Northern Ireland, but the first two are worth at least a brief mention. What about Eddy Shah himself? He is perhaps best known for taking on the National Graphical Association (NGA) print union in the Messenger dispute in Warrington in 1983. Here, according to his admirers, the union tactic of mass picketing was finally defeated and the Thatcher anti-trade union laws, that inflicted a succession of massive fines on the NGA, culminating in the sequestration of its funds, finally turned the tide against union power. Shah became, according to one account, 'a symbol of the Thatcher era'.[21] He went on to launch the *Today* newspaper in March 1986 but had overextended himself. The paper fell into the hands of Rupert Murdoch, who later closed it. Now the great entrepreneur has found the time to turn out a succession of thrillers.

In the first of his SAS thrillers, *Ring of Red Roses*, Mark Duncan of the SAS finds himself involved in an attempt by the Russian president to restore Tsarism! He intends to instal the great grandson of the last Tsar's younger brother, Mikhail, as a constitutional monarch in an attempt to bind the country together. KGB chief, General Dmitry Vashinov, pervert and sadist, rapist and murderer, is determined to prevent the restoration by any means necessary. Shah's portrayal of Vashinov is interesting because it introduces readers to one of the hallmarks of his fiction: episodes in which he provides graphic descriptions of sexual acts of various kinds, usually but not always involving sadism. Vashinov's degraded tastes contrast starkly with Duncan's virile manliness, a manliness that women find irresistible. Duncan rescues the KGB prostitute, Vera Kasynova, both physically and morally: 'they made love. It was gentle, a loving that neither had known before. He came four times and never lost his hardness ...' The SAS are hard men in more than one sense of the word![22]

In his next SAS thriller, *The Lucy Ghosts*, Shah has SAS hero Adam Nicholson foiling a neo-Nazi attempt to take over in Germany. Once again, the book has its ration of sexual titillation, although nothing quite as perverse as *Ring of Red Roses*. He dedicates this book to the scabs who stood by him during the Warrington dispute.[23]

Much more substantial than either of these two books is his Northern Ireland thriller, *Fallen Angels*. In this novel, a team of former SAS officers launches a campaign of torture and assassination against the IRA and its sympathisers in order to force them to the negotiating table. They seem to be putting into effect a top secret contingency plan, Operation Cartel, that was developed in the mid-1980s, but never put into effect. The political consequences would have been too damaging. Now the fear is that rogue elements within the British secret state might have activated it and be running out of control. Sam Richardson, ex-SAS himself, now with MI6, is charged with hunting them down, and, if there is any official connection (there is!), making sure it never comes to light. The killings carried out by the so-called 'Fallen Angels' are often gruesome: one IRA man is brutally tortured and then after he has been killed, his lips are cut off and placed around his penis. This is the style of the South American death squad. One of the SAS killers, George Fleet, is gay. He is 'a man to whom evil and cruelty came naturally, a sort of in-built revenge against the world for having made him gay'. In one particularly unsavoury episode, Fleet kills a Protestant paramilitary while having anal sex with him, cutting the man's throat as they both orgasm. He leaves the body with the knife stuck up its anus. This sort of stuff is obviously what Shah and his publishers believe his readership wants. The Angels' last atrocity involves the kidnapping of Fergal Baxter, the IRA Director of Intelligence. He is horribly tortured into providing enough information for the security forces to inflict a serious setback on the IRA and hopefully force it to the negotiating table. Baxter is left completely insane by the unbearable pain he has suffered. By now though, Richardson has tracked them down to a final confrontation in the Florida Everglades. Significantly, at the end of the novel he lets the surviving Angel escape.

Throughout *Fallen Angels*, Shah contrives to give a quite remarkable airing to the view that a campaign of counter-terror, assassination and torture is the only way to bring the IRA to the negotiating table. The novel promotes the idea that if the British took the gloves off and fought fire with fire then the war in Northern Ireland would have been over long ago. The men who would carry out this campaign might well be disturbed individuals like George Fleet, but these are the sort of men you need to wage 'a dirty war'. This strategy is endorsed by a number of characters in the book and in the end receives the hero's endorsement when he lets the last Angel go.

Unfortunately for Shah, by the time the book was coming out, the IRA had declared their ceasefire. This made the counter-terror option seem somewhat over the top. Moreover, it was the British government that was rejecting talks without preconditions, not the IRA. The book has a hastily-written foreword where he goes some way to dissociating himself from its contents. Nevertheless, he notes that should the war restart there are 'many of the public who would support any such defensive action against future terrorists'. He piously hopes that 'there will never be the need for individuals and groups to react for vengeance and retribution'. Together, with John Lennon, all he is saying is 'give peace a chance'. One can only admire the nerve of someone who can preface such a tale of killing and torture with such a sentiment.[24]

Soldier A to Z SAS

The Iranian Embassy siege and the Falklands War inspired an early series of SAS novels, 'The Fighting Saga of the SAS', all written by James Albany. These volumes celebrated 'that breed of soldier ... forged into the world's most feared fighting force'. The first volume, *Warrior Caste*, appeared in 1982. It was a conventional novel of Second World War heroics aimed very much at the bottom end of the market for popular war fiction. Its central characters, Lieutenant Jeff Deacon, Sergeant Buz Campbell and Corporal P.B. McNair only join the SAS in the last chapter, almost as an afterthought. It was followed by *Mailed Fist, Deacon's Dagger, Close Combat, Marching Fire, Last Bastion* and *Borneo Story*, the last appearing in 1984. These books were cheaply produced, poorly written and of shortlived interest.[25]

Much more substantial has been the 'A to Z' series, a major publishing phenomenon that was inspired by the Gulf War. It took as its model the 1989 memoir, *Soldier 'I' SAS*, written by Michael Paul Kennedy, that was in fact reprinted as part of the series. It was launched in 1993 by 22 Books, a subsidiary of Little Brown, with the publication of Shaun Clarke's *Soldier A SAS: Behind Iraqi Lines* and *Soldier B SAS: Heroes of the South Atlantic*. These were to be 'thrilling factoid adventure' stories, fictionalisations of actual SAS operations, telling it like it was. The series was launched with the slogan: 'Most men can only dream about such adventures – the SAS live them!' The astonishing success of the series, which at the time of writing has reached 'Soldier W', is demonstrated by the launching of a number of companion series, 'Marine A to Z SBS' which is up to the letter H, 'Mercenary' which has reached volume 11, and 'Soldier of Fortune' which has reached volume 9, at the time of going to press.[26]

There is not space here to look at the whole series, which has included novels on SAS exploits in wartime North Africa and France, in Malaya and Borneo, in Aden and the Gulf, in Vietnam and the Falklands, in Kazakhstan and Colombia, in Samarkand and the Gambia, in Gibraltar and on the streets of London, in Bosnia and Ethiopia, and, of course, in Northern Ireland. Instead, we will look at five novels: *Soldier R SAS: Death on Gibraltar* by Shaun Clarke, *Soldier T SAS: War on the Streets* by Peter Cave, *Soldier U SAS: Bandit Country* by Peter Corrigan and *Soldier K SAS: Mission to Argentina* and *Soldier O SAS: The Bosnian Inferno* both by David Monnery. These vary widely in quality from straightforward hackwriting to quite substantial thrillers, but all striving after a pseudo-authenticity.

First Shaun Clarke's *Soldier R SAS: Death on Gibraltar* (1994). This is a fictional reconstruction of the Loughall ambush of May 1987 in Northern Ireland and of the Gibraltar shootings of March 1988. The real names of the IRA volunteers are used throughout. The book opens with 15 men from G Squadron SAS being transported from Stirling Lines, Hereford, to RAF Brize Norton from where they are to be flown to Northern Ireland. Clarke strives after authenticity, not by describing their emotional states or recounting their thought processes, but by a detailed description of their clothing, weapons and equipment. They are all, we are told, dressed in standard DPM windproof, tight-weave cotton trousers and olive green cotton battle smocks with British Army boots and maroon berets. They are armed with L7A2 7.62mm general-purpose machine-guns (GPMGs), 7.62mm Heckler and Koch G3-A4K 20-round assault rifles with LE1-100 laser sights, and 5.56mm M16 30-round Armalite rifles. They have many attachments for their various weapons, including bipods, telescopic sights, night-vision aids, and M203 40mm grenade-launchers. Each man also carries a 9mm Browning High Power handgun holstered at his hip. They all carry ammunition, water, rations, a medical pack, spare clothing and batteries packed in their square frame Cyclops bergens. With uncharacteristic restraint, he does not give us the exact weight of their loads. But there is more! Accompanying them are crates of high-tech communications and surveillance equipment including Nikon F-801 35mm SLR cameras with David Minimodulux hand-held image intensifiers for night photography, a PRC319 microprocessor-based tactical radio, Pace Communications Ltd Landmaster 111 handheld transceivers and Radio Systems Inc. walkie-talkies.

This sort of detailed description of weaponry and equipment is a feature of many SAS thrillers, but it is carried to extremes in the A to Z series. The paraphernalia and accoutrements of combat have become crucial to the pornography of war, fetish objects to be obsessively and lovingly cherished and admired. These are instruments of power.

The 15 heavily armed SAS men arrive in the Province where they join up with another 24 already stationed there. They proceed to set up the Loughall ambush in which eight IRA volunteers and one innocent bystander are to be killed. The real names of all these men are used in the book. Patrick Kelly, the IRA commander, was hit several times 'with blood spreading out from a fatal head wound', Jim Lynagh and Patrick McKearney 'died in a hail of bullets', Donnelly in 'the same rain of bullets', Arthurs and Eugene Kelly as they took cover behind 'the bullet-riddled Toyota', Gormley 'was cut down by heavy SAS gunfire' and O'Callaghan 'was cut to pieces'. The unfortunate bystander, Oliver Hughes, who drove onto the killing ground, was killed 'outright', while his brother Andrew was badly wounded, 'three rounds in the back and one in the head'. This is the factoid style exemplified. It pretends to report an event rather than to tell a story. In fact, it is a fictionalised account of the official SAS version of the ambush presented absolutely uncritically.

This documentary style of writing is not sustained throughout. When the novel comes to deal with its three main characters, Mairead Farrell, Sean Savage and Danny McCann, members of the IRA unit sent to Gibraltar, it does attempt some psychological exploration. Savage is a romantic dreamer, Farrell a woman embittered by the death of her lover, while McCann is a psychopath, a mad dog. There are quite sympathetic accounts of Savage and Farrell, but Mad Dan McCann, we are told, had a 'blood-chilling enthusiasm for extortion, knee-capping and other forms of torture and, of course, assassination'. He did not 'torture, maim and kill for the IRA cause; he did it because he had a lust for violence and a taste for blood'. He is portrayed as a brutal, coarse, stupid pig of a man, despised and feared by his own comrades, ready to commit any atrocity. It is worth remembering that Clarke is not writing about a fictional character here, but about a man who was shot down, unarmed, by the SAS in broad daylight!

Clarke's actual account of the Gibraltar shootings once again follows the official SAS version. While walking along the road, Mad Dan looks over his shoulder and spots the two plainclothes SAS men approaching from behind. His 'right arm moved across the front of his body' and so he was shot down, twice in the back and twice in the head. Mairead Farrell, walking alongside him, 'grabbed for the bag under her arm' and was promptly shot seven times. Sean Savage, some distance away and walking in the opposite direction, was challenged but 'reached down instinctively to his jacket pocket, forgetting that he did not have a pistol'. Big mistake! He was shot 17 times ('his body was riddled with bullets, his head had been virtually pulverised, and he appeared to be losing blood from every pore'). In a 'Postscript', Clarke acknowledges that this was 'the most contentious' operation in the regiment's history. He briefly reviews some of the controversy; nevertheless it has to be insisted that up to that point the book presents the SAS version of events as fact.[27]

A number of other books in the series are similar fictional reconstructions of actual SAS operations, but most are, in fact, straightforward fictions that merely lay claim to be the ultimate in authenticity. A good example is *Soldier U SAS: Bandit Country* by Peter Corrigan published in 1995. Set in Crossmaglen, South Armagh, the novel tells the story of an SAS undercover operative, Captain John Early, who is sent in to the town to try to identify a sniper, 'the Border Fox', who has killed nine British soldiers in 18 months. The novel presents a brutal view of the Northern Ireland conflict with neither side looking particularly good. Corrigan describes a night-time army raid in the town that serves as cover for the insertion of an SAS covert observation post in the loft of an empty house:

> There was uproar in Crossmaglen that night ... sledgehammers smashed down doors and soldiers piled into houses amid a chaos of cursing and shouting, breaking glass, screaming children. Households were reduced to shambles as the Security Forces searched house after house ... carpets were lifted up, the backs of televisions wrenched off, the contents of dressers and wardrobes scattered and trampled ... Finally, their work done, the army and police withdrew, leaving behind them a trail of domestic wreckage and huddles of people staring at the chaos of their homes. It had gone like clockwork.

This sort of portrayal of British soldiers brutalising the local population is not what one normally expects from SAS thrillers.

In another episode, Corrigan describes the SAS ambush of an IRA arms cache: Lieutenant Charles Boyd is desperate for a 'clean' kill. He wants the two IRA men visiting the cache shot dead with guns in their hands. There is no warning given. The two men are simply shot to pieces at close range, but unfortunately neither of the weapons they had removed from the cache were loaded. This is soon remedied, however. 'That's more fucking like it. No one will whinge about civil liberties now.' Boyd, a very gung-ho figure, is, predictably enough, strongly in favour of counter-terror, of the systematic assassination of known terrorists. Only 'a few tiny special interest groups and some downright traitors' could possibly object. Sometimes the failure to carry out such a policy made him almost uncontrollably angry. Boyd, one cannot help feeling, is, in his own way, as much part of the problem in Corrigan's Northern Ireland as the IRA leader, Eugene Finn, a bully and a killer, quite prepared to torture men he believes to be informers or agents.

Early falls in love with Maggie Lavery, the sister of the landlord of the pub he is staying at in Crossmaglen. She is the widow of Patrick Kelly, one of the men killed by the SAS at Loughall. Only when he finally kills the Border Fox does he discover to his horror that it is her!

While Corrigan's novel does, as one would expect, celebrate SAS expertise and is actually dedicated to a company of the Royal Irish Rangers, his Northern Ireland has more the character of a brutal and brutalising tragedy than of a simplistic conflict between good and bad, right and wrong. The British Army is caught in a thankless position, doing a dirty job that leaves everyone soiled. What we do not get from this or any other SAS novel, however, is any serious questioning of the shoot-to-kill methods that the SAS are alleged to have used. These methods are not condemned as illegal or as counter-productive, prolonging the conflict, but are a shared secret between the author and his readers, who believe that this is how it really is despite official denials. The SAS are never shown killing innocent civilians, something that has happened all too often in Northern Ireland. Nevertheless the book has a power that one would not expect from the blurb on the back cover.[28]

Before passing on to David Monnery's two novels, let us first look briefly at Peter Cave's *Soldier T SAS: War on the Streets* (1995). This is by no means one of the better novels in the series, but it is interesting in that it portrays the SAS in action on the streets of London, combating public disorder and terrorism. Their opponents are not the IRA, striking miners, Arab terrorists or protesting students, but far right neo-Nazis. Moreover, a key figure in the SAS team pitted against them is Cave's black Barbadian, Sergeant Andrew Winston, a man with 'a quiet unshakeable pride – both as a man and as a black man'. What we have here is an SAS thriller that takes a quite overt stand against the neo-Nazi danger that is threatening to spread to Britain from the Continent. In one incident, a Nazi who is being arrested by the SAS goes to give the Hitler salute as a gesture of defiance and is promptly shot dead because he made a 'threatening hand movement'. This sort of hostile exposé of the contemporary fascist revival is not what one expects from an SAS thriller.[29]

What is clear by now is that while the A to Z series is packaged as so many gung-ho war books, celebrating the factoid adventures of a warrior elite, a number of volumes are, in fact, something more than this. There are volumes that are quite straightforward celebratory accounts of SAS heroism and expertise at taking down Britain's enemies, uncomplicated militarist fantasies, but there are other volumes that take a more complicated view of the world and some that without any exaggeration attempt to lean to the left. This brings us to David Monnery's two volumes.

First *Soldier K SAS: Mission to Argentina* (1994). A novel about SAS operations on the Argentine mainland during the Falklands War would seem positively to lend itself to an uncritical endorsement of Margaret Thatcher's warlike prowess as prime minister. Monnery manages to avoid this quite nicely, not by an overtly anti-Conservative stand but by a variety of devices. His main character, James Docherty, is the son of a Glaswegian trade union leader who regarded his son's joining the SAS as 'about as kosher as screwing Margaret Thatcher and enjoying it'. Despite everything, Docherty remains his father's son. Of the other members of the patrol he leads into Argentina, one, Hedge, joined the army as an alternative to the dole or prison, while another, 'Razor' Wilkinson, has a mum who brought him up as a single parent, working as a nurse in Walthamstow. Razor fumes about her life: 'she worked so bloody hard for next to nothing. It made him angry just thinking about it. Fucking government.' Even more significant than these carefully developed character studies is the fact that the British agent who is their contact in Argentina is a former leftwing guerrilla. Isabel Fuentes was a member of the Popular Revolutionary Army (ERP) and took part in kidnappings and bank robberies. The guerrillas were defeated in the so-called 'dirty war', a campaign of counter-terror, wholesale torture and secret executions, an extreme example of what a number of SAS thrillers flirt with as a solution to the Northern Ireland conflict. She was captured and tortured while her lover was killed in front of her. She has no regrets about her revolutionary past, in fact she is still 'proud of everything they had tried to do'. She is a most unlikely agent for MI6 to choose ever to make use of but serves as a device to try to rescue the war from the purposes of Conservative propaganda. It does not, indeed cannot, succeed, but it is quite remarkable that the attempt is made. The Falklands War was not a war against Argentinian fascism, but a war to save the Thatcher government, a government, moreover, which had been quite happy to have good relations with the junta prior to the war. A successful radical novel on the Falklands would have to have recognition of this reality at its centre, would have had to oppose the war.[30]

By the time of *Soldier O SAS: The Bosnian Inferno* (1994), Docherty and Isabel Fuentes are married and have two children. He is still emotionally a man of the left, for the underdog, even though a long-serving member of the regiment. Monnery confronts this paradox:

> In the public mind, and particularly on the liberal left, the Regiment was assumed to be a highly trained bunch of right-

wing stormtroopers. There was some truth in this impression, particularly since the large influx during the eighties of gung-ho paras – but only some. Men like Docherty, who came from families imbued with the old labour traditions, were also well represented among the older hands, and among the new intake of younger men, the SAS emphasis on intelligence and self-reliance tended to militate against the rightist bias implicit in any military organisation.

It would be nice to think so. There is just no evidence to substantiate it and the regiment's whole record, since it re-formed, points the other way. In Malaya, Oman, Aden, Dhofar and elsewhere, the SAS has been an instrument of counter-revolution. The courage and skill of its soldiers have been used in ruthless campaigns against national liberation movements throughout the world. This is the reality. Monnery continues the anti-Conservative jibes of the Argentina volume: Sarajevo is described as having 'more dyed-in-the-wool bastards per square foot ... than you'd find anywhere outside a Conservative Party conference'. But this attempt to give the SAS thriller a left twist is just not convincing.

Docherty's mission in Bosnia is to extract an SAS soldier, John Reeve, an old friend, from the town of Zavik where he has assumed command of the Bosnian militia who are holding off the Serbs. The novel is written with a passionate sympathy for the plight of the Bosnians, fighting against a murderous Serb enemy guilty of mass rape and wholesale massacre. There is no pulling punches with regard to Serb atrocities: Muslim villagers crucified to the side of a barn, the sniping and shelling of civilian targets, Muslim women held prisoner in Serb military brothels and regularly raped by their captors. With the assistance of Hajrija Mejra, a woman sniper in the Bosnian militia, the SAS team finally get through to Zavik. Instead of bringing Reeve back, they do what they can to help the townspeople defend themselves and return with a lorry-load of wounded children. The SAS are avenging angels on a mercy mission. The book is written with both passion and humour and, once again, like the Argentine volume, has strong women characters among its protagonists. Monnery has, against all the odds, attempted to write a radical, progressive, SAS thriller, but in the end the effort is futile and the project misconceived. The weight of reaction is just too much. Such a novel can only be written against the SAS, not for them.[31] Having said this, in the unlikely event of the series ever tackling the SAS presence in Cambodia, it would be very interesting to see what Monnery would make of it. Unfortunately, *Soldier Z SAS: The Cambodian Scandal* with the SAS acting as Thatcher's stooges, helping train Pol Pot's mass murderers, is not a novel we are likely to see.

The Unromantic SAS

There are only a handful of novels that present an unsympathetic view of the SAS. As early as 1974 Marshall Pugh portrayed them as the British state machine's assassins, 'the Frighteners', in his thriller, *A Dream of Treason*. More recently, in Julian Rathbone's *Dangerous Games* (1991), the psychopath Cranmer is a former SAS man, and similarly in Jack Curtis's *Sons of the Morning* (1991), the psychopathic sniper who has London in a grip of terror, is ex-SAS, although Curtis does not make anything of this. It explains why he is a good shot, rather than why he is a psychopath. These critical references are few and far between, though, and the overwhelming weight of thriller and war literature celebrates the regiment and its men.[32] The most important exception is Derek Robinson's outstanding novel, *A Good Clean Fight* (1993), which presents a determinedly unromantic and often blackly comic view of SAS exploits in North Africa during the Second World War. This is a sequel to his Battle of Britain novel, *A Piece of Cake*, but it combines the continuing RAF storyline with an SAS one.

A Good Clean Fight follows the parallel adventures of 'Fanny' Barton's embattled Tomahawk squadron and Captain Jack Lampard's SAS patrol. Robinson is a fine novelist, writing fiction of some distinction. He presents a grim, unromantic and anti-heroic view of the war in the desert with men's lives being wantonly put at risk and sacrificed at the whim of their senior officers. Lampard, for example, while a personally fearless and often brilliant soldier, is personally unstable, continually taking unjustified risks with his men's lives. The man is 'an addict', one of his subordinates complains. 'He's got to have his dose of glory ... I think his brakes have failed.' Lampard's excesses are mirrored by those of Fanny Barton. To avoid having his squadron withdrawn from frontline duties, he leads them on increasingly dangerous, indeed suicidal, operations until all but a gallant few are dead. In Lampard's case, his moral weakness is brought out by his practice of seducing the widows of deceased fellow officers. While on leave, he finds out which young officers have been recently killed and if they had wives staying in Cairo. If so, he presents himself as a friend of their dead husbands, come to offer his condolences. Robinson's cynical view of human weakness is made fully apparent by the knowing readiness with which these young women are prepared to forget their husbands and jump into bed with the handsome but unscrupulous Lampard.

For Robinson, the war is not an exercise in heroics, instead it is little more than organised murder. Towards the end of the novel, he describes a fight between Lampard's heavily armed jeeps and two German lorries:

There was a very brief point-blank battle between the double pair of Vickers Ks in his jeep and the machine-gunner in the second truck aided by a dozen rifles. The German soldiers had been well drilled; they got off a useful volley of shots and the machine gunner fired over their heads. But the Vickers Ks erupted with a blast of two hundred bullets in five seconds ... It was a mismatch, the dream of every soldier, to find the enemy exposed and out-gunned and to overwhelm him, kill him ten times over, give him not the fraction of a chance. The fight was over in the time a man might hold his breath ... The second truck caught fire. Its fuel tank exploded with a gentle, almost apologetic boom.

The fight leaves Lampard with three of his own men dead. They are sprawled on the ground in the uncomfortable attitudes of battlefield corpses. Already, the flies are beginning to feast. 'It would', Robinson writes, 'be a great day in fly history.'

This is a marvellous account of the futility of war, of young men being led to their deaths by vain fools. It is all the more impressive for the way it confronts the myth of the SAS, taking the regiment as one of its exemplars. Unfortunately, A Good Clean Fight stands alone among SAS fiction.[33]

Conclusion

In the Introduction to this book, the SAS was referred to as 'the last symbol of British national virility'. This assertion might well prove to be somewhat optimistic in its use of the word 'last', but it remains the case that the incredible explosion of popular interest in the SAS in the 1980s and 1990s constitutes a significant cultural phenomenon: a massive assertion of British masculinity in a troubled and dangerous world. The enormous body of material celebrating the regiment and its exploits is testimony to this. It has to be seen as an aspect of a new popular militarism that was given its first important impetus by the storming of the Iranian Embassy, the Falklands War and the IRA hunger strikes. The soldier hero was back in fashion with a vengeance. Margaret Thatcher made use of these episodes as one of the ideological cornerstones of her particularly rabid brand of Conservatism, as part of her own warlike pose as the modern Boudicca, the Iron Lady, a leader of men. This popular militarism has had its most recent triumph with the freeing of Paratrooper Lee Clegg, convicted of murdering a Catholic teenager in Northern Ireland. An unprecedented campaign by the rightwing press forced John Major's government into legal manoeuvres that put at risk the Northern Ireland 'peace process'. At the very centre of this popular militarism, indeed, exemplifying it, has been the SAS.

Myth

One of the concerns of this book has been the extent to which the attention focused on the SAS in recent years has involved the celebration of myth rather than reality. In the Second World War, the SAS was merely one of a number of irregular clandestine military units active on the British side. Certainly, it displayed considerable courage, skill and endurance whether it was in the deserts of North Africa or alongside the resistance in France and Italy. Many SAS soldiers were to face torture and execution at the hands of the Nazis. Nevertheless, it has to be insisted, the SAS never played a decisive role in campaigns that were in fact decided by the clash of great mass armies. They harassed the enemy while conventional forces dealt the decisive blows. This is not to denigrate the bravery of the SAS but to take their activities out of the realm of romance and to place them in the context of total war. Moreover, a good case can be made that other irregular formations, in particular the Chindits in Burma and the Special Operations Executive (SOE) in all the various theatres of war, played a more important part than the SAS in the final achievement of victory.

The immediate postwar years saw the veterans of all these organisations and units produce memoirs recounting their exploits, recalling the endurance, the suffering, the heroism displayed in the struggle. The popularity of these books lay in the way they portrayed the war as an enterprise in which individual bravery and skill could actually make a difference. While the activities of a dozen men might not affect the outcome of the battles of El Alamein, Kohima or Normandy, they did decide whether the raid on a German airfield or the ambush of a German convoy was a success. These tales made industrial war human, validated the sacrifice of the individual and served as a necessary myth. At this time, the SAS memoirs did not stand out from those of members of the Long Range Desert Group, the Chindits or SOE.

In the postwar period, the SAS was re-formed for deep jungle patrolling during the Malayan Emergency and survived afterwards as a specialised counter-insurgency unit. Its counter-revolutionary activities in Malaya, Oman, Borneo, Aden and South Arabia, and Dhofar, were not the subject of celebration at the time. The regiment operated without publicity, keeping out of the public eye, attempting to keep its activities, as far as possible, secret. This secrecy was to be preserved with considerable success until the early 1980s when the storming of the Iranian Embassy led to the celebration of the SAS as a band of military supermen, the best of British manhood. One aspect of this was the systematic exaggeration of the role of the SAS in Britain's post-1945 colonial wars. The regiment's mopping-up role in Malaya was identified as the turning point in the campaign against the Communist guerrillas, while the five-hour battle of Mirbat became the decisive moment in the Dhofar war.

For the 1980s, however, the SAS were the men who could take on terrorists and beat them at their own game. The faceless assassins and bombers would themselves be cut down by the British government's own terminators, by Margaret Thatcher's own men-in-black. While the SAS was never allowed to unleash a campaign of counter-terror against the Irish republican movement, 'disappearing' its leaders, rank-and-file activists and supporters on Argentinian lines (despite the wishes of many of its men), it was given an effective carte blanche in the sense that when up against members or suspected members of the IRA the SAS were not required to take prisoners. Indeed, they were encouraged to act as de facto executioners whether or not their opponents offered resistance, whether or not they were armed. Far from such activities shortening the conflict in Northern Ireland, they actually contributed to its protracted character, maintaining the cycle of violence, raising the level of tension in the province and sustaining the IRA's popular support. What is certain is that for all their vaunted superhuman military skills, the SAS failed to defeat the IRA.

For the SAS, the Falklands War was a disappointing conflict, with the glory being captured by the hard men of the Royal Marines and the Parachute Regiment. There was an absolute determination that this would not be the case in the Gulf. General Sir Peter de la Billière led the way in celebrating the heroics of the SAS, operating behind Iraqi lines, turning the technological massacre of Saddam Hussein's troops into a *Boys' Own* adventure. This version of the Gulf War was consolidated by Andy McNab and Chris Ryan's bestselling war memoirs. The marginal role the SAS actually played in the war was overwhelmed by the triumphant celebration of British pluck, determination, courage and endurance. The British soldier was worth any number of Iraqis.

Masculinity

The regiment's emergence into the full glare of publicity in the 1980s has produced a deluge of histories and illustrated histories, handbooks, memoirs and novels. What we are confronted with here is a publishing phenomenon without any precedent. The torrent of printed material has been accompanied by TV programmes, most notably the notorious 1996 Carlton series, *SAS: The Soldiers Story* and a number of videos proclaiming the regiment's prowess. So far there has, thankfully, been only one feature film, the appalling *Who Dares Wins*.

At the moment, the demand for SAS material seems insatiable. Why is this? Why is there this compelling need for many, primarily young, men to validate their masculinity and their national identity with the help of the SAS? In the words of the 'Soldier A to Z SAS' series of novels, the SAS are the men who do what other men can only dream of. The violent warrior masculinity celebrated in books and on TV is the last human activity at which the British male can claim to excel. Our elite killers are, we are told, the best in the world.

A number of factors have contributed to this development. The fascination with the SAS, with 'men behaving militarily', can be usefully seen as part of the male backlash against feminism and the women's movement. At a time when changing patterns of employment are contributing to the undermining of the certainties of traditional masculinity, of male self-confidence, the reassertion of a warrior masculinity restores men to their proper place in the

order of things. Women are effectively excluded from this male make-
believe world of camaraderie, toughness, endurance, suffering and,
of course, violence. Here men can be themselves, dressing up in
military fetish-wear and equipping themselves with phallic toys of
enormous destructive potential. Women only intrude here to
provide a home for the hero to return to and occasional sexual relief;
not sex as part of a relationship, but sex as the periodic demonstration
of male potency. Even sex in this universe comes second to the
military virtues of toughness, endurance and the capacity for
violence. Of course, this remains (thankfully) a fantasy, an imaginary
exercise, for the great majority of young men, only partially
overlapping with the actual world they inhabit. What it does,
however, is enable them to avoid confronting the real predicament
(unemployment, low pay, casualisation) in which they find
themselves. It is a consolation, a reactionary substitute for control
over their own lives and destinies. History can be ignored, society
disappears, and what remains is being tough and brave and macho
and having mates who share this identity. The huge amount of SAS
material that has appeared over the last ten to fifteen years has,
without any doubt, both encouraged and satisfied this male need.

Bolstering up the masculine identity of young men is not the only
need the SAS boom has addressed. It also constitutes an intervention
in the contemporary crisis over British national identity, a crisis that
has torn the Conservative Party apart. Apparently irreversible
decline, the end of empire, economic failure and loss of national
self-confidence seemed to be Britain's fate at the end of the 1970s.
Thatcherism provided a powerful response to this crisis and the
SAS first entered the public arena as part of this response. Britain
might have been on the defensive, but the SAS were there to help
turn the tide. Far from being a push-over for international terrorists,
whether Arabs or Irish, the SAS provided a salutary terminal lesson
of the dangers involved in messing with the Brits. Race and nation
were vindicated by the exploits of the soldier heroes, white supermen,
able to take on any odds and emerge victorious. Even the disastrous
Bravo Two Zero patrol during the Gulf War was transformed into
a triumph of British masculinity over the brutal Iraqis. 'Our boys'
could take whatever the 'ragheads' could dish out and still emerge
defiant. This was what being British was all about.

This popular militarism has deep roots in British culture. It is
very much part of our imperial heritage. The celebration of the soldier
heroes who had established the empire on which the sun never set
and the blood never dried were a central component of British
national identity by the nineteenth century. From Wellington to
Gordon, from Garnett Wolseley to Kitchener, from Baden-Powell
to Lawrence of Arabia, British soldiers marched and fought over
most of the world. Africa, China, South America, India, the Middle

East, Russia and Europe, the British have shed foreign blood over them all, killing for queen and country. Even the Dalai Lama had to be taught the fearful consequences of defying the British Lion when the Younghusband expedition invaded Tibet in 1904, slaughtering his poorly armed troops with their machine guns and artillery. These imperial exploits fed into popular culture via memoir, history, biography, fiction, newspaper report, exhibition, and, in the twentieth century, film. Children's and juvenile fiction, in particular, became the vehicle for the imperial adventures with the *Boys' Own* hero intrepidly upholding the honour of the white race in the face of the savage hordes. The racist charge of this literature made an important contribution to the fostering of imperial self-confidence.

What we see today, however, is a revived popular militarism that does not sustain empire, but compensates for its loss. The SAS are not celebrated as imperial warriors but rather as the exemplars of a narrower Britishness, a still-white Britishness, that sidesteps the multiracial nature of British society today, and confronts all foreigners with the certainty of violent and bloody retribution if they, in Michael Portillo's words, 'mess with Britain'. Britain might be in decline, relegated to the second (or third) division, but *the British* are still people to reckon with. The race that conquered an empire have not vanished from the earth. They are still there. The SAS is the proof.

While Thatcher was able to enlist this popular militarism in her own service, under her successor it escaped out of control. The bestselling memoirs by 'other ranks', by the likes of McNab, Ryan and McCallion, have given it a powerful boost, but at the expense of considerable embarrassment to the regiment itself. The memoirs of ex-public-school officers, telling of how they led their working-class soldiers into battle, were comfortable tales of class hierarchy and harmony. The common soldiers knew their place. The memoirs written by the lower ranks have seriously shaken this upper-class utopia, revealing widespread contempt for officers and dissatisfaction with aspects of army life and security policy. Such dissident voices cannot be tolerated. Indeed, the 1990s' boom in SAS material, instead of being in the service of Thatcherism, seemed almost to be a response to the collapse in belief in her supposed miraculous transformation of Britain.

The SAS

Of course, this fascination with the SAS will inevitably come to an end sooner or later. The popular taste for the memoirs, novels, handbooks and videos will decline, assisted by the efforts of the

Ministry of Defence to return the regiment to clandestinity. But while the popular militarism of the 1980s and 1990s is likely to go into decline and will probably become confined to the far right, the SAS itself will continue its activities into the twenty-first century. The regiment will play its part in the inevitable future conventional wars, counter-insurgency campaigns and anti-terrorist operations that Britain will be involved in, as well as in advising and training the armed forces of 'friendly' foreign governments and the bodyguards of 'friendly' foreign rulers. It will continue to provide personnel for the British security services and mercenaries for private enterprise security firms such as Executive Outcomes, with a considerable degree of overlap between the two. All this will, if they have their way, be done in secret as the soldier heroes are returned to the shadows and the myth of the SAS becomes an interesting episode in the cultural history of contemporary Britain's decline. Meanwhile the SAS will remain dangerous men, a counter-revolutionary elite, to be deployed against the enemies of the state, both at home and abroad.

Notes

Introduction

1. James Adams, *Secret Armies* (London: Hutchinson 1988) pp. 169, 170.
2. John le Carré, 'Siege', *Observer Review*, 1 June 1980.
3. Patrick Bishop and John Witherow, *The Winter War* (London: Quartet 1982) p. 108.
4. Graham Dawson, *Soldier Heroes* (London: Routledge 1994) pp. 1, 4.
5. Peter de la Billière, *Looking for Trouble* (London: Harper Collins 1994); Andy McNab, *Bravo Two Zero* (London: Bantam 1993); Chris Ryan, *The One That Got Away* (London: Century 1995); Jenny Simpson, *Biting the Bullet: Married to the SAS* (London: Harper Collins 1996).

Chapter 1

1. Virginia Cowles, *The Phantom Major* (London: Guild Publishing 1985) pp. 11–25.
2. For a sympathetic account of this fiasco see John Strawson, *A History of the SAS Regiment* (London: Grafton Books 1986) pp. 51–5.
3. See Peter C. Smith, *Massacre at Tobruk* (London: William Kimber 1987).
4. Mike Langley, *Anders Lassen of the SAS* (London: New English Library 1988) pp. 176–7; Roy Bradford and Martin Dillon, *Rogue Warrior of the SAS* (London: John Murray 1987) pp. 49–50, 135–6.
5. Philip Warner, *The Special Air Service* (London: William Kimber 1971) pp. 79–80.
6. John Strawson, *A History of the SAS Regiment*, p. 129.
7. John Strawson, *The Battle for North Africa* (London: Batsford 1969).
8. Barrie Pitt, *The Crucible of War: Year of Alamein 1942* (London: Jonathan Cape 1982) pp. 27, 203–4.
9. See Strawson, *History*, pp. 137–99; Warner, *The Special Air Service*, pp. 123–82.
10. Roy Farran, *Winged Dagger* (London: Collins 1948) and *Operation Tombola* (London: Collins 1960).
11. Bradford and Dillon, *Rogue Warrior of the SAS*, pp. 207–8.
12. Warner, *The Special Air Service*, p. 172.
13. James Ladd, *SBS: The Invisible Raiders* (London: Arms and Armour Press 1983) pp. 94–5.
14. Farran, *Winged Dagger*, p. 340.
15. For a discussion of the Farran affair see David Charters, 'Special Operations in Counter-Insurgency: The Farran Case, Palestine 1947', *Journal of the Royal United Services Institution* 124, 2 (June 1979).

16. See Cheah Boon Kheng, *Red Star Over Malaya* (Singapore: Singapore University Press 1983) and Michael Stenson, 'The Ethnic and Urban Bases of Communist Revolt in Malaya' in John Wilson, ed., *Peasant Rebellion and Communist Revolution in Asia* (Stanford: Stanford University Press 1974).

17. Cheah Boon Kheng, *The Masked Comrades* (Singapore: Singapore University Press 1979) pp. 63–72.

18. For the conduct of the Emergency see in particular Anthony Short, *The Communist Insurrection in Malaya 1948–1960* (London: Muller 1975) and Richard Stubbs, *Hearts and Minds in Guerrilla Warfare* (Oxford: Oxford University Press 1989).

19. For the SAS in Malaya see in particular, Alan Hoe and Eric Morris, *Re-Enter the SAS* (London: Leo Cooper 1994). On Woodhouse: Denis Healey, *The Time of My Life* (London: Penguin Books 1990) p. 230.

20. Peter de la Billière, *Looking for Trouble* (London: Harper Collins 1994) p. 107.

21. John Coates, *Suppressing Insurgency: An Analysis of the Malayan Emergency* (Boulder, Colorado: Westview Press 1992) pp. 165–6. For a recent account of SAS activities with regard to the aboriginal population see John D. Leary, *Violence and the Dream People* (Athens, Ohio: Ohio University Press 1995).

22. One of the British Army's foremost experts on jungle warfare, John Cross, has emphasised the political foundations of the British success: *In Gurkha Company* (London: Arms and Armour Press 1986) p. 23.

23. Michael Dewar, *Brush Fire Wars* (London: Robert Hale 1984) p. 85.

24. Frank Kitson, *Bunch of Five* (London: Faber 1980) p. 201.

25. Sir David Lees, *Flight from The Middle East* (London: HMSO 1980) pp. 131–3.

26. David Smiley, *Arabian Assignment* (London: Leo Cooper 1975) p. 89.

27. De la Billière, *Looking for Trouble*, pp. 150–1.

28. James H. Wyllie, *The Influence of British Arms* (London: George Allen and Unwin 1984) p. 68.

29. Strawson, *History*, pp. 264–73. See also Peter Dickens, *SAS: The Jungle Frontier* (London: Arms and Armour Press 1983).

30. For the Gurkhas in Borneo see Cross, *In Gurkha Company*, and Christopher Bullock, *Journeys Hazardous* (Worcester: Square One 1994). For an excellent discussion of the Gurkhas see Lionel Caplan, *Warrior Gentlemen: Gurkhas in the Western Imagination* (Oxford: Berghahn 1995).

31. Anthony Kemp, *The SAS: Savage Wars of Peace* (London: John Murray 1994) pp. 71–2.

32. Healey, *The Time of My Life*, 287–90.

33. Peter Dickens, *SAS: The Jungle Frontier* (London: Arms and Armour Press 1983); Tony Geraghty, *Who Dares Wins* (London: Arms and Armour Press 1980).

34. For British involvement in the Yemen see Smiley, *Arabian Assignment*, pp. 103–237; Xan Fielding, *One Man in his Time* (London: Macmillan

1990) pp. 130–55; and Johnny Cooper, *One of the Originals* (London: Pan 1991) pp. 147–86.

35. Alan Hoe, *David Stirling* (London: Little Brown 1992) pp. 432–65.

36. For an account of this episode see de la Billière, *Looking for Trouble*, pp. 218–22 and for the reminiscences of a member of the patrol see Peter Stiff, *See You in November* (Alberton: Galago 1985) pp. 35–8.

37. Thomas Mockaitis, *British Counterinsurgency in the Post-Imperial Era* (Manchester: Manchester University Press 1995) p. 55.

38. Charles Allen, *The Savage Wars of Peace* (London: Michael Joseph 1990) p. 163.

39. For the 'Keeni-Meeni' squads see Geraghty, *Who Dares Wins*, pp. 100–3.

40. De la Billière, *Looking for Trouble*, p. 263.

41. Tony Jeapes, *SAS: Operation Oman* (London: William Kimber 1980) p. 11.

42. Fred Halliday, *Arabia Without Sultans* (London: Pelican 1974) pp. 343, 351.

43. Allen, *The Savage Wars of Peace*, p. 198; de la Billière, *Looking for Trouble*, p. 277; Jeapes, *SAS: Operation Oman*, p. 157.

44. Kemp, *The SAS: Savage Wars of Peace*, p. 107.

45. Michael Dewar, *Brush Fire Wars*, p. 174.

46. For the closing stages of the Dhofar war see in particular Ken Perkins, *A Fortunate Soldier* (London: Brassey's 1988) and John Akehurst, *We Won a War* (Salisbury: Michael Russell 1982).

47. De la Billière, *Looking for Trouble*, p. 289.

48. See John Pilger, *Distant Voices* (London: Vintage 1992) pp. 184–95.

49. Geraghty, *Who Dares Wins*, pp. 222–37.

50. James Adams, Robin Morgan and Anthony Bambridge, *Ambush: The War Between the SAS and the IRA* (London: Pan 1988) pp. 62–3.

51. The supposed use of the media by terrorists has been exhaustively 'studied' but the far more potent use of the media by government and the security services is a seriously neglected area. The creation of the 'terrorist scare' and its role in bolstering the political right requires urgent study. A vital starting point for such investigation is Philip Schlesinger, Graham Murdock and Philip Elliott, *Televising Terrorism* (London: Commedia 1983).

52. For an account by one of the SAS men involved see Barry Davies, *Fire Magic* (London: Bloomsbury 1994).

53. Gary Murray, *Enemies of the State* (London: Simon and Schuster 1993) p. 222.

54. Harry McCallion, *Killing Zone* (London: Bloomsbury 1995) pp. 173–7.

55. Jenny Simpson, *Biting the Bullet: Married to the SAS* (London: Harper Collins 1996) pp. 33–4.

56. Sunday Times Insight Team, *The Falklands War* (London: Andre Deutsch 1982) p. 214.

57. For a discussion of this see my 'From Counter-Insurgency to Internal Security: Northern Ireland 1969–1992', *Small Wars and Insurgencies* 6, 1 (Spring 1995).

58. Paddy Devlin, *Straight Left* (Belfast: Blackstaff Press 1994) p. 134.

59. Mark Urban, *Big Boys' Rules: The Secret Struggle Against the IRA* (London: Faber 1992) pp. 171–2. For a useful discussion see also Stephen Dorril, *The Silent Conspiracy* (London: Heinemann 1993) pp. 83–6.
60. For Margaret Thatcher's attitude see my 'Thatcher, *The Downing Street Years* and Northern Ireland', *Irish Studies Review* 7 (Summer 1994).
61. Mark Urban, *UK Eyes Alpha* (London: Faber 1996) p. 270.
62. Simpson, *Biting the Bullet*, p. 67.
63. On Brian Nelson see Brendan O'Brien, *The Long War* (Dublin, O'Brien Press 1993) pp. 230–1 and Martin Dillon, *The Enemy Within* (London: Doubleday 1994) pp. 185–92.
64. Peter de la Billière, *Storm Command* (London: Harper Collins 1992) p. 11.
65. Margaret Thatcher, *The Downing Street Years* (London: Harper Collins 1993) p. 825–6.
66. De la Billière, *Storm Command*, pp. 3–4.
67. Urban, *UK Eyes Alpha*, pp. 174–5.
68. Andy McNab, *Bravo Two Zero* (London: Bantam 1993) and Chris Ryan, *The One That Got Away* (London: Century 1995).
69. Norman Schwarzkopf, *It Doesn't Take a Hero* (London: Bantam 1992).

Chapter 2

1. J. Glenn Gray, *The Warriors* (New York: Harper & Row 1970) pp. 29–51.
2. John Hislop, *Anything but a Soldier* (London: Michael Joseph 1965) p. 7.
3. Harold Challenor with Alfred Draper, *Tanky Challenor: SAS and the Met* (London: Leo Cooper 1990) p. 116. Challenor is best known as the police sergeant who in July 1963 'planted' pieces of brick on demonstrators arrested while protesting against Queen Frederika of Greece's visit to London. He escaped prison on the grounds of mental illness.
4. Hislop, *Anything but a Soldier*, pp. 122–3.
5. J. Fraser McLuskey, *Parachute Padre* (Stevenage: Spa Books 1985) p. 78; Derrick Harrison, *These Men are Dangerous* (London: Blandford Press 1988) p. 16.
6. Roy Farran, *Winged Dagger* (London: Collins 1948) p. 164.
7. Challenor, *Tanky Challenor*, p. 39.
8. Malcolm James (Pleydell), *Born in the Desert: With the SAS in North Africa* (London: Greenhill Books 1991) pp. 134–5, 193.
9. Ian Wellstead, *SAS with the Marquis* (London: Greenhill Books 1994) p. 87; Johnny Cooper, *One of the Originals* (London: Pan 1991) pp. 92–3. For an account of the torture and execution of SAS prisoners see Serge Vaculik, *Air Commando* (London: Jarrolds 1954). A Czech, serving in the SAS, Vaculik was captured in France in 1944 and handed over to the Gestapo. He was brutally tortured (beaten, hand crushed in a press and his fingernails pulled out, plunged into alternating baths of boiling and freezing water, cigarettes stubbed out

on him) and taken into the woods to be shot along with his comrades. They made a break for it and Vaculik and one other man got away to join up with the resistance. The rest were killed.

10. Harrison, *These Men are Dangerous*, pp. 183–7.
11. Challenor, *Tanky Challenor*, p. 59.
12. Farran, *Winged Dagger*, p. 217.
13. Hislop, *Anything but a Soldier*, pp. 158–9.
14. Farran, *Winged Dagger*, pp. 88–9, 96, 239–40, 243–4.
15. Roy Farran, *Operation Tombola* (London: Collins 1960) pp. 245–6.
16. Farran, *Winged Dagger*, pp. 221, 254–5.
17. James (Pleydell), *Born in the Desert*, pp. 317–20.
18. John Verney, *Going to the Wars* (London: Collins 1955) p. 148.
19. Peter de la Billière, *Looking for Trouble* (London: Harper Collins 1994) pp. 78–84, 125, 144, 242, 315. While de la Billière was very much concerned to honour his beloved regiment in his two books, his losses as a Lloyds' name, believed to be in the region of £400,000, were also a factor in publication.
20. Charlie Beckwith and Donald Knox, *Delta Force* (London: Arms and Armour Press 1984) pp. 14–15. Beckwith had a reputation for racism and, according to one account of Delta Force, he 'required Delta candidates to pass a strenuous swimming test "to keep out them goddamn niggers". Blacks tend to be bad swimmers and as an unrepentant racist, Beckwith believed that they tended to make bad, lazy soldiers and didn't want them in Delta. "The problem with blacks", says British SAS man Lofty Wiseman, who worked closely with Beckwith, "is that their big muscles burn up too much oxygen. Their frame and large pores make them poor swimmers because they get waterlogged"': from Martin Arostequi, *Twilight Warriors* (London: Bloomsbury 1995) p. 109.
21. 'Lofty' Large, *One Man's SAS* (London: William Kimber 1987).
22. Michael Paul Kennedy, *Soldier 'I' SAS* (London: Bloomsbury 1989) pp. 93–4, 199–200.
23. Barry Davies, *Fire Magic* (London: Bloomsbury 1994); Souhaila Andrawes and Barry Davies, *Shadow of the Dove* (London: Bloomsbury 1996). Souhaila Andrawes has since been extradited to Germany, tried, found guilty and sentenced to twelve years imprisonment.
24. Andy McNab, *Bravo Two Zero* (London: Bantam 1993) pp. 363–4.
25. Chris Ryan, *The One That Got Away* (London: Century 1995).
26. Peter Stiff, *See You in November* (Alberton, South Africa: Galago 1985) pp. 49–51, 54, 129–30, 187, 333–4. 'Taffy' is mentioned by Tony Geraghty in his account of the notorious Radfan patrol: *Who Dares Wins* (London: Arms and Armour Press 1980) p. 76. For the Rhodesian SAS see Barbara Cole, *The Elite* (Amanzimtoti: Three Knights Press 1984).
27. Harry McCallion, *Killing Zone* (London: Bloomsbury 1995) pp. 28, 30, 32, 194, 204–5.
28. Kennedy, *Soldier 'I' SAS*, p. 121.
29. Michael Asher, *Shoot to Kill* (London: Guild Publishing 1990) pp. 32, 120, 151.

30. Andy McNab, *Immediate Action* (London: Bantam 1995) pp. 65, 159, 243, 265.
31. Paul Bruce, *The Nemesis File* (London: Blake Publishing 1995).
32. Jenny Simpson, *Biting the Bullet: Married to the SAS* (London: Harper Collins 1996) pp. 33, 43, 109, 138, 142–3, 174, 277–8, 280. According to a report in the *Sunday Times* on 4 August 1996, Andy McNab's third wife, Frances, is due to publish her own memoirs with Blake Publishing early in 1997. This apparently will reveal that the SAS 'are the sexiest men and most wonderful lovers in the world'.
33. Executive Outcomes, a mercenary organisation, was apparently established in early 1993 by two former SAS soldiers, Anthony Buckingham, now an important international businessman, and Simon Mann. It has, in a very short time, established a presence in some 30 countries, mainly in Africa, but also in Asia. Such organisations are likely to become increasingly important as we move into the next century. See Khareen Pech and David Beresford, 'Corporate dogs of war who grow fat amid the anarchy of Africa', *Observer* 19 January 1997.

Chapter 3

1. Virginia Cowles, *The Phantom Major* (London: Guild Publishing 1985) p. 12.
2. Philip Warner, *The Special Air Service* (London: William Kimber 1971) pp. 193, 245–6.
3. Jennifer Shaw, ed., *Ten Years of Terrorism* (London: RUSI 1979).
4. Tony Geraghty, *Who Dares Wins* (London: Arms and Armour Press 1980) p. 181.
5. John Strawson, *A History of the SAS Regiment* (London: Martin, Secker and Warburg 1984) pp. 342, 343–4.
6. Peter Dickens, *SAS: The Jungle Frontier* (London: Arms and Armour Press 1983); Robin Hunter, *True Stories of the SAS* (London 1985); William Seymour, *British Special Forces* (London: Sidgwick and Jackson 1985); James Ladd, *SAS Operations* (London: Robert Hale 1986); James Adams, *Secret Armies* (London: Hutchinson 1988); James Adams, Robin Morgan and Anthony Bambridge, *Ambush: The War Between the SAS and the IRA* (London: Pan 1988); Eric Morris, *Guerrillas in Uniform* (London: Hutchinson 1989); Raymond Murray, *The SAS in Ireland* (Dublin: Mercier Press 1990); Anthony Kemp, *The SAS at War 1941–1945* (London: John Murray 1991); Mark Urban, *Big Boys' Rules* (London: Faber 1992); Anthony Kemp, *The SAS: Savage Wars of Peace* (London: John Murray 1994); Alan Hoe and Eric Morris, *Re-enter the SAS* (London: Leo Cooper 1994); Martin Arostegui, *Twilight Warriors* (London: Bloomsbury 1995); Paul McCue, *Operation Bulbasket* (London: Leo Cooper 1996); Charles Whiting, *Death on a Distant Frontier* (London: Leo Cooper 1996); Patrick Marrinan, *Colonel Paddy* (Belfast: Ulster Press 1960); Roy Bradford and Martin Dillon, *Rogue Warrior of the SAS* (London: John Murray 1987); and Alan Hoe, *David Stirling* (London: Harper Collins 1992).

7. Adams, *Secret Armies*, pp. 9, 34, 392.
8. Adams, Morgan and Bambridge, *Ambush*, p. 189. For the *Sunday Times* assault on the 'Death on the Rock' documentary and its motives, see in particular Roger Bolton, *Death on the Rock and Other Stories* (London: W.H. Allen 1990) and David Miller, *Don't Mention the War: Northern Ireland, Propaganda and the Media* (London: Pluto 1994).
9. Raymond Murray, *The SAS in Ireland*, pp. 333–48.
10. Mark Urban, *Big Boys' Rules*, pp. 171–2, 196–205, 238–47.
11. Tony Geraghty, *This is the SAS* (London: Arms and Armour Press 1982); Peter Macdonald, *The SAS in Action* (London: Sidgwick and Jackson 1990); Steve Crawford, *The SAS at Close Quarters* (London: BCA 1993) and *The SAS Encyclopaedia* (London: Simon and Schuster 1996); Mike Robinson, *Fighting Skills of the SAS* (London: Sidgwick and Jackson 1991); Peter Darman, *SAS: The World's Best* (London: Sidgwick and Jackson 1994) and *A-Z of the SAS* (London: Sidgwick and Jackson 1992); Craig Philip and Alex Taylor, *Inside the SAS* (London: Bloomsbury 1992); Barry Davies, *SAS: The Illustrated History* (London: Virgin Books 1996); Steve Crawford, *SAS: Gulf Warriors* (London: Simon and Schuster 1995).
12. Crawford, *The SAS at Close Quarters*, pp. 9, 63, 78.
13. Macdonald, *The SAS in Action*, p. 149.
14. Robinson, *Fighting Skills of the SAS*, pp. 86–7.
15. Darman, *SAS: The World's Best*, pp. 171–83.
16. Crawford, *SAS: Gulf Warriors*.
17. Davies, *SAS: The Illustrated History*, p. 6.
18. John Wiseman, *The SAS Personal Trainer* (London: Headline 1996) and *The SAS Survival Handbook* (London: Collins Harvill 1986); Barry Davies, *The SAS Escape, Evasion and Survival Manual* (London: Bloomsbury 1996); Andrew Kain and Neil Hanson, *SAS Security Handbook* (London: Heinemann 1996).
19. Wiseman, *The SAS Personal Trainer*, pp. 114, 144, 181, 190.
20. Wiseman, *The SAS Survival Handbook*.
21. Davies, *SAS Escape, Evasion and Survival Manual*, pp. 34, 270.
22. Kain and Hanson, *SAS Security Handbook*, pp. 42, 94, 97, 141, 149, 165.
23. *The Story of the SAS*, Castle Communications 1995.
24. *The SAS*, DD Video 1993.
25. Peter Crossland, *Victor Two* (London: Bloomsbury 1996) pp. 82, 128–9, 132.
26. Peter Beaumont, 'Sadistic and Salacious', *Observer*, 9 June 1996.
27. *SAS: The Complete Soldiers' Story*, director Andrew Piddington, Carlton 1996.
28. *The Rock*, director Michael Bay, Buena Vista 1996.
29. *Sea of Sand*, director Guy Green, Rank Tempean 1958; *Tobruk*, director Arthur Hiller, Universal 1967; *Play Dirty*, director Andre de Toth, United Artists 1969.
30. *Who Dares Wins*, director Ian Sharp, Sturla Leasing 1982.
31. *The Odd Angry Shot*, director Tom Jeffrey, Sanson Productions 1978.

32. Gilbert Adair, *Hollywood's Vietnam* (London: Heinemann 1989)
     p. 143.

Chapter 4

1. Gavin Lyall, *Uncle Target* (London: Hodder and Stoughton 1988)
    p. 11. This is the third novel featuring Lyall's SAS hero, Harry
    Maxim. The previous two are *The Secret Servant* (London: Hodder
    and Stoughton 1980) and *The Conduct of Major Maxim* (London:
    Hodder and Stoughton 1982).
2. James Follett, *The Tiptoe Boys* (London: Corgi 1982).
3. Terence Strong, *Whisper Who Dares* (London: Coronet 1982).
4. Terence Strong, *The Fifth Hostage* (London: Coronet 1983); *Conflict
    of Lions* (London: Coronet 1985); *The Last Mountain* (London:
    Coronet 1989); *The Sons of Heaven* (London: Coronet 1990); *This
    Angry Land* (London: Coronet 1992).
5. Terence Strong, *Stalking Horse* (London: Coronet 1993) pp. 45–6,
    153–4, 393.
6. Frederick Forsyth, *The Fist of God* (London: Corgi 1994) pp. 620–2.
7. Gerald Seymour, *Harry's Game* (London: William Collins 1975);
    Archangel (London: William Collins 1982); *Song in the Morning*
    (London: William Collins 1986).
8. Gerald Seymour, *In Honour Bound* (London: William Collins 1984)
    p. 182.
9. Gerald Seymour, *The Fighting Man* (London: Harper Collins 1993).
10. Gordon Stevens, *Provo* (London: Harper Collins 1993).
11. Gordon Stevens, *Kennedy's Ghost* (London: Harper Collins 1994).
12. Gordon Stevens, *Kara's Game* (London: Harper Collins 1996)
    pp. 80–1.
13. Shaun Clarke, *The Exit Club* (London: Simon and Schuster 1996).
14. Barry Davies, *Going Hostile* (London: 22 Books 1995).
15. Ranulph Fiennes, *The Feather Men* (London: Bloomsbury 1991).
    According to Stephen Dorril, while 'the SAS reacted with undisguised
    fury at this tale of scurrilous goings-on ... there may be a grain of truth
    in Fiennes' pot-boiler'. He goes on to report allegations of a secret
    assassination unit, Group 13, made up of former SAS members that
    over the last twelve years has 'carried out a number of contract
    killings on behalf of the British government through contacts in
    MI6', including killings in Britain itself. See Stephen Dorril, *The Silent
    Conspiracy* (London: Heinemann 1993) p. 273.
16. Chris Ryan, *Stand By, Stand By* (London: Century 1996) pp. 75, 77.
17. Stephen Leather, *Hungry Ghost* (London: Harper Collins 1991).
18. Stephen Leather, *The Chinaman* (London: Hodder and Stoughton
    1992); *The Long Shot* (London: Hodder and Stoughton 1994); *The
    Double Tap* (London: Hodder and Stoughton 1996).
19. Simon Weston, *Cause of Death* (London: 22 Books 1995); *Phoenix*
    (London: Bloomsbury 1996).
20. Conor Cregan, *With Extreme Prejudice* (London: Hodder and
    Stoughton 1994) pp. 26, 69, 389.

21. David Goodhart and Patrick Wintour, *Eddie Shah and the Newspaper Revolution* (London: Coronet 1986) p. xiv. For a good account of the Messenger dispute see Mark Dickinson, *To Break a Union* (Manchester: Booklist 1984).
22. Eddy Shah, *Ring of Red Roses* (London: Doubleday 1991) p. 31.
23. Eddy Shah, *The Lucy Ghosts* (London: Doubleday 1992).
24. Eddy Shah, *Fallen Angels* (London: Doubleday 1994) pp. 8, 376.
25. All 'The Fighting Saga of the SAS' books were published by Pan between 1982 and 1984.
26. The full list of Soldier A to Z SAS so far is:
Soldier A SAS: Behind Iraqi Lines
Soldier B SAS: Heroes of the South Atlantic
Soldier C SAS: Secret War in Arabia
Soldier D SAS: The Colombian Cocaine War
Soldier E SAS: Sniper Fire in Belfast
Soldier F SAS: Guerrillas in the Jungle
Soldier G SAS: The Desert Raiders
Soldier H SAS: The Headhunters of Borneo
Soldier I SAS: Eighteen Years in the Elite Force
Soldier J SAS: Counter-insurgency in Aden
Soldier K SAS: Mission to Argentina
Soldier L SAS: The Embassy Siege
Soldier M SAS: Invisible Enemy in Kazakhstan
Soldier N SAS: The Gambian Bluff
Soldier O SAS: The Bosnian Inferno
Soldier P SAS: Nightfighters in France
Soldier Q SAS: Kidnap The Emperor!
Soldier R SAS: Death on Gibraltar
Soldier S SAS: The Samarkand Hijack
Soldier T SAS: War on the Streets
Soldier U SAS: Bandit Country
Soldier V SAS: Into Vietnam
Soldier W SAS: Guatemalan Adventure
27. Shaun Clarke, *Soldier R SAS: Death on Gibraltar* (London: 22 Books 1994) pp. 9–12, 30, 237–40, 243.
28. Peter Corrigan, *Soldier U SAS: Bandit Country* (London: 22 Books 1995) pp. 27, 54.
29. Peter Cave, *Soldier T SAS: War on the Streets* (London: 22 Books 1995).
30. David Monnery, *Soldier K SAS: Mission to Argentina* (London: 22 Books 1994) pp. 47, 84.
31. David Monnery, *Soldier O SAS: The Bosnian Inferno* (London: 22 Books 1994) pp. 9–10, 42.
32. Marshall Pugh, *A Dream of Treason* (London: André Deutsch 1974); Julian Rathbone, *Dangerous Games* (London: William Heinemann 1991); Jack Curtis, *Sons of the Morning* (London: Bantam 1991).
33. Derek Robinson, *A Good Clean Fight* (London: Harvill 1993) pp. 454, 523–4.

Select Bibliography

Adams, James, Morgan, Robin, and Bambridge, Anthony, *Ambush: The War Between the SAS and the IRA* (London: Pan 1988)

Adams, James, *Secret Armies* (London: Hutchinson 1988)

Akehurst, John, *We Won a War* (Salisbury: Michael Russell 1982)

Arostegui, Martin, *Twilight Warriors* (London: Bloomsbury 1995)

Asher, Michael, *Shoot to Kill* (London: Guild Publishing 1990)

Beckwith, Charlie and Knox, Donald, *Delta Force* (London: Arms and Armour Press 1984)

Bishop, Patrick and Witherow, John, *The Winter War* (London: Quartet 1982)

Bolton, Roger, *Death on the Rock* (London: W.H. Allen 1990)

Bradford, Roy and Dillon, Martin, *Rogue Warrior of the SAS* (London: John Murray 1987)

Bruce, Paul *The Nemesis File* (London: Blake Publishing 1995)

Caplan, Lionel, *Warrior Gentlemen: Gurkhas in the Western Imagination* (Oxford: Berghahn, 1995)

Challenor, Harold with Draper, Alfred *Tanky Challenor: SAS and the Met* (London: Leo Cooper 1990)

Coates, John, *Suppressing Insurgency* (Boulder, Colorado: Westview Press 1992)

Cooper, Johnny, *One of the Originals* (London: Pan 1991)

Cowles, Virginia, *The Phantom Major* (London: Guild Publishing 1985)

Crawford, Steve, *SAS: Gulf Warriors* (London: Simon and Schuster 1995)

Crossland, Peter, *Victor Two* (London: Bloomsbury 1996)

Cross, John, *In Gurkha Company* (London: Arms and Armour Press 1986)

Curtis, Mark, *The Ambiguities of Power: British Foreign Policy Since 1945* (London: Zed Books 1995)

Davies, Barry, *Fire Magic* (London: Bloomsbury 1994)

Davies, Barry, *Shadow of the Dove* (London: Bloomsbury 1996)

Dawson, Graham, *Soldier Heroes* (London: Routledge 1994)

de la Billière, Peter, *Storm Command* (London: Harper Collins 1992)

de la Billière, Peter, *Looking for Trouble* (London: Harper Collins 1994)

Dewar, Michael, *Brush Fire Wars* (London: Robert Hale 1984)

Dickens, Peter, *SAS: The Jungle Frontier* (London: Arms and Armour Press 1983)

Dillon, Martin, *The Enemy Within* (London: Doubleday 1994)

Farran, Roy, *Winged Dagger* (London: Collins 1948)

Farran, Roy, *Operation Tombola* (London: Collins 1960)

Fielding, Xan, *One Man in his Time* (London: Macmillan 1990)

Geraghty, Tony, *Who Dares Wins* (London: Arms and Armour Press 1980)

Geraghty, Tony, *This is the SAS* (London: Arms and Armour Press 1982)

Glenn Gray, J., *The Warriors* (New York: Harper and Row 1970)

Halliday, Fred, *Arabia Without Sultans* (London: Pelican 1974)

Harrison, Derrick, *These Men are Dangerous* (London: Blandford Press 1988)

Healey, Denis, *The Time of My Life* (London: Penguin Books 1990)

Hislop, John, *Anything but a Soldier* (London: Michael Joseph 1965)

Hoe, Alan, *David Stirling* (London: Little Brown 1992)

Hoe, Alan and Morris, Eric, *Re-enter the SAS* (London: Leo Cooper 1994)

James, Malcolm, *Born in the Desert* (London: Greenhill Books 1991)

Jeapes, Tony, *SAS: Operation Oman* (London: William Kimber 1980)

Kemp, Anthony, *The SAS: Savage Wars of Peace* (London: John Murray 1994)

Kennedy, Michael Paul, *Soldier '1' SAS* (London: Bloomsbury 1989)

Kheng, Cheah Boon, *The Masked Comrades* (Singapore: Singapore University Press 1979)

Kheng, Cheah Boon, *Red Star Over Malaya* (Singapore: Singapore University Press 1983)

Kitson, Frank, *Bunch of Five* (London: Faber 1980)

Ladd, James, *SBS: The Invisible Raiders* (London: Arms and Armour Press 1983)

Langley, Mike, *Anders Lassen of the SAS* (London: New English Library 1988)

Leary, John D., *Violence and the Dream People* (Athens, Ohio: Ohio University Press 1995)

Lees, Sir David, *Flight from the Middle East* (London: HMSO 1980)

McCallion, Harry, *Killing Zone* (London: Bloomsbury 1995)

McInnes, Colin, *Hot War, Cold War: The British Army's Way in Warfare 1945–95* (London: Brassey's 1996)

McNab, Andy, *Bravo Two Zero* (London: Bantam 1993)

McNab, Andy, *Immediate Action* (London: Bantam 1995)

Miller, David, *Don't Mention the War: Northern Ireland, Propaganda and the Media* (London: Pluto 1994)

Mockaitis, Thomas, *British Counterinsurgency in the Post-Imperial Era* (Manchester: Manchester University Press 1995)

Murray, Gary, *Enemies of the State* (London: Simon and Schuster 1993)

Murray, Raymond, *The SAS in Ireland* (Dublin: Mercier Press 1990)

O'Brien, Brendan, *The Long War* (Dublin: O'Brien Press 1993)

Perkins, Ken, *A Fortunate Solder* (London: Brassey's 1988)

Pilger, John, *Distant Voices* (London: Vintage 1992)

Pitt, Barrie, *The Crucible of War: Year of Alamein 1942* (London: Jonathan Cape 1982)

Ryan, Chris, *The One That Got Away* (London: Century 1995)

Short, Anthony, *The Communist Insurrection in Malaya 1948–1960* (London: Muller 1975)

Simpson, Jenny, *Biting the Bullet: Married to the SAS* (London: Harper Collins 1996)

Smiley, David, *Arabian Assignment* (London: Leo Cooper 1975)

Smith, Peter C., *Massacre at Tobruk* (London: William Kimber 1987)

Stiff, Peter, *See You in November* (Alberton: Galago 1985)

Strawson, John, *The Battle for North Africa* (London: Batsford 1969)

Strawson, John, *A History of the SAS Regiment* (London: Grafton Books 1986)

Stubbs, Richard, *Hearts and Minds in Guerrilla Warfare* (Oxford: Oxford University Press 1989)

Sunday Times Insight Team, *The Falklands War* (London: Andre Deutsch 1982)

Thatcher, Margaret, *The Downing Street Years* (London: Harper Collins 1993)

Urban, Mark, *Big Boys' Rules* (London: Faber 1992)

Urban, Mark, *UK Eyes Alpha* (London: Faber 1996)

Vaculik, Serge, *Air Commando* (London: Jarrolds 1954)

Verney, John, *Going to the Wars* (London: Collins 1955)

Warner, Philip, *The Special Air Service* (London: William Kimber 1971)

Wellstead, Ian, *SAS with the Marquis* (London: Greenhill Books 1994)

Wilson, John, ed., *Peasant Rebellion and Communist Revolution in Asia* (Stanford: Stanford University Press 1974)

Wyllie, James H., *The Influence of British Arms* (London: George Allen and Unwin 1984).

Index